Easy Oracle Automation

Oracle10g Automatic Storage, Memory and Diagnostic Features

Easy Oracle Series

Dr. Arun Kumar R.

I dedicate this book to my loving and understanding wife Karthika Devi and daughter Anjitha, whose relentless support made this book possible. I also dedicate this book to my parents, all my teachers, and the almighty GOD.

- Arun Kumar

Easy Oracle Automation

Oracle10g Automatic Storage, Memory and Diagnostic Features

By Arun Kumar R.

Printed in the United States of America.

Published in Kittrell, North Carolina, USA.

Easy Oracle Series: Book 1

Series Editor: Don Burleson

Editors: Janet Burleson and John Lavender

Production Editor: Teri Wade

Cover Design: Bryan Hoff

Printing History: December, 2004 for First Edition

ISBN: 0-9745993-6-0

Library of Congress Control Number: 2004096475

Table of Contents

Using the Online Code Depot

Purchase of this book provides complete access to the online code depot that contains the sample code scripts.

All of the code depot scripts in this book are available for download in zip format, ready to load and use and are located at the following URL:

rampant.cc/auto_dba.htm

If technical assistance is needed with downloading or accessing the scripts, please contact Rampant TechPress at info@rampant.cc.

Conventions Used in this Book

It is critical for any technical publication to follow rigorous standards and employ consistent punctuation conventions to make the text easy to read.

However, this is not an easy task. Within Oracle there are many types of notation that can confuse a reader. Some Oracle utilities such as STATSPACK and TKPROF are always spelled in CAPITAL letters, while Oracle parameters and procedures have varying naming conventions in the Oracle documentation. It is also important to remember that many Oracle commands are case sensitive, and are always left in their original executable form, and never altered with italics or capitalization.

Hence, all Rampant TechPress books follow these conventions:

Parameters - All Oracle parameters will be lowercase italics. Exceptions to this rule are parameter arguments that are commonly capitalized (KEEP pool, TKPROF), these will be left in ALL CAPS.

Variables – All PL/SQL program variables and arguments will also remain in lowercase italics (dbms_job, dbms_utility).

Tables & dictionary objects – All data dictionary objects are referenced in lowercase italics *(dba_indexes, v$sql)*. This includes all *v$* and *x$* views (*x$kcbcbh*, *v$parameter*) and dictionary views (*dba_tables*, *user_indexes*).

SQL – All SQL is formatted for easy use in the code depot, and all SQL is displayed in lowercase. The main SQL terms (select, from, where, group by, order by, having) will always appear on a separate line.

Programs & Products – All products and programs that are known to the author are capitalized according to the vendor specifications (IBM, DBXray, etc). All names known by Rampant TechPress to be trademark names appear in this text as initial caps. References to UNIX are always made in uppercase.

Acknowledgments

I would like to express my sincere thanks to Don Burleson for giving me an opportunity to publish a work along with his team of well-known authors and industry leaders. Special thanks to Don and Mike Ault for letting me use material from their articles as reference. I would also like to thank the Beta Team at Oracle Corporation, Arup, Tony, and other SELECT Journal team members for their appropriate support.

I wish to acknowledge the tremendous amount of support received from my wife Karthika, daughter Anjitha, parents - Prof. RK Nair and Prof. Anandavally, and family during the six months that this authoring venture was paralleling a very busy career and life. All of them provided great encouragement, offered support, and shared in the excitement of seeing a major piece of work become a reality.

I would like to express my sincere appreciation to Cingular Wireless and the management (Stan, Thaddeus, Victor, Joe, Greg, and Dan) and colleagues for all their support for this book and my authoring ventures. I would like to express my thanks to Elliot and DBTA magazine team for their help in promoting the book through my column. Thanks are also due to all my friends and members of IEEE Dallas section and Engineers' Association.

This type of highly technical reference book requires the dedicated efforts of many people. Even though I worked as the primary author, I got relentless support from Don, Mike, Janet, and the Rampant team.

In short, the author played a modest role in the development of this book, and I need to thank and acknowledge everyone who helped bring this book to fruition:

John Lavender, for the production management, including the coordination of the cover art, page proofing, printing, and distribution.

Linda Webb, for all the author coordination work including getting timely reviews from reviewers and for her expert page-proofing services.

Teri Wade, for her help in the production of the page proofs.

Janet Burleson, for her assistance with the web site and for creating the code depot and the online shopping cart for this book.

Richard Stroupe, for his expert technical review of the content and his wife Tina, son Trey and newborn Audrey, for letting him finish his excellent reviewing efforts.

I would like to offer this work at the Lotus Feet of GOD, who has been instrumental in providing my family, all the successes, and help us sail over the rough seas of life.

I would like to get readers' comments on this book at autodba@dbatrends.com. Your comments and recommendations will help me improve this book over future editions.

With my sincere thanks,

Arun Kumar

Dr. Arun Kumar R.

Preface

Oracle Databases command significant clout in the enterprise database market. With every major release, the Oracle adds new functionality, which makes the databases seem difficult to administer. Oracle Database 10g made a major break-through over all hurdles with its ease of installation and administration.

Oracle has brought the latest version of its premier database product to the mass market in a way that benefits very small companies to large enterprises. DBAs can easily set up and administer their databases on traditional UNIX and Windows platforms as well as the cheaper and robust Linux.

With over 153 manuals in the Oracle Database 10*g* Documentation Library and over 25 books from major publishers, novice database users as well as experienced administrators find it difficult and confusing to find a reliable, single source of information on 10g to start. Also the sheer volume of material presented in these books, makes it tedious for any user to get the essential knowledge and to get acquainted with the database.

Smaller IT organizations as well as large businesses find that there is no single source of knowledge to judge how easily and reliably they can set up or convert their databases to Oracle Database 10g. This book is the culmination of dedicated effort to address all these challenges and help the Oracle reader with a one-stop resource guide.

This book will cater to the needs of all the database enthusiasts who want to learn about the powerful automatic database administration features and get their feet wet with Oracle Database 10g. It has comprehensive coverage of all major features, installation guidelines, and automatic features for simpler database administration and enables the reader to install a complete ready-to-use Oracle database in less than a day. Enough screen shots with lucid explanations are given to guide the novice users at each step of the learning process.

For the more experienced readers and practicing Oracle professionals, this book has a special "Guru Conversation" section at the end of each major chapter to provide information about the Oracle10g *v$* views and internal mechanisms behind these automatic tuning and configuration tools.

Sincerely,

Arun Kumar

Dr. Arun Kumar R.

Oracle Grid Computing

CHAPTER

"Looks like a cache fusion problem".

Introduction

The fundamental idea of Grid computing relies on the notion that computing can be considered as a utility analogous to the electric power grid or the telephone network. The utilities are meant to be unbreakable and highly available. If a customer needs more energy, the electric grid can provide it without affecting other customers. Likewise, if a generator goes down, the utility company is able to shift the load to other power generating stations over the grid and maintain availability of its resources.

Similarly, the key initiative for computing at organizations is improving affordability and availability of enterprise systems. Companies are looking at ways to improve their system's availability, process efficiencies and ease operation at reduced expenses. This is the client side view on utility computing.

Oracle 10g is committed to using the latest technology.

From a server side view, Grid computing is the way to achieve this goal by consolidating islands of hardware and using centralized tools to allocate and manage resources effectively. From a server utilization perspective, resources are not sitting idle and all requests for resources are answered promptly. High availability of such resources ensures that companies get optimum performance at reduced expense.

Oracle Corporation has embraced the idea of Grid technology to provide seamless availability solutions through its database products. The idea of grid computing began in the academic and research communities.

The concept of Grid has been in development for several years at Oracle, although some of the features were first available in Oracle 9i. Oracle 9i has the key differentiating technologies for building the Grid such as Oracle Streams, Oracle transportable tablespaces and Oracle Real Application clusters.

It has the portability, security, scalability and manageability needed for Grid technology. Oracle has matured this technology with the introduction of Oracle Database 10g. Some other key reasons behind this initiative are availability of cheaper, faster and affordable hardware along with better evolution of traditional operating systems and newer open source software like Linux.

Benefits of Using Grid technology

What follows is a brief review of some of the technical challenges which led to the development of Grid technology. In the early part of the 1990s, the focus of IT organizations was to use smaller, cheaper and dedicated UNIX and MS-Windows servers instead of costlier mainframes. However, organizations soon realized the higher expense of maintaining multiple servers, and the over-allocated hardware spread over the enterprise was causing organizations to think of better and cheaper alternatives.

Every company is interested in saving money on hardware and software, resource allocation and utilization, and getting better, quicker results on investments. Grid computing is the best-proven way to achieve all these and more at overall lower costs.

Grid computing changes the way that enterprises look at resources. Companies can buy resources for all their needs and allocate them judiciously among different applications depending on the demand. For example, while the payroll application is running every 2 weeks at night, other business intelligence applications can part their resources to speed up the payroll processing.

During daytime, the resources from overnight batch jobs can be allotted for adhoc queries. These are just a few of the scenarios where a company can shift the resources, yet run all the applications at peak performance at the lowest possible cost. This also results in reduction of development, deployment, and maintenance costs of database applications.

For users of Grid computing, the mystery of computing resources is completely eliminated. All they have to know is that resources are available to address their needs and perform their commands satisfactorily. This is analogous to using a hair dryer or microwave oven without consulting the utility company before operating the appliance. The users do not have to worry about availability of resources.

The personality of your Oracle database can change quickly!

Now that resource availability has been addressed, it is time to move on to the initiatives Oracle has put in motion to promote Grid Computing.

Oracle and Grid Computing Initiatives

Oracle is a leading member of the Enterprise Grid Alliance (EGA), a consortium of leading vendors and customers for enterprise grid computing. The focus of the EGA is on promoting tools and standards for developers and users, and fostering understanding and adoption of grid computing within the enterprise. Oracle's focus with the EGA is to promote grid computing in enterprises and provide support of enterprise computing via grid technologies and database architectures.

Code Depot Username = book, Password = check

Oracle has provided grid features at no additional cost to the customers. It has also provided the Grid SDK (Software Development Kit) free of charge to support this initiative. Oracle provides distributed SQL features to transparently query or update data in other Oracle databases or non-Oracle databases using transparent gateways, and makes it appear local. Oracle Transportable tablespaces allow Oracle datafiles to be copied from one server to a different one, even across different operating systems.

Oracle Streams can share data between databases or database nodes automatically, enabling efficient communications between applications on a grid. The Grid Infrastructure will be addressed in the next few paragraphs.

How Does Grid Infrastructure Work?

In the last decade, availability and affordability of super fast computers, storage devices and networking devices has improved dramatically. By using the increased efficiencies of processes and systems, grid computing can be achieved as in any utility grid. To explain this further, please refer to Figure 1.1. By putting all the hardware and applications together, islands of under utilized resources are eliminated.

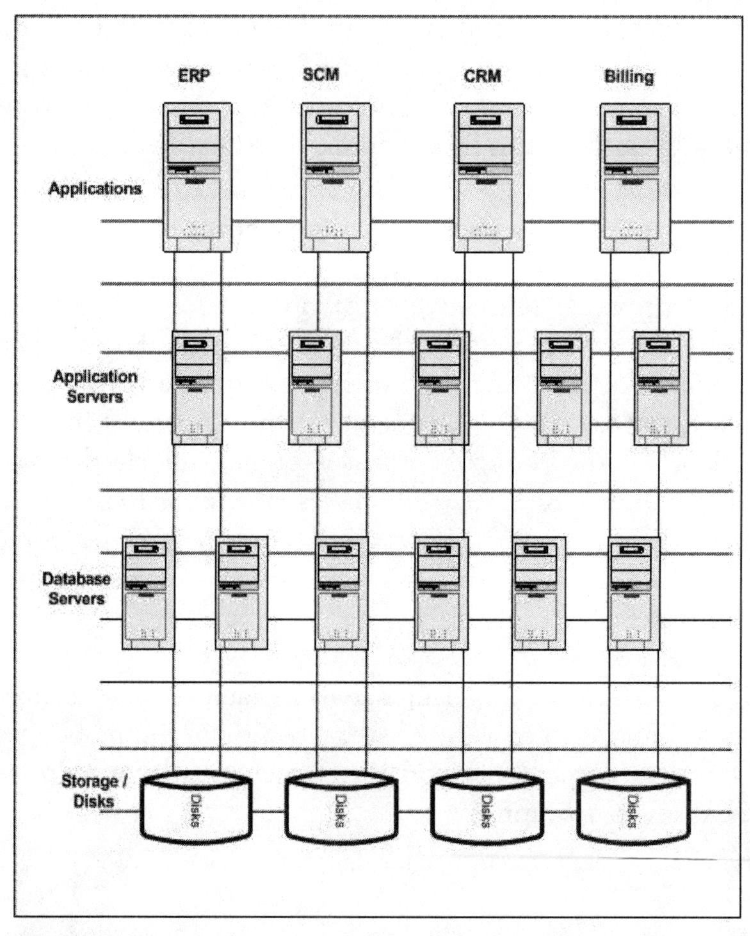

Figure 1.1 *Grid Infrastructure*

Hardware vendors are selling cheaper and faster machines, server blades, networking equipment, etc., which was unheard of ten years ago. A server blade is a circuit board with memory, CPU and hard disk to be mounted on a rack. They offer the lowest cost of computing that is scalable, efficient and reliable. Blade farms or groups of fast computers are the basis of clustering technology and grid computing.

On the software side of computing, Linux continues to attract more companies by providing an inexpensive and reliable operating system. Linux runs very well on blades and smaller machines up to four CPUs. This CPU constraint is assumed to be overcome in the near future. When considering a blade farm or server farm running on Linux, the cost advantage is much higher than in a Symmetric MultiProcessor (SMP) environment.

When a grid environment similar to the one in Figure 1.1 is deployed, users cannot determine where the server is located and where the data is being stored. The experience to the users is a faster, seamless operation of their applications.

Oracle started leveraging grid technology with the introduction of Real Application Clusters (RAC) in Oracle 9i Release 1. Oracle 9i has proven its scalability on Linux clusters with up to 32 nodes, though theoretically there is no architectural limit. RAC enables the utilization of blade farms. The RAC technology enables applications to choose the blades depending on the need for resources. This capability has matured in Oracle Database 10g to the Automatic Storage Management solution. In addition, the introduction of BigFile tablespaces, etc., has just extended the storage limits, which was unimaginable in earlier Oracle releases and with competing database vendors. In fact, BigFile tablespaces can support up to 8 exabytes, which is 8 million terabytes.

Companies with multiple databases on heterogeneous, dedicated hardware can use grid computing to consolidate the hardware resources, improve utilization and efficiency of resources, and manage a larger environment with less administrative overhead.

Oracle's portability across multiple operating systems and hardware platforms can be used as an advantage for supporting heterogeneous grids. These heterogeneous grids will allow use of all existing hardware and major operating systems. Applications developed for one operating system can be run on another without any changes. Over the last few years, flexible storage accessible over storage area networks has become very popular, enabling multiple servers to access the same set of disks in a distributed environment.

Oracle Database 10g has introduced the grid control functionality to have centralized management of databases and application servers running on multiple grids. This feature is useful in small as well as large enterprises, when managing tens to hundreds of database servers. All these databases can be linked on the grid to ensure automated database administration of various tasks and data movements among them.

The Automatic Storage Management solution will be reviewed in this book along with the many other new database features. All these features enable the database administrator to expand the existing databases without any storage limits. This book is more focused on easy database administration of the database and not on installing a grid solution using multiple computers. The reader is advised to consult *Oracle Enterprise Manager Grid Control Installation and Basic Configuration manual- 10g Release 1 (10.1) (Part No. B12012-02)* for more details.

Oracle provides distributed SQL features that make the data seem local regardless of the actual location of the database. Also,

Oracle allows access to non-Oracle databases and any ODBC compliant databases by means of transparent gateways and makes the data appear as it does in Oracle databases. This topic will be explored during a review of transportable tablespaces in a later chapter.

Streams is an Oracle feature that adds to the abilities of grid computing by providing a uniform framework for information sharing, message queuing, replication, data movement, data warehouse loading, etc. Oracle Streams helps the grid to keep one or more databases in sync, even when updates are made only on one database. Streams automatically captures database changes and propagates them to subscribing nodes, applies the changes and resolves any conflicts. Oracle 10g extends Streams support by adding the streams pool in the SGA

In a nutshell, grid computing allows flexible management and deployment of the computing resources of the organization that easily adapts to organizational changes.

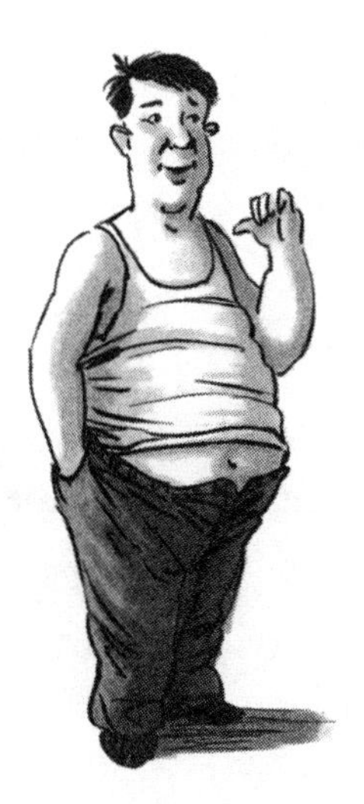

"I'm your new executive DBA manager."

Conclusion

In this chapter, the evolution of Grid technology and Oracle's Grid technology initiatives has been explored. Here are a few of the key points:

- Grid computing relies on the notion that computing can be considered as a utility, which improves the affordability and availability of systems.
- For users of Grid computing, the network appears faster and with more seamless operation of end-user applications.
- Oracle's portability across multiple operating systems and hardware can be used as an advantage for supporting heterogeneous grids.
- Oracle 9i has the key differentiating technologies for building the Grid like Oracle Streams, Oracle transportable tablespaces and Oracle Real Application clusters.
- Oracle Database 10g has come up with a slew of novel changes to its 9i architecture to provide grid technology adaptability.
- Oracle has provided the Grid SDK (Software Development Kit) free of charge to support the grid ethnology initiatives.
- Oracle provides distributed SQL features that make the data seem local to the users instead of its actual location.
- Grid computing allows flexible management and deployment of the computing resources of the organization to easily adapt to organizational changes.

In chapter 2, the focus will be on the major architectural changes made to Oracle Database 10g over the terminal release of Oracle 9i, and how they help to improve the manageability and adaptability of enterprise databases.

Architecture Changes in a Nutshell

CHAPTER 2

Even a child can manage an Oracle10g database!

What's new in the 10g Architecture?

Until Oracle 9i, database administrators used to spend a good deal of time on database monitoring, identifying problem areas and performance bottlenecks and trying to improve the database performance. These tasks focused on the following areas.

Storage management - disk configuration, I/O monitoring, disk sizing, stripes and disk contention.

Space Management – database file sizing, monitor space utilization and chaining.

System Resources – CPU utilization and database buffers.

Application and SQL tuning - statistics, indexes, etc.

Backup and Recovery Management –Backing up database, recovery planning and strategies, testing of recovery methods, MTTR etc.

Oracle Database 10g comes with a slew of novel changes to its architecture over the previous versions. It is this author's opinion that Oracle Database 10g is the most complex and powerful database ever created among competing database technologies. By making the database more sophisticated and powerful, Oracle has automated many of the traditional administrative functions, making Oracle Database 10g suitable even for small businesses. For a small business, it means getting away with handling costly DBA operations in-house, while maintaining the same functionality as in larger businesses.

The irony of Oracle Database 10g is that it is both extremely simple to manage than previous database releases and most other databases on the market and has the most complex engines known to relational database architectures. Oracle Database 10g has automated features which control most of the DBA activities including storage management, memory management and performance management. Plus, the senior database administrator has more than 100 new dynamic performance tables to experiment with to tune the system. Database professionals and organizations enjoy the power of Oracle Database 10g. Some of these notable revisions to the database architecture are briefly reviewed in this chapter.

Next will be an examination of the performance improvement features in this flagship database release.

Summary of Performance Improvement Features

The new and improved performance features in Oracle Database 10g, Release 10.1.0.2, will be introduced next. In the following chapters, they will be explored in greater detail. Here is a summary of the new performance features:

- Automatic diagnosis of performance problems, potential or real, and subsequent correction is a novel feature in Oracle Database 10g. This is done by Automatic Statistics Collection and Retention, Automatic Database Diagnostic Monitor (ADDM), Automatic SQL Tuning, and Automated Space Management (ASM). The Automatic Statistics Collection is handled by the new Automatic Workload Repository (AWR). AWR collects the data, processes it, and maintains performance statistics for use by ADDM and other advisors for problem detection and automatic self-tuning.
- The optimizer statistics collection feature automates the process of getting optimizer statistics for objects. Objects with stale statistics or no statistics are automatically analyzed. Remember that DBAs used to analyze large objects in earlier versions of Oracle databases for up-to-date statistics and performance improvement. Also Rule-based Optimization (RBO) functionality is no longer supported. It still exists in Oracle Database 10g Release 1, but is no longer supported. Oracle supports only the query optimizer, and all applications using Oracle Database 10g (10.1) should make use of that optimizer.
- Automatic Shared Memory Management (ASMM) helps the DBA by simplifying management of System Global Area (SGA) parameters through self-tuning algorithms. ASMM also ensures the optimal utilization of available memory resources and improves overall database performance.

- Automatic Storage Management (ASM) helps with the management of space needed by various objects in the database. Simply add a disk and let Oracle manage the various objects that will use it. Also, it is possible to add and remove storage as needed and improve the I/O on various disks. ASM will be explored in more detail in a later chapter.
- Automatic SQL Tuning features are offered by SQL Tuning Advisor and SQL Access Advisor. More details on these tuning advisors are also given in a later chapter.

The Making of Oracle Database 10g

Oracle Database 10g is the result of research and development of around 200 developers and architects for over 3 years as stated by Oracle press releases. What does it mean to a database administrator or an end user? In simple terms, Oracle has tried to take the pains out of administering the databases by automating as much functionality as possible and by making administration more scalable. During this process, changes have been made to memory structures, resource management, storage handling, data types, improved SQL tuning, faster data loading, faster recovery, just to name a few.

Beware of Oracle developers who speak fluent Klingon.

The following is an examination of some of the key new features of Oracle Database 10g.

Changes to Memory Structures

The major memory structures associated with an Oracle instance are System Global Area (SGA) and Program Global Area (PGA). SGA is shared by all server and background processes, while PGA is exclusive to the server and background processes.

System Global Area (SGA)

System Global Area (SGA) is a group of shared memory structures that contain data and control information for one Oracle database instance. When multiple users are connected to the same instance, the data in the SGA is shared by all users. This is why it is called the Shared Global Area.

An Oracle instance is made of the SGA and Oracle processes. Oracle allocates memory for the SGA when the database instance is started and returns the memory when the instance is shut down. The maximum size of the SGA is determined by *sga_max_size* initialization parameter in the *initInstanceName.ora* file or server parameter (SPFILE) file.

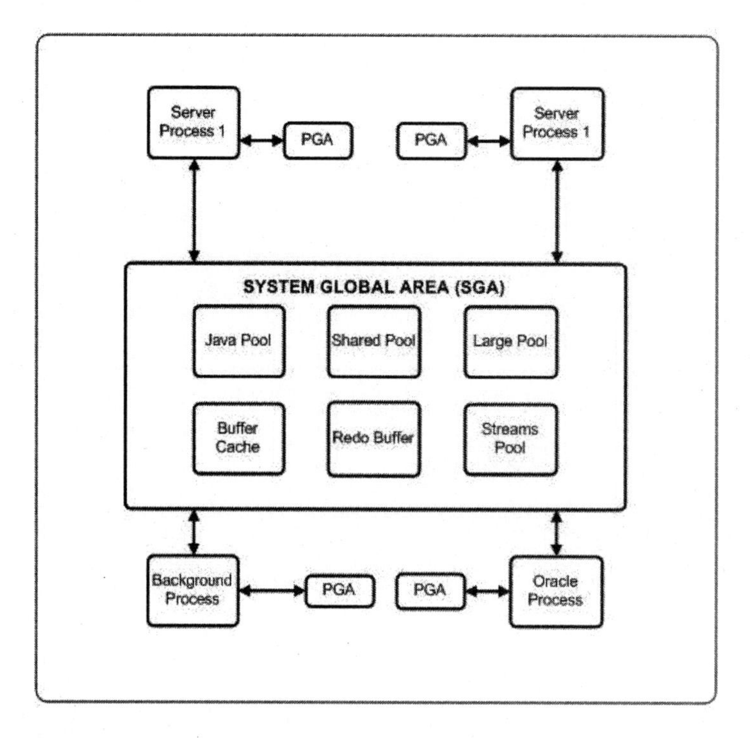

Figure 2.1 *Oracle Database 10g Memory Structures*

The SGA contains the following data structures:

Database Buffer Cache - The Database Buffer Cache is the portion of the SGA that holds copies of data blocks read from data files. All concurrent user processes share access to the database buffer cache. The size of the database buffer cache is set by the initialization parameter file *db_block_size*. Usual values are from 2K to 32K. This standard block size is used by the SYSTEM tablespace.

Redo Log Buffer – Redo Log Buffer is a circular buffer in the SGA that holds information relating to changes made in the database in the form of redo entries. The background process, LGWR, writes the redo log buffer to the active redo log file or group on disk.

Shared Pool – Shared Pool contains the library cache, the dictionary cache, buffers for parallel execution and control structures. It is sized by *shared_pool_size* parameter.

Java Pool – Java Pool is used in memory for all session-specific java code and data within the JVM (Java Virtual Machine). The Java pool advisor provides information on how the size of the Java pool can affect the parse rate.

Large Pool (Optional) – Large Pool is a large optional memory area used to provide memory allocations for memory requests larger than the size of shared pool.

Data Dictionary Cache – Data Dictionary Cache, also known as row cache is a special location in memory to hold data dictionary data. The Data dictionary is a collection of database tables and views containing reference information about the database, its structures, and its users.

Streams pool – Streams pool controls the Streams memory.

Database Buffer Cache – Oracle supports multiple block sizes in a database. The sizes and numbers of non-standard block size buffers are specified by the following parameters.

- *db_2k_cache_size*
- *db_4k_cache_size*
- *db_8k_cache_size*
- *db_16k_cache_size,* and
- *db_32k_cache_size.*

If the cache is large, a request for data is more likely to find the information, resulting in a cache hit.

Other information - The SGA contains general information about the database and the instance, which is accessed by the background processes. This part is called fixed SGA.

All SGA components allocate and deallocate memory in units called granules. The granule size is determined by the total SGA size and the operating system. It is 4 MB if the total SGA is less than 1 GB and 16MB if the SGA is over 1 GB. For 32bit Windows, the granule size is 8MB for a SGA larger than 1 GB.

The size of the SGA is determined by several initialization parameters, of which the following are of higher relevance.

- *db_cache_size* – size of the cache of standard blocks
- *log_buffer* – number of bytes allocated for the redo log buffer
- *shared_pool_size* – size in bytes of the area for shared SQL and PL/SQL
- *large_pool_size* – size of the large pool (default = 0)
- *java_pool_size* – size of the Java Pool.
- *db_nk_cache_size* – size of non-default block size cache

In previous database versions, the DBA had to manually specify different SGA component sizes by setting the above parameters. Oracle Database 10g has the Automatic Shared Memory Management (ASMM) feature to simplify this memory management process. ASMM methods will be explored in a later chapter.

Program Global Area

Program Global Area (PGA) is a memory area that contains data and control information for a server process. Access to the PGA is exclusive to server processes and software code acting on its behalf.

The contents of PGA memory vary depending on how the instance is running, whether the shared server or dedicated server option is in effect. But generally, the PGA memory can be classified into the following areas: Private SQL Area, Cursors and SQL Areas, and Session Memory

Private SQL Area – A Private SQL Area has data on bind information and runtime memory structures. Every session or user that issues an SQL statement has a private SQL area. Many private SQL areas can be associated with the same shared SQL area. The private SQL area of a cursor is divided into the persistent area, which is freed only when the cursor is closed, and the run-time area, which is freed when the execution is terminated.

The actual location of a private SQL area depends on the session's connection. For a session connected through a dedicated server, private SQL areas are located in the server process's PGA. If a session is connected through a shared server, part of the private SQL area is kept in the SGA.

Cursors – A cursor is a handle or name for a private SQL area, which is used as a named resource throughout the execution of the program. The number of private SQL areas that a user process can allocate is limited by *open_cursors* parameter. The default value is 50.

Session memory – Session memory is the memory allocated to hold a session's variables and other information related to the session. For a shared server, the session memory is shared and not private.

This section has reviewed the Oracle memory structures, namely the System Global Area (SGA) and the Program Global Area (PGA) and introduced some of the new features that affect them in Oracle 10g. The next section will introduce some of the new features in Oracle 10g.

Details of New Feature Upgrades

This section will provide an introduction to the major feature upgrades in Oracle Database 10g, compared to Oracle 9i releases.

SYSAUX Tablespace

SYSAUX tablespace provides storage for all non SYS-related tables and indexes that would have otherwise been placed in the SYSTEM tablespace. This is required in all Oracle Database 10g databases and therefore must be created along with new installs or upgrades.

The SYSAUX tablespace is an auxiliary tablespace to the SYSTEM tablespace. Many database components use SYSAUX as their default location to store data. The SYSAUX tablespace is mandatory and is always created along with a new database or database upgrade. Creating any other schema tables in SYSAUX is not recommended.

The SYSAUX tablespace reduces the number of tablespaces that are created by default in the seed database and user-defined database. In a RAC environment with RAW devices, a RAW device is created for every tablespace, which makes RAW device management difficult. By consolidating these tablespaces into the SYSAUX tablespace, the number of RAW devices can be reduced.

The SYSAUX tablespace and its occupants are created when the CREATE DATABASE command is executed in 10g. When a database is upgraded to 10g, the CREATE TABLESPACE command is used, The CREATE TABLESPACE SYSAUX can be called only in a migrate mode.

Ensure there is enough space for the SYSAUX tablespace and note that SYSDBA privilege is needed to create SYSAUX. Attempts to alter the mandatory attributes of the SYSAUX tablespace are not allowed and will result in an error.

After SYSAUX is created, the DBA can monitor the space usage for each occupant by querying the *v$sysaux_occupants* table. This view has the following information about the occupants of the SYSAUX tablespace - occupant's name, occupant description, schema name, move procedure and current space usage. Oracle Enterprise manager has a GUI interface to assist in the relocation of any occupant using too much space in the SYSAUX tablespace. The *wksys.move_wk* procedure can be used to manually move occupants in and out of the tablespace.

Automatic Storage Management

Automatic Storage Management (ASM) is a new database service for efficient management of disk drives with 24/7 availability. It helps keep the DBA from potentially having to manage thousands of database files across multiple database instances by creating disk groups. The disk groups are comprised of disks and the files that reside on them.

ASM will not eliminate any existing database functionalities with file systems or raw devices and Oracle Managed Files (OMF) as in previous versions. With it, the DBA needs to manage a smaller number of disk groups. ASM also serves as a cluster file system for RAC configurations.

BigFile Tablespace

Gone are the days of smaller tablespaces in the range of a few megabytes. Database tables of today are hungry for storage. A BigFile Tablespace (BFT) is a tablespace containing a single, very large data file. With the new addressing scheme in 10g, four billion blocks are permitted in a single data file and file sizes can be from the 8 Terabytes to 128 Terabytes range. To distinguish a regular tablespace from a BFT, a regular tablespace is called a small file tablespace. Oracle Database 10g can be a mixture of small file and BigFile tablespaces.

Rename Tablespace

Another new feature exclusive for Oracle Database 10g is the provision to rename tablespaces. In older versions, you would have to create a new tablespace, copy the contents from the old tablespace and drop the old tablespace. The benefits of this feature are more simplified processing of tablespace migration within a database and ease of transporting a tablespace between two databases. You can rename a tablespace SALES_HIST to SALES_HISTORY using the following command:

```
ALTER TABLESPACE SALES_HIST RENAME TO SALES_HISTORY;
```

The rename tablespace feature applies only to databases with a compatibility level of 10.0.1 and higher. In addition, an offline tablespace, a tablespace with offline data files, and tablespaces owned by SYSTEM or SYSAUX cannot be renamed.

Cross-Platform Transportable Tablespaces

In previous releases of Oracle database, the Transportable Tablespace feature enabled a tablespace to be moved across different Oracle databases running on the same platform architecture. Oracle Database 10g has dramatically changed this functionally to allow the movement of data across different platforms.

This means that in selected heterogeneous platforms or operating system environments, Transportable Tablespaces can be used to move data from one environment to another. Using this feature, a database can be migrated from one platform to another by rebuilding the database catalog and transporting the user tablespaces. By default, the converted files are placed in the new flash recovery area which was also introduced in Oracle Database 10g. A list of fully supported platforms can be found in *v$transportable_platform.*

A new data dictionary view called *v$transportable_platform* lists all supported platforms, along with platform ID and endian format information. The *v$database* dictionary view has two new columns, PLATFORM_ID and PLATFORM_NAME, to support this feature.

```
SQL> desc v$transportable_platform
Name                              Null?          Type
------------------------------ -------- ----------------------
PLATFORM_ID                                     NUMBER
PLATFORM_NAME                                   VARCHAR2(101)
ENDIAN_FORMAT                                   VARCHAR2(14)
```

Endianness is the pattern for byte ordering in native types for data files. There are two main patterns – big endian and little endian. In big endian format, the most significant byte comes first while in little endian, the least significant byte comes first.

For transportable tablespaces to work, the source and target database must use the same character set and national character set. If the platforms are of different endianness, an additional step is needed on either source or target database to match the target endianness format. Here is the information from *v$transportable_platform* on a typical server.

```
PLATFORM_ID        PLATFORM_NAME                        ENDIAN_FORMAT
----------------------------------------------------------------------
          1        Solaris[tm] OE (32-bit)              Big
          2        Solaris[tm] OE (64-bit)              Big
          7        Microsoft Windows IA (32-bit)        Little
         10        Linux IA (32-bit)                    Little
          6        AIX-Based Systems (64-bit)           Big
          3        HP-UX (64-bit)                       Big
          5        HP Tru64 UNIX                        Little
          4        HP-UX IA (64-bit)                    Big
         11        Linux IA (64-bit)                    Little
         15        HP Open VMS                          Little
          8        Microsoft Windows IA (64-bit)        Little
          9        IBM zSeries Based Linux              Big
         13        Linux 64-bit for AMD                 Little
         16        Apple Mac OS                         Big
         12        Microsoft Windows 64-bit for A       Little
```

Automated Memory Management Using AWR and ADDM

Automatic Workload Repository (AWR) provides background services to Oracle Database 10g to collect, maintain, and utilize the statistics for problem detection and self-tuning. The AWR has an in-memory statistics collection facility, which is useful for 10g components to collect statistics. These metrics are stored in memory for performance reasons. The memory version of these statistics is written to disk regularly by a new background process called MMON (Memory Monitor). Oracle captures and retains this historical data without DBA intervention. The historic data can be used for analysis of performance problems that occurred in a certain timeperiod and to do trend analysis.

Automatic Database Diagnostic Monitor (ADDM) is one of the most important advisor features in Oracle Database 10g. It analyzes the system using information collected in AWR, identifies potential and current problems and provides recommendations for fixing these issues. It also invokes other advisors. ADDM does analysis of snapshots taken periodically and writes results to AWR. It uses the wait and time statistics method, which analyzes activities with high time consumption on a priority basis. More details on ADDM can be found in later chapters.

Drop Database Command

With this new release of Oracle database, there is finally a great feature to drop the entire database with a single command. The new DROP DATABASE command deletes all database files, all online log files, control files and the server parameter (spfile) file. This command will not remove archive logs or backups, which have to be deleted manually.

Automated SQL Tuning Features

Oracle Database 10g has provided a handful of new features like Automatic Workload Repository (AWR), Automatic Database Diagnostic Monitor (ADDM), SQL Tuning Advisor and SQLAccess Advisor for tuning the SQL statements or application code. While AWR and ADDM render services to support automatic SQL tuning, SQL Tuning Advisor and SQLAccess Advisor are the actual tuning tools.

SQL Tuning Advisor provides tuning advice for SQL statements without modifying any statement. It takes one or more SQL statements as input and invokes the automatic tuning optimizer to perform SQL tuning without actually modifying any statement. The output is a series of advice or recommendations along with the rationale behind each recommendation and its expected benefits. These recommendations will prompt the user to collect statistics on the affected objects, create new indexes or restructure the statements.

For complex applications and large databases, SQLAccess Advisor comes in very handy. SQLAccess Advisor is a tuning tool that provides advice on indexes, materialized views and materialized view logs for a given work load. It also provides advice on database schema issues and determines optimal data access paths.

For both the tuning tools, a task is created, the Advisor is run which generates recommendations, and the recommendations may or may not be implemented. The recommendations given by these tools can then be accepted or rejected. These Advisor tools are available through Oracle Enterprise Manager 10g (OEM) and from SQL command prompt. More about the SQL tuning Advisor and SQLAccess Advisor will be provided in a later chapter.

Data Pump Utilities

Oracle Database 10g has a new high-speed infrastructure for data and metadata movement called Data Pump. The Data Pump infrastructure provides dramatic improvement in performance over the original export and import utilities. It also provides high-speed data load and unload capability to existing tables. Using a robust proprietary format, platform independent flat files can be moved between multiple servers. It is also possible to use the new network mode to transfer data using database links. Although the commands to Export and Import are similar, they are separate products.

One benefit of Data Pump Export and Import is the ability to detach from a long running job and reattach without affecting the job. Another benefit of Data Pump is remapping of data during the export and import processes. Using Data Pump, the names of source data files, source schema names, and source tablespaces can be changed to different names at the target system. Data Pump also supports fine-grained object selection using the *exclude*, *include* and *content* parameters.

Backup and Recovery – Flashback, RMAN

Flashback query was introduced in Oracle 9i. In Oracle Database 10g, the functionality of the AS OF clause has been expanded from 9i. All Flashback features rely on undo information to recreate a state in the past. The DBA can use the VERSIONS BETWEEN clause to retrieve all versions of the rows that existed between two time points. Flashback Versions Query retrieves all committed occurrences of the rows.

The Flashback Transaction Query is a diagnostic tool to view the changes made to the database at the transaction level. This feature will help to diagnose problems, analyze and audit transactions, and recover from user or application errors. The undo SQL generated by the flashback transaction query can be used to rollback the changes made by a transaction. The Flashback versions Query and Flashback Transaction Query can be used in tandem to determine the appropriate flashback time

The Flashback Table allows the DBA to recover database tables to a specific point in time without restoring from a backup. With this feature, the data in the tables and all associated objects, including indexes, constraints, and triggers, etc., are restored. This statement is executed as a single transaction. All the tables must be flashed back successfully or the entire transaction is rolled back. This is significantly better than media recovery in terms of speed, availability and ease of recoverability.

In Oracle Database 10g, flashback functionality has been extended for the entire database. Using this, a database can be reverted to a past state at a particular point in time. This will help to recover form changes due to user errors or logical data corruptions. It is faster than point in time recovery using backups and redo log files. The database must be mounted in an exclusive state to perform the flashback operation. More details on flashback operations are available in a later chapter.

Globalization Development

Oracle Database 10g provides a Globalization Development Kit (GDK) with comprehensive programming APIs, tools and documentation to aid the design, development and deployment issues with creating global applications. The Oracle NLS definition files, which include language, territory, linguistic sort and character set, have become platform independent. This reduces the need to regenerate new binary files on each platform where developers are using these capabilities. The database also has expanded locale coverage with support for new languages and territories and support for Unicode 3.2.

For a small Oracle shop, the DBA may never need to use these features, but this GDK definitely helps to address any design issues for global applications.

This section has reviewed some of the new features available in the 10g Database upgrade. The next section will focus on upgrades to the Oracle Enterprise Manager.

Changes to Oracle Enterprise Manager

Oracle has vastly improved the Enterprise Manager Console to manage all aspects of the hardware and software environment, including the Grid control. Oracle Enterprise Manager can be invoked from a Web browser, from client installation, or from the database server itself. The Database Control is installed with every Oracle Database 10g system and can be used to monitor and administer single or multiple database instances.

The Enterprise Manager framework monitors the entire Oracle environment and provides detailed system monitoring for timely detection and notification of problems. It makes use of metrics and thresholds for each monitored parameter and uses alerts to provide information. Metrics are units of measurement defined to assess the health of the system being monitored.

Every target has a set of predefined metrics with thresholds associated with them. Thresholds are the boundary values against which the metric values are compared. Once a value reaches its threshold, an alert is generated. Alerts are also generated when a significant change is noted by clearing of a previous alert, change in availability of a monitored service, or when a specific error condition or database action occurs.

The Enterprise Manager provides aggregate information of all monitored targets and collects aggregate performance and availability data over time. Metrics can be compared to determine trends in performance across various subsets of data.

Since this chapter is not meant to be a detailed explanation of all of the Enterprise Manager features, readers are requested to refer to the *Enterprise Manager Concepts* guide and *Enterprise Manager Advanced Configuration* guide for more details. Installation and setup of Oracle Enterprise Manager will be reviewed in the next chapter.

Conclusion

This chapter has reviewed the major architectural changes including performance improvement, storage management, space management, system resources, application tuning and backup and recovery management on Oracle 10g. The topics included:

- Automatic diagnosis of performance problems and correction being facilitated by ADDM and AWR.
- Rule-based optimization (RBO) being de-supported.
- SYSAUX tablespace providing storage to all non SYS-related objects that would have been placed in the SYSTEM tablespace.
- Automatic Storage Management (ASM) providing efficient management of disk drives.
- Cross-platform transportable tablespaces enabling the DBA to migrate tablespaces across different platforms.
- Automatic SQL Tuning being done by SQL Tuning Advisor and SQLAccess Advisor.
- Data Pump utilities providing a high speed infrastructure for data and metadata movement unheard of using export/import utilities.
- Flashback functionality being extended to the database level.
- Oracle Enterprise Manager managing all hardware and software environments including Grid control.

With a glimpse of all the new features of Oracle Database 10g in mind, the next step will be reviewing the installation process for a database.

Installation and Database Creation

CHAPTER 3

Installing Oracle used to be a fight.

Setup Oracle Database 10g

In this chapter, the installation of Oracle software and a starter database using Oracle Universal Installer OUI will be examined. Readers are also requested to refer to the appropriate reference platform-dependent manuals for more details. Oracle Universal Installer (OUI) is the Graphical User Interface (GUI) tool that allows installation and removal of the software on appropriate platforms.

Oracle Database 10g Prerequisites

Oracle Universal Installer (OUI) checks the environment to verify that it meets the minimum requirements for successful installation. This early analysis for potential problems with the system setup reduces any chances of problems during the installation process.

OUI performs all pre-requisite checks defined for the installation process before installing any software. These checks include OUI-specific verifications and those defined for a specific product for the particular operating system on which OUI runs. All pre-requisite check parameters must be defined in the *oraparam.ini* file or another user-defined *.ini* file. All results are logged in the *installActions<timestamp>.log* file.

OUI does the pre-requisite checking in one of the following three ways:

- Automatically when the user runs the OUI executable during an installation,
- Silent Mode, when checks are run and managed from the command line for a silent installation, and
- Standalone when checks are run without completing an installation.

For silent installations, OUI performs as many pre-requisite checks as possible, alerts all errors to the DBA and provides the location of the *installActions<timestamp>.log file* before exiting the installation.

A Word on Silent Installation

A silent installation runs in the background and does not require any inputs from the DBA. The interactive dialogs normally seen by the DBA are not displayed. Instead of prompting the DBA to select a series of installation options, OUI installs the software using a pre-defined set of options stored in a response file or passed on the command line.

A response file is a specifications file with necessary installation information which would normally be provided by the DBA through the OUI user interface during an interactive installation session. Each answer is stored as a value for a variable identified in the response file. The response file template for the database installation can be found in the stage directory (on CD-ROM) under the *<root of CD>/response* directory as follows:

```
<Products.xml_Location>/Response/<product>.<installtype>.rsp
```

The silent install method applies only to the base release of the database software. It cannot be used for already patched software. Silent installation will not be reviewed here as it is beyond the scope of this book. In addition, silent installation is not recommended for installations using ASM.

Continuing the review of the installation prerequisites, necessary inputs to the checking process are listed in the *prerequisite.xml* file located in the *oraInventory/logs* directory. After the checker is run, its results, along with the pre-defined inputs, are written to the *prerequisite_results.xml* file in the same location. The *prerequisite_results.xml* file can be reused as an input file for later executions of the checker process.

Regardless of the platform being used, minimum system requirements exist:

- A minimum of 512 MB of memory
- Sufficient paging Space and Disk space
- Operating system with up-to-date service packs or patches

- Correct file system format

The installer software will adjust any operating system variables needed for the Oracle database server. The OUI will provide guidance through a series of questionnaires and accept responses on software installation and database creation. The following questions apply to all the platforms.

What Database Product Do You Want to Install?

Oracle Enterprise Edition – Oracle's full featured database product with all bells and whistles for high-end applications.

Oracle Standard Edition - A scaled down, less expensive version of the enterprise edition for departmental level applications.

Custom Install - This choice allows for the customization of the Enterprise edition installation by electing to install or prevent installation of certain components.

Figure 3.1 displays an image of the Select Installation Type screen.

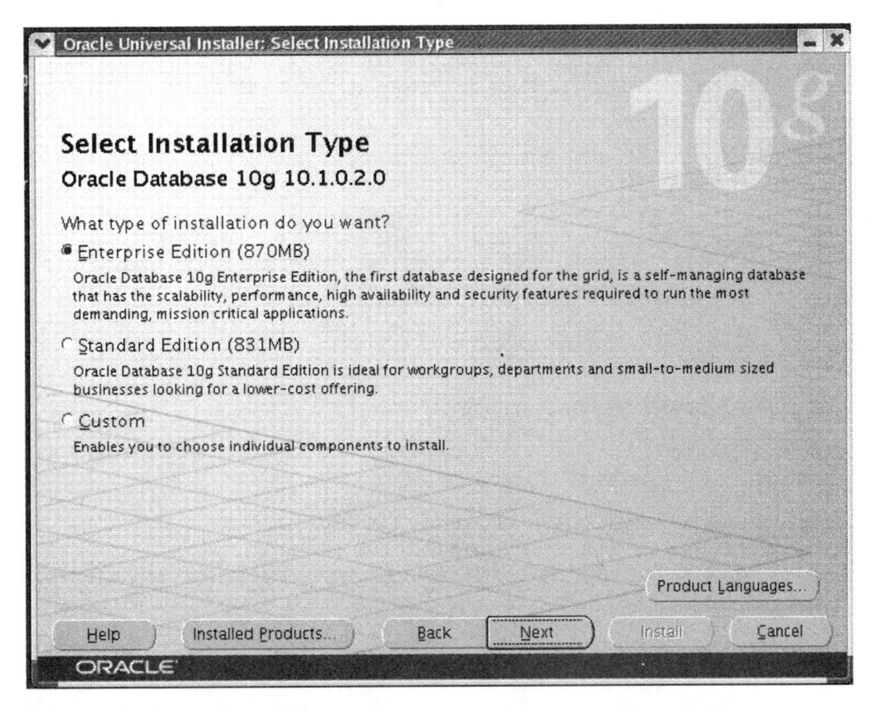

Figure 3.1 *Oracle Universal Installer – Select Installation Type*

Do You Want a Starter Database along with Oracle Software?

For a starter database, the installer automatically launches the Database Configuration Assistant (DBCA) at the end of installation. To have Oracle create a pre-configured database, choose among the following database types:

- General Purpose
- Transaction Processing
- Data Warehouse
- Choose Advanced install for creating a custom database.

The Select Database Configuration screen is displayed in Figure 3.2

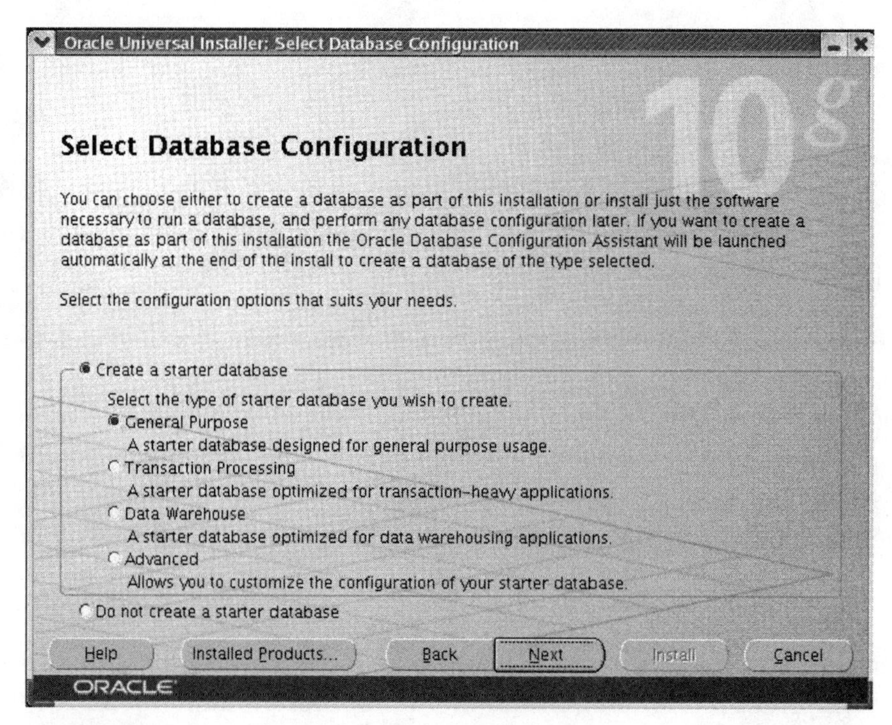

Figure 3.2 *OUI – Select Database Configuration*

Installing a database at this time is not required. The Database Configuration Assistant (DBCA) can be invoked later in order to complete the process. More details on using DBCA will be given later in this chapter. Figure 3.2 displays the Select Database Configuration screen without the Create a starter database option selected.

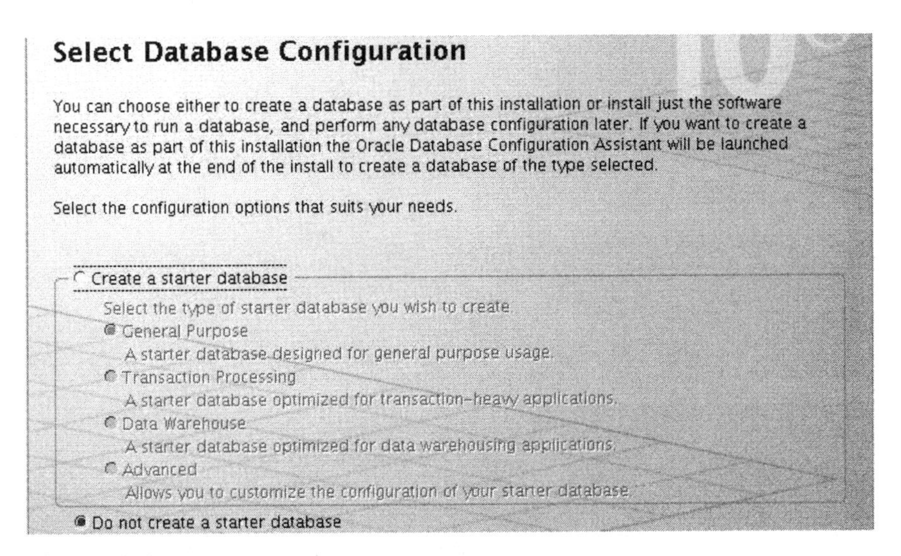

Figure 3.3 *OUI – Select Database Configuration*

What Database Product Do You Want to Install?

Database configuration options are Global Database Name, Oracle System Identifier (SID) and sample schemas. The Global Database Name is the full name of the database, which distinguishes it from other databases. For example, TEST10G.US.ASCENTIKA.COM. In this example, the database name is TEST10G, and the database domain name is US.ASCENTIKA.COM. The database name and database domain name when joined together will make up the global database name.

Oracle recommends the use of example schemas for testing examples in their documentation. The author advises using them only if there is not any other database ready for testing.

During the install, there will be prompts for passwords for preloaded database schemas like SYS and SYSTEM, which enable administration of the database.

It's not a good idea to allow your Systems Administrators to install Oracle.

What Are the Database Storage Options?

A typical Oracle database consists of datafiles which store user data, database metadata, control files with information required to run and recover the database, and logfiles, etc.. In Oracle Database 10g, there are 3 choices for the storage sub system:

- File System that creates database files managed by the Operating system's file system. Oracle will create and manage these files in directories specified by the DBA.
- Raw Devices, which enable management of storage devices outside the operating system with unformatted physical disk space. This is preferred for Oracle Real Application Clusters (RAC). This method is not explained in detail here as it is not widely used for general database applications. For more details, please refer to Oracle Documentation.
- Automatic Storage Management (ASM), which is a new functionality to define a pool of storage or disk group in which Oracle Database 10g automatically manages database file placements and naming. This option simplifies file management, database administration and improves

performance in large environments. Automatic Storage Management requires a separate database instance to configure and manage disks. All disk management techniques like mirroring and striping are handled automatically by ASM.

For the installation reviewed in this chapter, the default selection of File System was chosen. The author recommends this method as ASM managed files can be added to the database at a later stage. Use ASM files only if comfortable with doing disk management commands as root or when help can be obtained to accomplish those tasks. Almost all companies are likely to have both File System managed and ASM managed files in their databases for a foreseeable future.

Using the ASM file method will be reviewed briefly in the DBCA section of this chapter and examined in more detail in Chapter 5. Figure 3.4 displays an image of the Storage Options screen with the File System option selected.

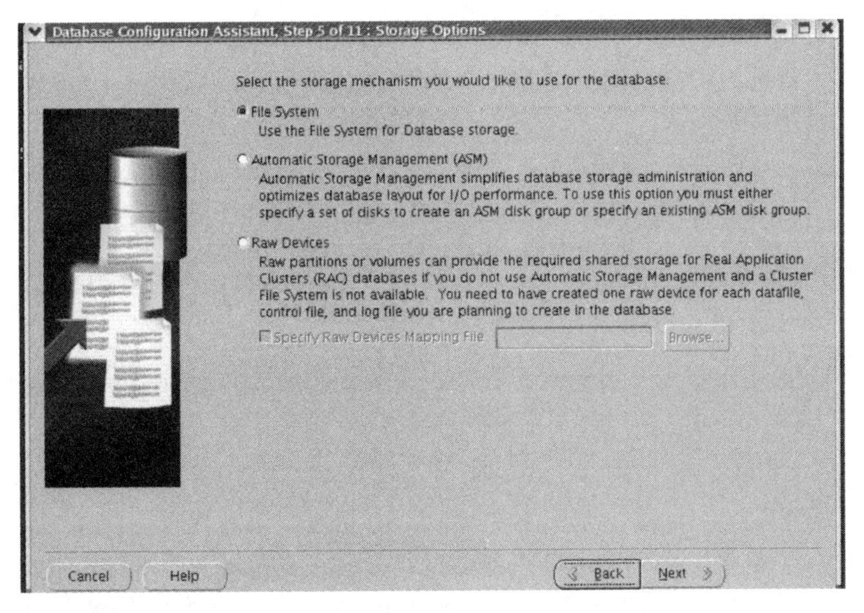

Figure 3.4 - *Oracle Universal Installer – Storage Options*

What are The Database Management Options?

Oracle will prompt for whether to manage databases centrally or locally. The central deployment mode allows for management of multiple databases and application servers from a single console by using a special agent on the database machine. The local deployment mode manages only a single database instance.

Local deployment mode will be used throughout this book for novice users. Experienced DBAs who have more than one database to manage can choose the central deployment mode.

Installation of Oracle Software and Database

It is a good idea to refer to the specific operating system installation manual from Oracle or to online help while doing an install. Refer to documentation to set up users, groups and privileges for Oracle installation accounts. Seek the help of the system administrator if required.

1. Log on as a member of the administrative group, who has permissions to run the software.
2. Insert the distribution CD for the database into the CD drive. If using downloaded software, go to the appropriate Install directory under Disk1 and click or run the installer program. It will be necessary to mount the CD in non-Windows environments and set the DISPLAY.
3. The Oracle Universal Installer Welcome page appears. Select Next to begin installation.

For first time installs on UNIX and Linux, the following steps are needed:

1. Specify Inventory Directory – a directory for installation files and OS group with write permissions to that directory. This is

different from ORACLE_HOME, discussed later. Select Next to continue

2. A dialog page appears asking that *oraInst.sh* be run as root in a separate window. Run this and return to OUI page. Select Continue.

3. Specify File Locations is the next page where the Oracle Home name and directory path to install the software are entered. If there is already an existing installation on the server, choose a different name and path for the new installation. Select Continue.

4. Select Enterprise Edition or Standard Edition or Custom Install. Select Continue.

5. Select the type of pre-configured database to be installed – General Purpose or Transaction Processing or Data Warehouse. Do not choose Advanced. Select Continue.

6. Specify that a starter database is desired – or it will be necessary to run DBCA again after the installation is completed.

7. On the following screens, specify database choices for the installation - Global database name and SID, database character set (choose default) and database management choices.

8. For database management, choose Use Database Control for Database Management.

9. Choose Database Storage as discussed before.

10. Make selections for backup and recovery options - Enable automatic backups into a recovery area.

11. Set passwords for SYS and SYSTEM accounts.

12. Once the summary page is presented, click Install to start the installation. A progress bar will appear to track the installation process.
13. A dialog page appears in UNIX/Linux asking that *root.sh* be run in a separate window. When it finishes, choose Continue in OUI.
14. At the end of the install, the Configuration page appears. Allow the tools to install and Start configuring the network, netservice listener process, create database and management tools. Click Next.
15. When the database is created, an information page lists details about the database. Review the list. Click Password Management to unlock or change passwords on database accounts.
16. In the password management page, lock or unlock accounts and assign new password to unlocked accounts as needed.
17. A final End of Installation page appears with information on Web application port numbers.

Now that database installation is complete, use Enterprise Manger or a Web browser to connect to the database. At the prompt for user name and password, enter SYS and its password.

Database Configuration Assistant (DBCA)

If the decision was made not to choose the default database install, or if additional databases to work with are desired, use DBCA. DBCA can also be used to delete a database, add options to an existing database or manage templates. For assistance, please refer to an installation manual for a detailed description as this chapter is limited to essentials only.

To use DBCA in a Unix/Linux environment, type *dbca* at command prompt. DBCA is typically found in $ORACLE_HOME/bin.

For a Windows environment, from Programs, Oracle-home name, choose Configuration and Migration Tools and select Database Configuration Assistant. The Database Configuration Assistant window is displayed in Figure 3.5.

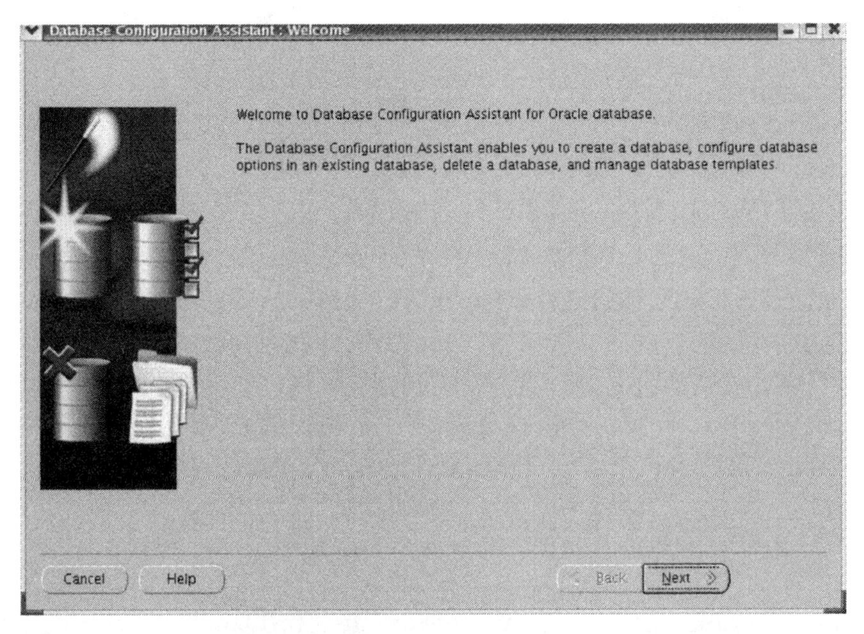

Figure 3.5 *Database Configuration Assistant – Welcome Screen*

Using DBCA to Create a Database

DBCA will provide a series of options like creating a database, deleting a database, etc. Choose Create a Database to begin the wizard that helps to create and configure the database. There will be a series of prompts for the database on the following topics:

- Database Templates
- Database Identification

- Management Options
- Database Credentials
- Storage Options
- Database File Options
- Recovery Configuration
- Database Content
- Initialization Parameters
- Database Storage
- Creation Options

Most of the prompts have a default setting. To accept all default parameters, click Finish at any step.

Database Templates

This prompt enables the selection of the type of database to create. By default, there are templates for Data Warehouse, General Purpose and Transaction Processing. These templates have settings optimized for workload. Click Show Details to see the configuration of each type of database.

For Complex environments, select Custom Database option. The interview for this option is much more extensive and subsequently it takes longer to create the database.

Database Identification

Database configuration options are Global Database Name, Oracle System Identifier (SID) and sample schemas. Enter the Global Database Name and the database domain name.

Management Options

This page allows the management of the database with Oracle Enterprise Manager (OEM). OEM provides web based management tools for individual databases as well as centralized management tools for entire Oracle environment. To use OEM, select Configure the Database with Enterprise Manager.

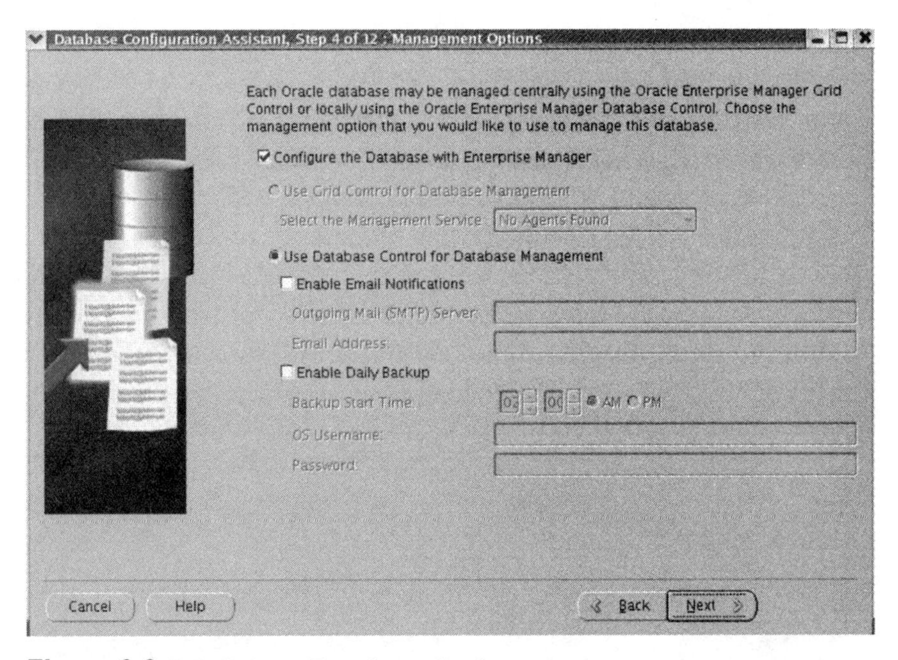

Figure 3.6 *DBCA – Database Configuration*

If Oracle Management Agent exists on the host computer, select Use GridControl for Database Management. Otherwise, select Use Database control for Database Management. In this option, enable e-mail Notifications and Enable Daily Backup can be set up.

Database Credentials

Here the passwords for accounts like SYS and SYSTEM, DBSNMP, and SYSMAN are specified. Although it is not recommended, to use the same password for all accounts, specify Use the Same Password for All Accounts.

Storage Options

In Oracle Database 10g, there are three choices for the storage sub system - File System, Raw Devices, or Automatic Storage Management (ASM). Make that choice here. Figure 3.7 displays the Storage Options screen. Setting up an ASM instance will be examined in more detail in a later chapter, and more details on possible problems with setting up ASM files in Linux will be provided later in this chapter. If the ASM option is chosen, the ASM managed disk(s) will appear in the selection to be added for storage.

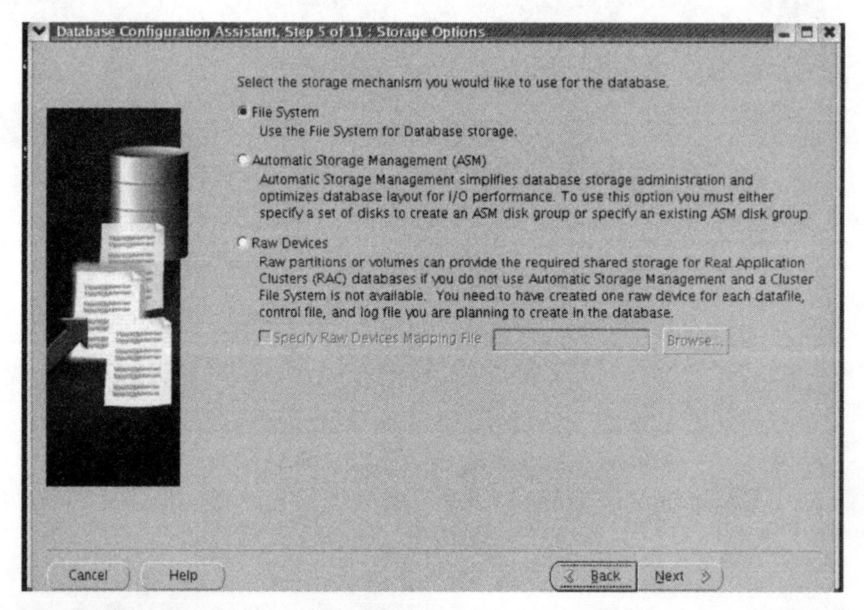

Figure 3.7 *DBCA – Storage Options*

Database File Options

Here the Oracle Home and directory path to install the Oracle software is specified. Choose one of the following options:

- Use Database File Locations from Template
- Use Common Location for All Database Files, or
- Use Oracle Managed Files.

For the first 2 choices, it will be necessary to make modifications to database file names and locations later. For Oracle Managed Files, specify a default location called database area for all files. Oracle automatically creates and deletes files from this location as required.

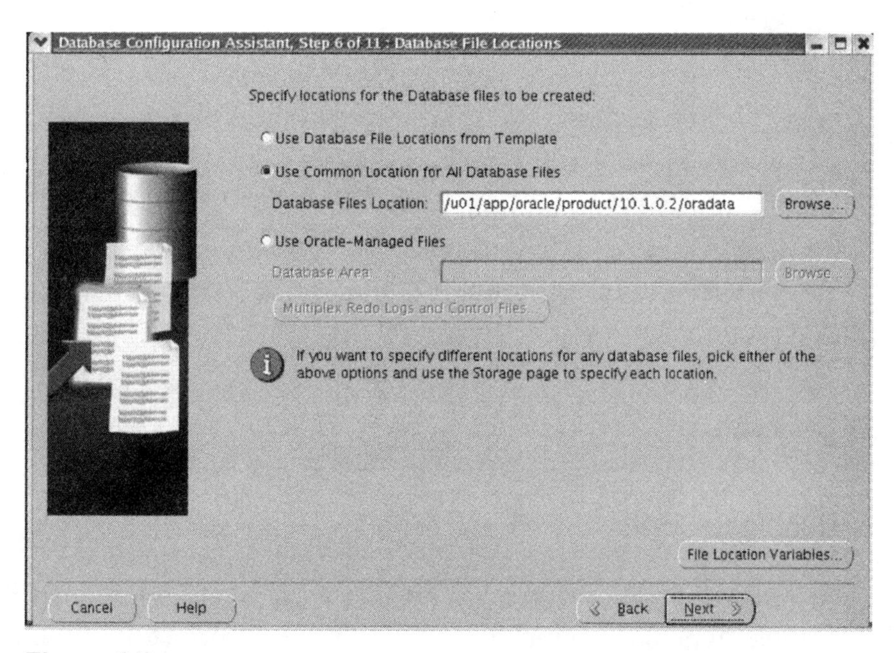

Figure 3.8 *DBCA – Database File Locations*

Recovery Configuration

When a new database is created be sure to plan for its recovery in case of any system failures. The Recovery Configuration screen is displayed in Figure 3.9. Use this page to specify Flash Recovery Area and also Enable Archiving. For Flash Recovery Area, specify the directory location and its size. If archiving is not enabled at this stage, it can be enabled later.

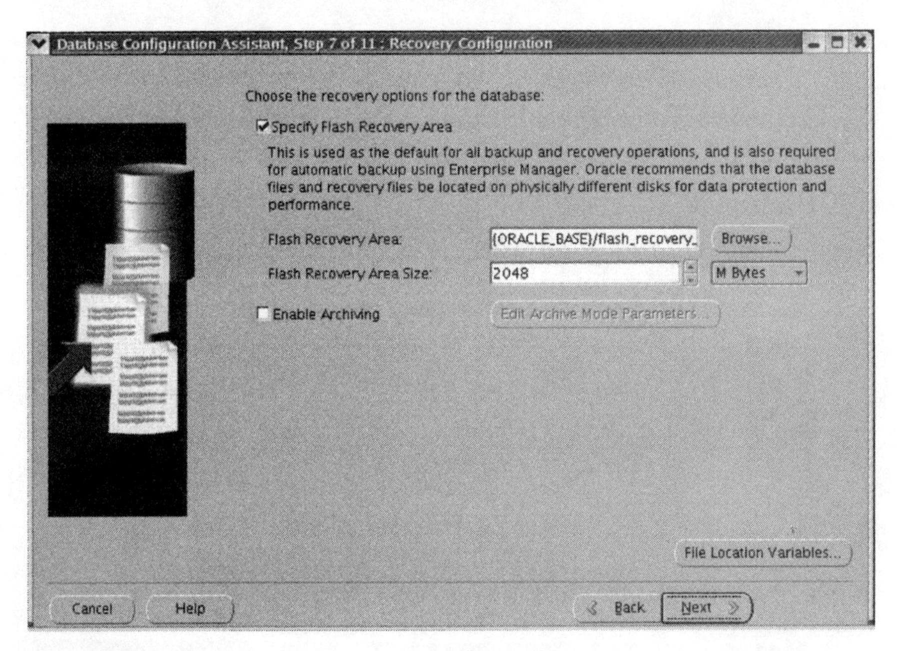

Figure 3.9 *DBCA – Recovery Configuration*

Database Content

In order to add sample schemas to the database, select the Sample Schemas option on the Sample Schemas property page. To specify scripts to be run, check Run the following scripts on the Custom Scripts property page. The default is No scripts to run.

Initialization Parameters

These parameters fall into the following categories:

- Memory
- Sizing
- Character Sets, and
- Connection Mode.

Use the Memory page to set the initialization parameters that control the memory usage of the database. Typical allots memory as a percentage of the total available physical memory and Custom dictates the values. The Initialization Parameters screen is displayed in Figure 3.10.

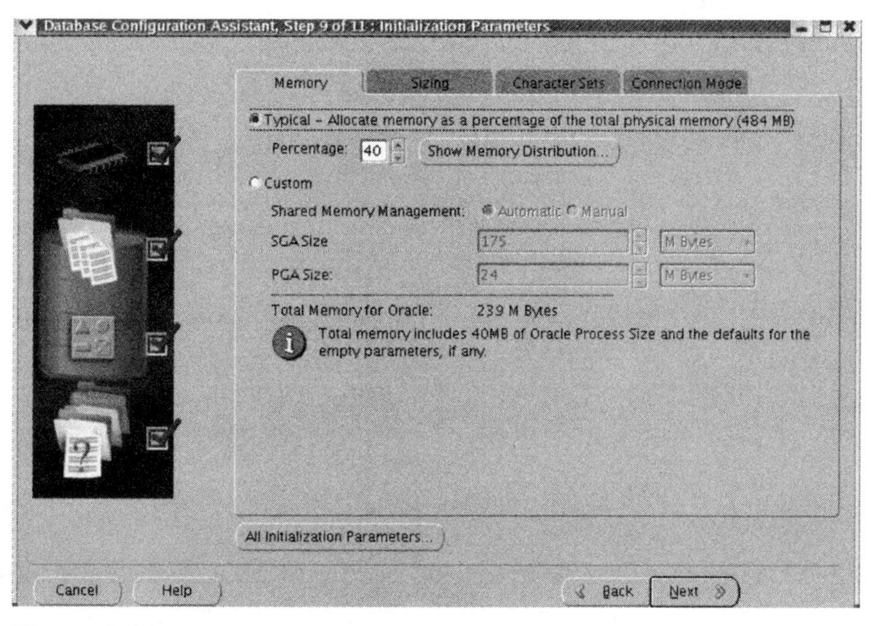

Figure 3.10 *DBCA – Initialization Parameters*

If selecting Custom, specify Automatic to allocate specific amounts to SGA and PGA or Manual to enter specific values for each SGA component. Refer to Figure 3.11 for an example.

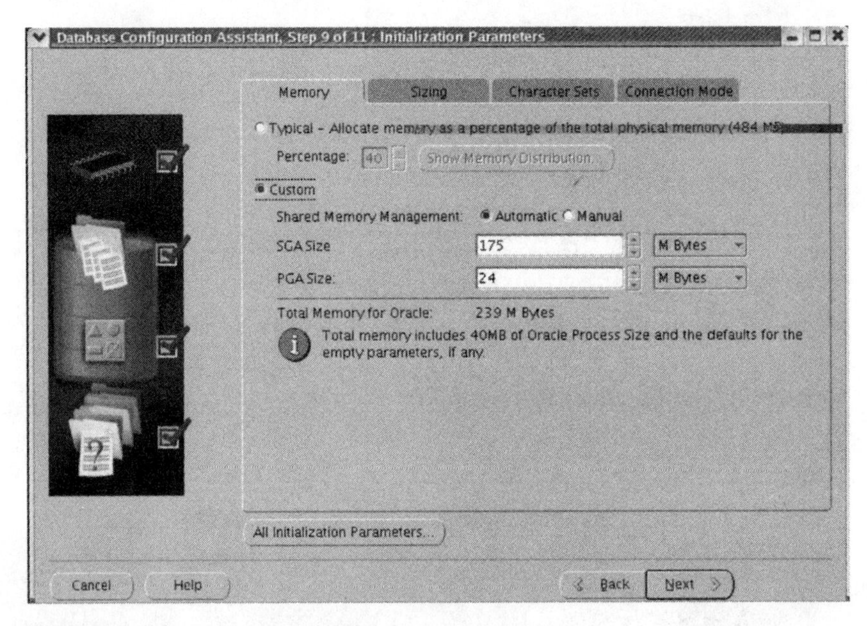

Figure 3.11 *DBCA – Initialization Parameters*

When sizing, specify the smallest block size (8K recommended) and the maximum number of operating system user processes that can connect simultaneously to the database (150 by default).

For Character Sets, select a character set that determines what languages can be represented in the database. Use the default if the only language that needs to be supported is the language of the operating system. Use Unicode (AL32UTF8) to support multiple languages for database users and applications.

To use any other non-default character sets used by the operating system, select the option Choose from the list of character sets. Select the National Character Set here or choose the default.

Similarly, select the default values from Default Language and Default Data Format according to location.

Database Storage

This tree listing shows the storage structure of the database. Objects can be Created or Deleted here. If one of the pre-configured templates is chosen, control files, datafiles or rollback segments cannot be added or removed.

Creation Options

At this time, you can save the database definition to a template or create the database or select both. Figure 3.12 displays the Confirmation screen.

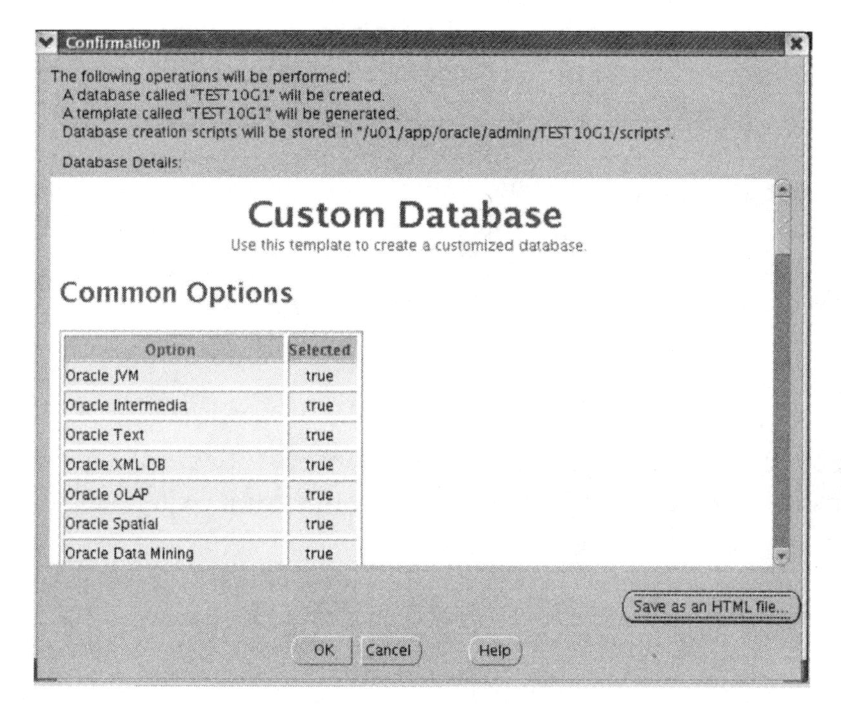

Figure 3.12 *Database Configuration Assistant – Confirmation*

Overview of Database Upgrade Assistant

If planning to upgrade an existing database, Oracle provides a tool called Database Upgrade Assistant (DBUA). It interactively steps through the upgrade process and configures the database for the new Oracle Database 10g release.

It can be invoked by *dbua* from the Unix/Linux prompts like *dbca*, or from Database Migration Assistant under Configuration and Migration Tools in a Windows environment. Please refer to *Oracle Database Upgrade Guide* for more details.

How to Set Up and Use OEM

Enterprise Manager is installed with a default super administrator account called SYSMAN. During the installation, there will be a prompt to provide a password for SYSMAN. This is needed for initial login to Enterprise Manager. SYSMAN account cannot be deleted or renamed.

Oracle recommends creation of an administrator account using the SYSMAN account for each administrator (DBA) on the system. This will help control access for every DBA working on the system in various roles and responsibilities.

The installation script for Enterprise Manager is located in the $ORACLE_HOME/bin directory in UNIX and Linux and is known as *emca.* It presents a series of questions on hostname, instance name, etc. as follows. These screens may vary depending on the operating system being used.

```
STARTED EMCA at Wed Feb 04 09:31:06 CST 2004

Enter the following information about the database to be configured
Listener port number: 1521
Database SID: TEST10G
Service name: TEST10G
Email address for notification:
```

```
Email gateway for notification:
Password for dbsnmp:
Password for sysman:
Password for sys:
Password for sys:
-----------------------------------------------------------------
You have specified the following settings
Database ORACLE_HOME
............/u01/app/oracle/product/10.1.0.2/db2
Enterprise Manager ORACLE_HOME
........../u01/app/oracle/product/10.1.0.2/db3
Database host name ................linuxhost
Listener port number ................ 1521
Database SID ................ TEST10G
Service name ................ TEST10G

Email address for notification ...............
Email gateway for notification ...............

-----------------------------------------------------------------
Do you wish to continue? [yes/no]: yes
...........
...........
..........
...........

... ...  <Your actual screen results may vary. The dotted lines
indicate the execution of various scripts in the process.>........

...........
...........
...........

The Enterprise Manager URL is: http://linuxhost:5500/em
```

Check the status of the OEM control by using the command:

```
$ emctl status dbconsole
```

Refer to the example in Figure 3.12.

```
[oracle@linuxhost bin]$ ./emctl status dbconsole
TZ set to US/Central
Oracle Enterprise Manager 10g Database Control Release 10.1.0.2.0
Copyright (c) 1996, 2004 Oracle Corporation.  All rights reserved.
http://linuxhost:5500/em/console/aboutApplication
Oracle Enterprise Manager 10g is not running.
-----------------------------------------------------------------
Logs are generated in directory /u01/app/oracle/product/10.1.0.2/linuxhost_TEST1
0G/sysman/log
```

Figure 3.12 *emctl status dbconsole*

Type *emctl* and Oracle will provide all options available with the command. Refer to Figure 3.13 for an example listing of *emctl* options.

```
[oracle@linuxhost bin]$ emctl
TZ set to US/Central
Oracle Enterprise Manager 10g Database Control Release 10.1.0.2.0
Copyright (c) 1996, 2004 Oracle Corporation.  All rights reserved.
Invalid arguments

Unknown command option
Usage::
   Oracle Enterprise Manager 10g Database Control commands:
       emctl start| stop| status dbconsole
       emctl secure <options>

       emctl set ssl test|off|on em
       emctl set ldap <host> <port> <user dn> <user pwd> <context dn>
emctl blackout options can be listed by typing "emctl blackout"
emctl config options can be listed by typing "emctl config"
emctl secure options can be listed by typing "emctl secure"
emctl ilint  options can be listed by typing "emctl ilint"
emctl deploy  options can be listed by typing "emctl deploy"
```

Figure 3.13 *emctl options*

To start the console, use the following command:

```
$ emctl start dbconsole
```

The status information shown in Figure 3.14 will be generated.

```
[oracle@linuxhost bin]$ ./emctl start dbconsole
TZ set to US/Central
Oracle Enterprise Manager 10g Database Control Release 10.1.0.2.0
Copyright (c) 1996, 2004 Oracle Corporation.  All rights reserved.
http://linuxhost:5500/em/console/aboutApplication
Starting Oracle Enterprise Manager 10g Database Control ....... started.
------------------------------------------------------------------
Logs are generated in directory /u01/app/oracle/product/10.1.0.2/linuxhost_TEST1
OG/sysman/log
```

Figure 3.14 *emctl status dbconsole*

Once the installation is complete, log onto it from the web interface is using UNIX, Linux, or Windows or use the OEM interface from Windows, Start Programs –Oracle Enterprise Manager Console environment. For those who are using the web browser version of OEM, type in the following address - http://<localhost>:port_numer/em

On the test server used in these examples, it is http://linuxhost:5500/em.

The port number can be changed by modifying *$ORACLE_HOME/install/portlist.ini.* This will invoke the OEM introductory screen, where the username and password are required to access the database. Refer to Figure 3.15.

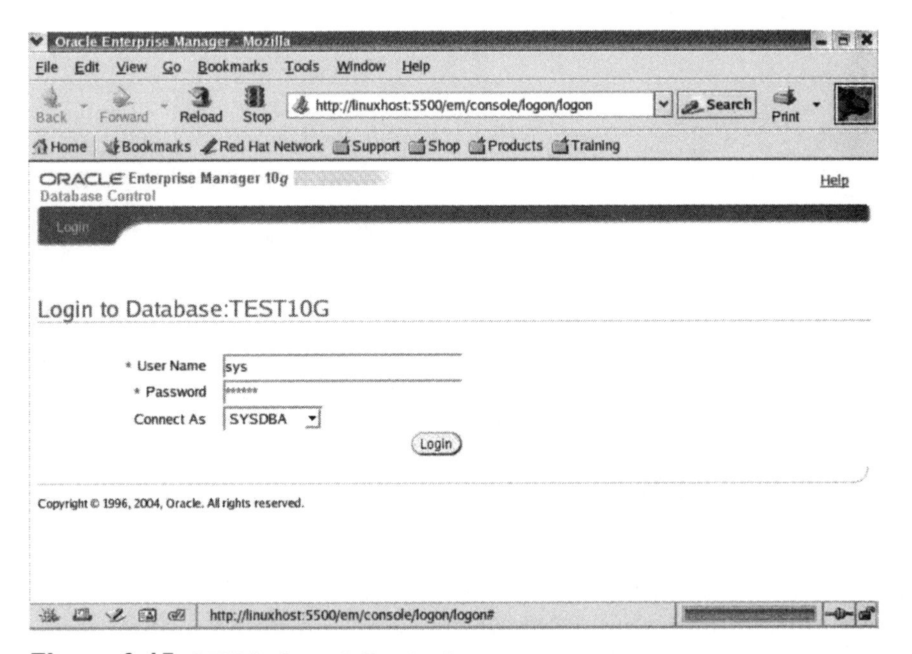

Figure 3.15 *OEM Console Login Screen*

Once the username and password are entered, the web interface will display the instance summary, which provides guidance through the rest of the instance administration tasks. The new look and feel of OEM provides a feature rich display that allows a DBA to drill down and scroll down to detailed reports on any metric. The default Home screen is shown in Figure 3.16.

Since the screen is long and has to be scrolled down to be viewed completely, it is presented here in multiple parts.

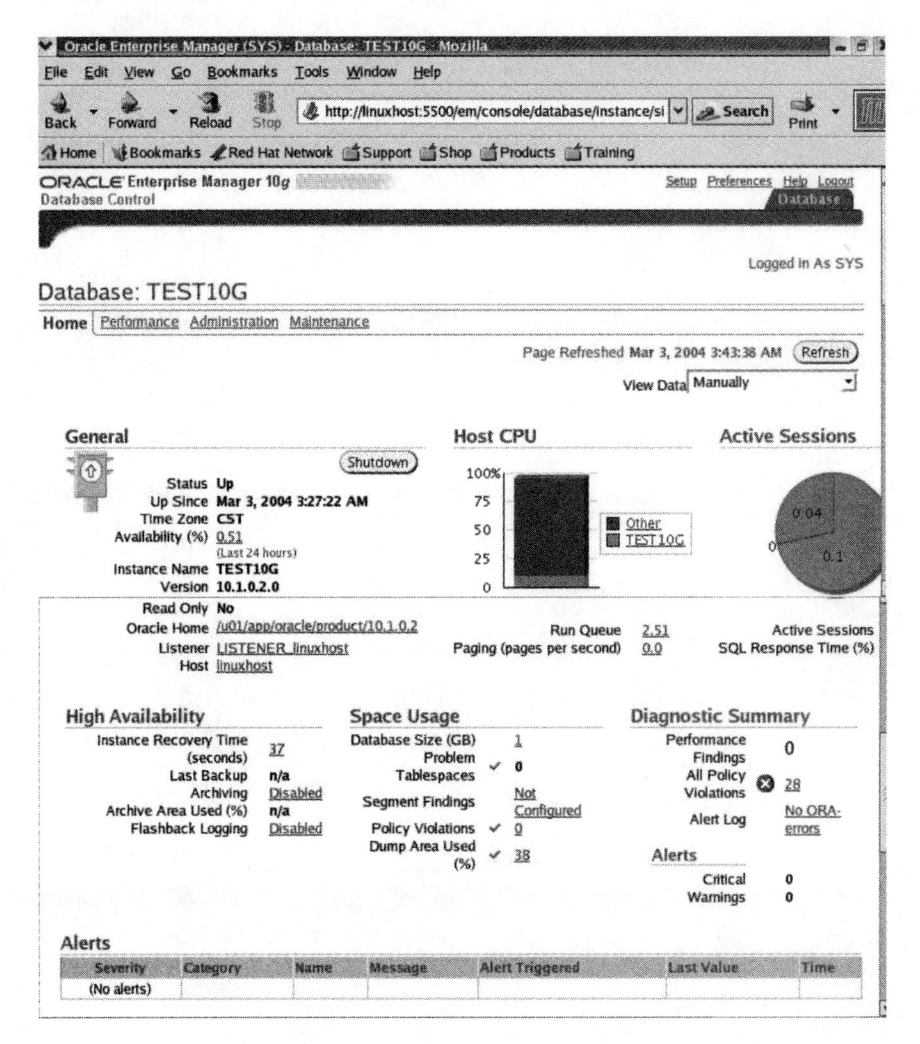

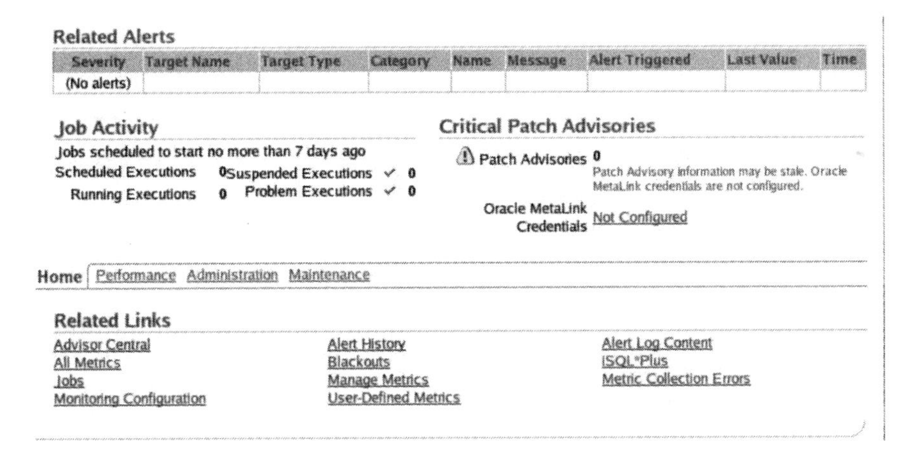

Figure 3.16 *OEM Home*

Additional screens are for Performance, Administration and Maintenance, and are similar to the images shown in the following Figures. Displays will differ depending on the instance configuration and number of databases being monitored.

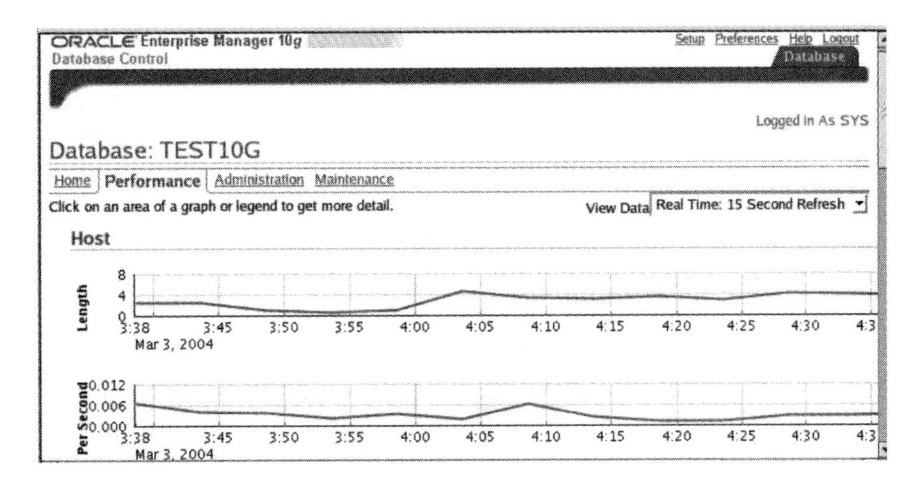

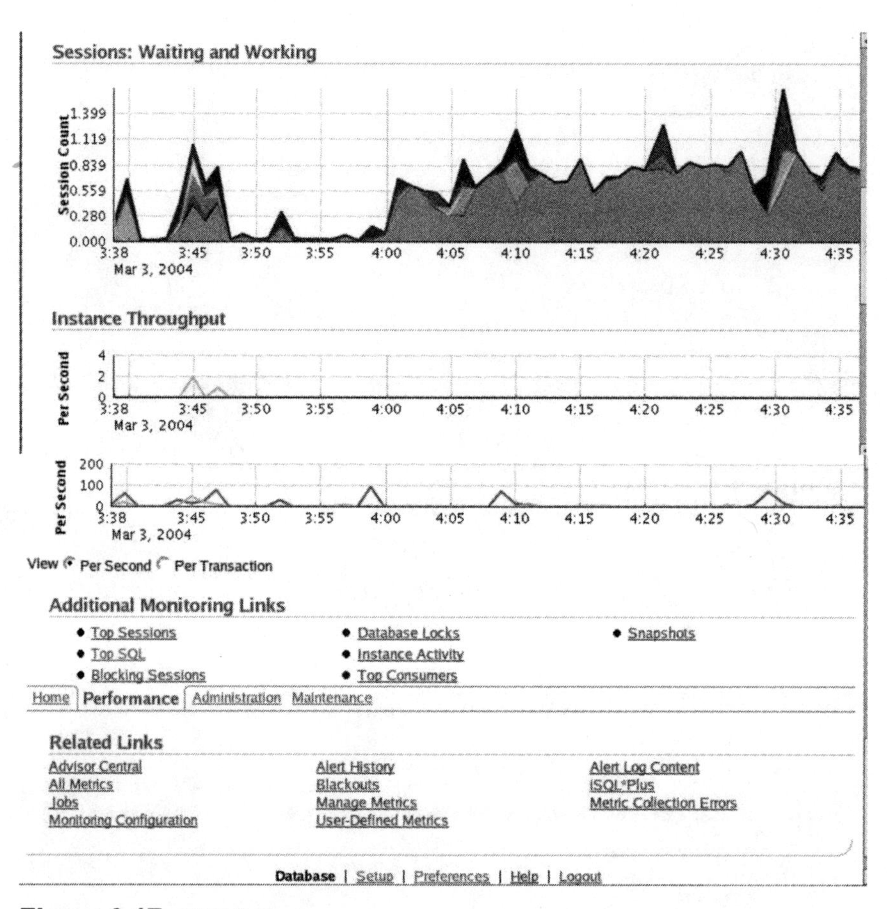

Figure 3.17 *OEM Performance*

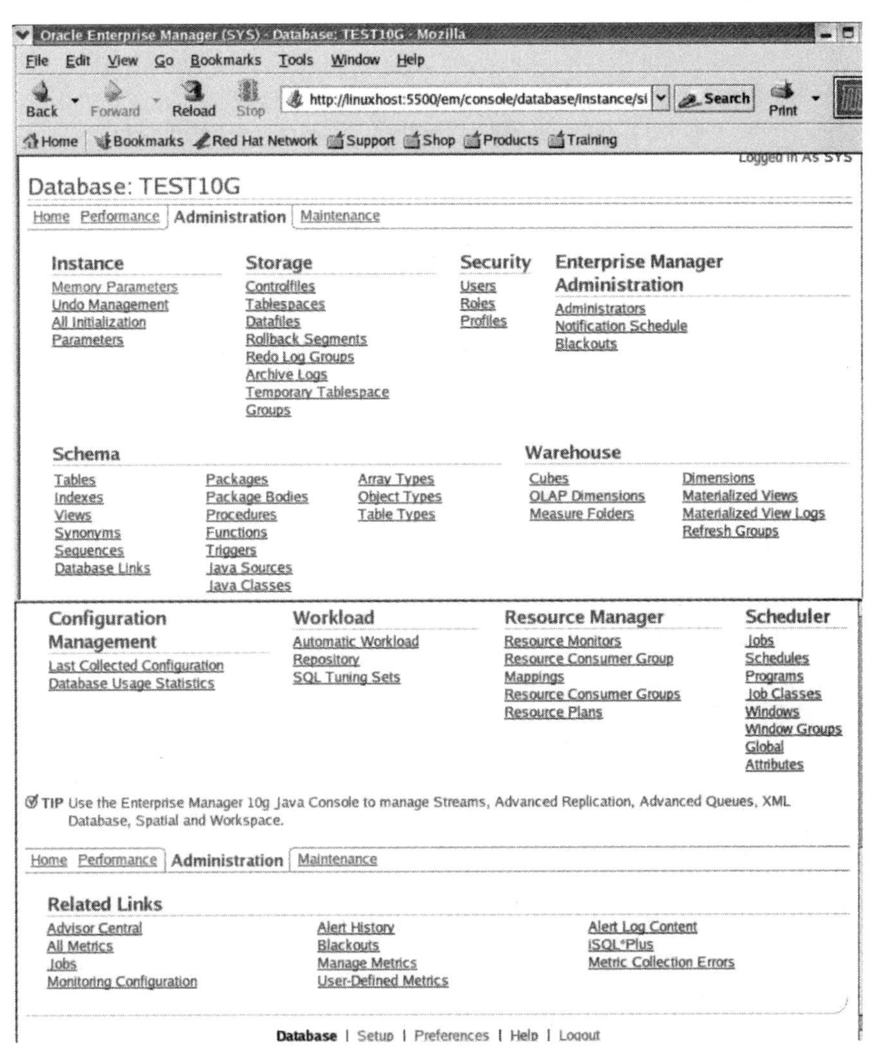

Figure 3.18 *OEM Administration*

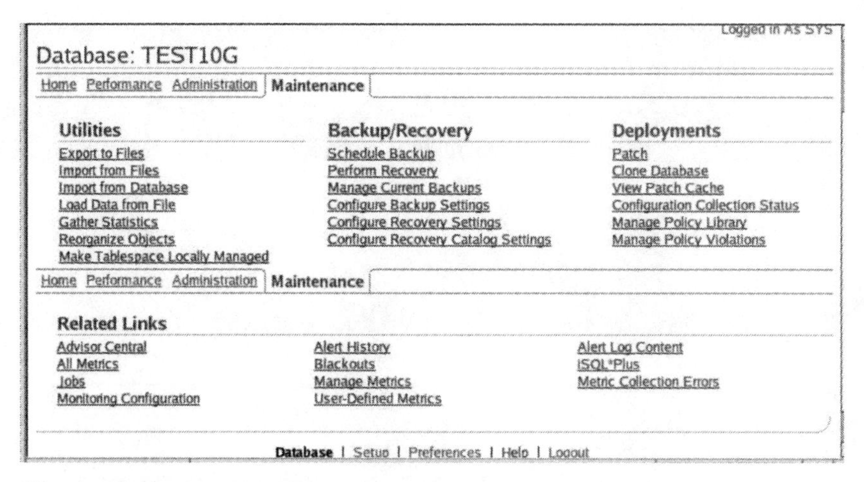

Figure 3.19 *OEM Maintenance*

Each of the Automatic DBA screens will be reviewed in detail in later chapters.

Conclusion

In this chapter, the important database installation procedures including checking for prerequisites, installation process, database editions, starter database types, storage options, use of DBCA and setting up of OEM have been examined. To summarize:

- Oracle database 10g needs a minimum of 512MB memory, regardless of the platform.
- Oracle Enterprise Edition, Standard Edition, and custom install are the 3 types of installation options available.
- Silent installation is not recommended for ASM installations.
- DBCA can be used to create the starter database at a later point, after the installation process.

- For storage subsystem, the DBA can choose between File system, Raw devices, or Automatic Storage Management (ASM) files.
- Enterprise Manager is installed using *emca* in $ORACLE_HOME/bin directory.

More about the automatic DBA will be examined in the following chapters. The next step in the journey is examining the Automatic Workload Repository and Automatic Database Diagnostic Monitor features.

Automatic Workload Repository and Automatic Database Diagnostic Monitor

"Yes, I was an Oracle DBA before I took this new job."

What is AWR?

Automatic Workload Repository (AWR) forms the central component of the new Oracle Database 10g manageability infrastructure. It provides services to the database to access, collect, process, and maintain performance statistics on various functionalities within the database. It is a built-in repository in every database.

During regular intervals, Oracle Database 10g takes snapshots of all vital statistics and workload data, and then stores them in the repository. This data is later used for analysis and as statistics for problem detection and self-tuning. By default the interval is 60 minutes and the data is stored for a period of seven days, after which it then gets purged. The interval and retention period can be altered. Please note that in *Oracle Database Concepts 10g* Release 1 (10.1) documentation, Part Number B10743-0114 under Manageability (Chapter 14), it is incorrectly stated that the snapshot interval is 30 minutes. The incorrect statement reads: "By default, the snapshots are made every 30 minutes, but you can change this frequency."

This captured data can be used for system level and user level analysis. This data is optimized to minimize overhead. In a nutshell, AWR is the basis for all self-management functionalities of the database. It helps with the historical perspective on database usage enabling accurate decisions to be made quickly.

The AWR infrastructure consists of two major components. They are as follows:

- **In-Memory Statistics Collection Facility** – This is useful for 10g components to collect statistics. These metrics are stored in memory for performance reasons and are accessible through *v$* performance views. The memory version of the statistics is written to disk regularly by a new background process called Memory Monitor or Memory Manageability Monitor (MMON).
- **AWR Snapshots** - represent the persistent portion of the facility. AWR snapshots can be viewed through data dictionary views.

The AWR statistics are kept in persistent storage to survive any database instance crashes and to provide historical data for baseline comparisons.

Now that the data has been collected, the next topic to cover is what can be done with it.

Uses of AWR

Automatic Workload Repository (AWR) helps with collection and retention of Oracle Database 10g statistics for self-tuning. Oracle Database 10g captures and retains this historical data without any DBA intervention.

The historic data is used for analysis of performance problems that occurred during a certain time period in the past and for trend analysis. After a problem had been reported in previous versions of Oracle, the DBA had no way of recreating the problem unless it had been written to alert logs. Using AWR, if there is a record of system events, the cause can be identified and solutions developed for problems that happened in the past.

STATSPACK is one of the manual ways for looking at historical data. However, this required the DBA to know when and where to get the information, and how to apply that information to the problem. STATSPACK is still available in Oracle database 10g.

Here are a few items and features of AWR to keep in mind when contemplating the switch from STATSPACK.

- In order to use the workload repository, application code will have to be changed.
- There is no supported path to migrate STATSPACK data into the workload repository.
- There is no view created on top of the workload repository to simulate the STATSPACK schema.
- Users who use AWR and STATSPACK at the same time will receive unwanted errors.

- AWR utilizes historic data to compare against the current performance data of the system to identify performance bottlenecks, predict future problems, and to help improve the performance.
- The AWR statistics data is accessible by DBAs, external users, and third party vendors to develop performance monitoring scripts and tools.
- AWR can be used to perform trend analysis.

The next section will examine the architecture of AWR by describing some of the many statistics that are collected.

Architecture of AWR

Automatic Workload Repository (AWR) provides a new infrastructure for collecting baseline statistics. Here is a partial list of the many statistics AWR in Oracle Database 10g collects:

- Time model statistics based on time spent by the activities.
- Object statistics that represent the access and usage statistics of database segments.
- Some session and system statistics retained in *v$sesstat* and *v$sysstat.*
- Some optimizer statistics for self-learning and tuning, ADDM, and Active Session History (ASH).

The following statistics are the most important ones used by AWR:

- **OS Statistics** - CPU and Memory using *v$osstat.*
- **Wait Classes** - CPU, application, commit, concurrency, scheduler, I/O, admin, configuration, commit, cluster, and network using *v$event_name.*

- **Time Model** - Connection management, PL/SQL compilation, parse, SQL execution, and PL/SQL execution using *v$sys_time_model.*
- **SQL Statistics** - SQL statistics (PL/SQL Java time, wait-class time), bind variables, efficient top SQL based on CPU, elapsed and parse statistics.

Active Session History will be reviewed briefly before moving on to AWR snapshots.

Active Session History

The Active Session History (ASH) contains recent session activity. The memory assigned to the ASH comes from the SGA and is fixed for the instance lifetime. Its size also cannot exceed 5% of the shared pool size and takes up 2MB per CPU within these limits.

The ASH works by sampling the *v$session* view every second and recording what events the sessions are waiting for. The sampling process accesses the database internal structures directly. During the sampling process, inactive sessions are ignored. The ASH is designed as a rolling buffer in memory by over-writing older information as needed. The *v$active_session_history* view is used to access the ASH statistics. This view will contain one row for every active session per sample.

Since ASH data is of high volume, flushing all ASH data is not advisable. Therefore, the data is filtered out by writing it to disk using MMON every 30 minutes and by MMNL (Memory Monitor Light) when the buffer gets full.

AWR Snapshots

The Automatic Workload Repository (AWR) is a collection of persistent system statistics stored in the system defined Workload Repository (WR) schema. The WR schema resides in the SYSAUX tablespace and is one of the main SYSAUX components.

A snapshot is a set of performance statistics captured at a certain time in the database. It is used for computing the rate of change of a statistic. Every snapshot is identified by a snapshot sequence number (*snap_id*) that is unique within AWR. Snapshots are generated every 60 minutes by default. The snapshot interval parameter can be used to change this frequency. This interval determines if snapshots of all major activities in the database are being obtained. Automatic snapshots are generated using an internal MMON task, which runs periodically. Manual snapshots can be taken by using the database control or a PL/SQL procedure.

To verify the frequency of these snapshots, issue the following command:

```
SQL>  select snap_interval, retention
          from dba_hist_wr_control;

SNAP_INTERVAL                RETENTION
---------------------------- ----------------------------
+00000 01:00:00.0            +00007 00:00:00.0
```

To change the settings for snapshot intervals of 30 minutes and a retention period of 30 days, issue the following command. The retention parameters are specified in minutes:

```
begin
   dbms_workload_repository.modify_snapshot_settings (
      interval => 30,
      retention => 30*24*60
   );
end;
```

Verify the new values by running the query on *dba_hist_wr_control.* For the above example the following results are obtained:

```
SNAP_INTERVAL              RETENTION
-------------------------- --------------------------
+00000 00:30:00.0          +00030 00:00:00.0
```

A manual snapshot can also be taken by calling the PL/SQL procedure *dbms_workload_repository.create_snapshot.* This procedure will immediately take a snapshot and record it in *wrm$_snapshot.* The metrics at the typical level are collected as the default. This will help to capture system behavior at specific points in time outside the monitoring interval. A high *interval* value may lead to missing workload spikes.

The following section examines the different types of statistics and metrics collected and at what frequency they can be collected.

Base Statistics, Metrics, and Statistics Levels

Base statistics represent the raw data that is collected. Metrics are secondary statistical data derived from base statistics. Most of the 10g metrics are used to track the rates of change of activities in the Oracle database. Metrics are used by internal components for system health monitoring, problem detection, and self-tuning. Oracle Database 10g has metrics for session, system, file, and wait-event statistics.

The advantage of having metrics is the ready availability of data for a component to compute the rate of change related to selected activities. In previous versions, statistics had to be gathered before and after running a job to compute the changed rate for base statistics. By using metrics, the information can be derived directly after running the job.

Statistics Levels can be captured by using the *statistics_level* initialization parameter. This parameter has three values: BASIC, TYPICAL, and ALL.

BASIC is the computation of the AWR statistics with metrics turned off. TYPICAL is the default value and collects only part of the statistics. It represents what is typically needed for 10g administration. Setting the parameter to ALL will retain all the statistics.

A baseline is defined on a pair of snapshots to tag sets of data for important time periods. Each baseline is unique for one and only one pair of snapshots. A baseline is identified by a user created name or a system generated identifier. A baseline can be manually named by running the *create_baseline* procedure and by specifying a name and a pair of snapshot identifiers.

A baseline identifier is assigned to the newly created baseline, which is unique for the life of the database. Baselines are used to retain snapshot data for comparison with current system behavior and the set up of threshold based alerts.

The MMON process purges all older snapshots on a nightly basis to make room for new statistics. Snapshots are removed in chronological order. Snapshots pertaining to baselines are retained until the baselines are removed. MMON tries to limit its purge task in the management window defined by the DBA. The amount of historical AWR statistics can be controlled by setting a retention period.

The *modify_snapshot_settings* procedure can be run to control the behavior of snapshots. The *retention* parameter determines how much AWR information is retained by the database. On a typical system, AWR collections require 200 MB to 300 MB of space if the data is kept for seven days. The default is seven days (10080) and the minimum is one day.

The space consumption depends mainly on the number of active sessions in the system, so adjust accordingly. If the retention value is set to 0, it will disable the automatic purging. If AWR detects that SYSAUX is out of space, it automatically deletes the oldest set of snapshots and reuses the space. Alerts will be sent to the DBA using the designated communication methods (email/pager) to inform them that SYSAUX is running out of space.

The *interval* parameter determines the frequency of snapshot generation. The minimum value is 10 minutes and the default is 60 minutes. Setting it to 0 will disable the automatic capturing of snapshots. Typical values are 10, 20, 30, 60, 120, etc.

Similar to STATSPACK, the AWR has a report generation mechanism to produce summary reports on statistics stored in the AWR repository. The analysis is done on statistics over a period of time and the reports are generated using the script *awrrpt.sql* in the $ORACLE_HOME/rdbms/admin directory. The script displays all the AWR snapshots available and prompts for options on how and where the reports are to be generated. The *awrrpt.sql* script produces two kinds of output. The default is HTML format with hyperlinks, and the other is in text format similar to STATSPACK reports. When the script is run, it prompts for the format of the report and the report name.

Alternatively, the *dba_hist_snapshot* table can be queried to retrieve the mapping between a *snap_id* and the actual clock time. The number of days can be entered to determine how many of the most recent days' snapshots are returned. The *wrm$snapshot* table can be queried to determine which *snap_id* to choose. The *begin_snap_id* and *end_snap_id* pair defines the time period over which the report is generated. The filename is the user-specified name given for the report.

The advantage of metrics is clear when it is possible for the DBA to begin analysis of snapshots based on when an activity was completed rather than having to redo the activity in order to start and stop data collection. The next section goes into more detail on the types of metrics that can be tracked using AWR.

Statistics Collection Process

Oracle Database 10g metrics can be tracked using AWR. The usage metrics are divided into two categories:

- Database feature usage
- High water mark (HWM) value of certain database attributes

These metrics are helpful in determining how often a particular feature is used, and helpful in determining resource usage within the database.

MMON tracks and records the database feature usage and HWM statistics on a weekly basis. The tracking is based on a sampling mechanism of the data dictionary. These statistics are recorded in AWR snapshots. The *dba_feature_usage_statistics* view and the *dba_high_water_mark_statistics* view can be queried to get these statistics. The Enterprise Manager can also be used to view the recorded statistics. Tables 4.1 and 4.2 describe the columns available in the *dba_feature_usage_statistics* view and the *dba_high_water_mark_statistics* view respectively.

COLUMN	DESCRIPTION
DBID	Database identifier
NAME	Feature Name (like Advanced Replication, Partitioning, Resource Manager etc)
VERSION	Database version

COLUMN	DESCRIPTION
DETECTED_USAGES	Number of times, the feature usage was detected
TOTAL_SAMPLES	Number of times the system checked for feature usage
CURRENTLY_USED	If usage was detected by the last system, check (TRUE) or not (FALSE)
FIRST_USAGE_DATE	First sample time of feature usage
LAST_USAGE_DATE	Last sample time of feature usage
AUX_COUNT	Feature-specific usage data in number format.
FEATURE_INFO	Feature-specific usage data in character format.
LAST_SAMPLE_DATE	Amount of time (in seconds) between last two usage times
LAST_SAMPLE_PERIOD	Amount of time (in hours) between the last two usage sample times
SAMPLE_INTERVAL	Sample interval
DESCRIPTION	Feature usage and usage detection logic

Table 4.1 – *dba_feature_usage_statistics view*

COLUMN	DESCRIPTION
DBID	Database identifier for which the high-watermark statistics are tracked
NAME	High-watermark statistic name
VERSION	Database version in which the high-watermarks were tracked
HIGHWATER	Highest value of statistic at sampling time
LAST_VALUE	Value of statistic at the last sampling time
DESCRIPTION	High-watermark statistic description

Table 4.2 – *dba_high_water_mark_statistics view*

Using statistics available in these two views, it is possible to gain a clearer understanding of how database features and resources are being used. When problems are encountered, alerts are generated. The next section will examine some of the server generated alerts.

Server Generated Alerts

Oracle Database 10g has features that help the DBA reduce the time spent on database monitoring tasks by automatically notifying the DBA of performance or resources allocation issues and suggesting remedial actions. A server generated alert is a notification message from the server of an impending problem.

Whenever a database metric does not match expected values or thresholds levels on different metrics are reached, an alert will be issued. This notification will contain the error/alert condition, and may contain suggestions for correcting the problem. Alerts are also generated when the problem condition has been cleared.

MMON helps by regularly scheduling monitoring actions. MMON can also be invoked when unusual conditions are detected in foreground processes by sending an alert. These alerts contain a description of the problem and advice on fixing the problem. OEM previously collected many of these alerts. Besides these alerts, by using the history of metric values in the workload repository, many database components self-tune.

The main difference between OEM alerts and server generated alerts is that with server generated alerts the metrics computation and threshold validations are performed by Oracle Database 10g and not by the OEM agent.

In Oracle 10g, the SGA can be accessed directly and the MMON wakes up every minute to compute the metric values. For those metrics with thresholds, MMON verifies these values and generates alerts as needed. Alerts based on threshold levels can be triggered at warning levels and critical levels. These levels can be internally set, customer defined, or customer altered from preset values.

There are two kinds of server generated alerts, threshold alerts and non-threshold alerts. Most alerts are configured by setting two threshold values on database metrics, a warning threshold and a critical threshold. These threshold alerts are also known as stateful alerts, which are automatically cleared upon fixing the alert condition. Stateful alerts are stored in *dba_outstanding_alerts* and are moved to *dba_alert_history* when cleared. Table 4.3 describes the structure of the *dba_outstanding_alerts* view

COLUMN	DESCRIPTION
SEQUENCE_ID	Sequence number for the Alert
REASON_ID	Alert reason ID
OWNER	Object owner for which the alert was issued
OBJECT_NAME	Object Name
SUBOBJECT_NAME	Sub-object Name
OBJECT_TYPE	Object type
REASON	Alert's Reason
TIME_SUGGESTED	Time of last update for the alert
CREATION_TIME	Time of first creation of the alert
SUGGESTED_ACTION	Recommended action
ADVISOR_NAME	Advisor name to be invoked for more information
METRIC_VALUE	Value of related metrics
MESSAGE_TYPE	Notification or Warning
MESSAGE_GROUP	Message group to which the alert belongs
MESSAGE_LEVEL	Severity level of the message (1 to 32)
HOSTING_CLIENT_ID	Client ID or security group to which the alert relates to

COLUMN	DESCRIPTION
MODULE_ID	ID of the module that originated the alert
PROCESS_ID	Process ID
HOST_ID	Originating host DNS name
HOST_NW_ADDR	IP or network address
INSTANCE_NAME	Originating instance name
INSTANCE_NUMBER	Originating instance number
USER_ID	User ID
EXECUTION_CONTEXT_ID	Threshold ID of execution
ERROR_INSTANCE_ID	Error instance ID plus a sequence number

Table 4.3 – *dba_outstanding_alerts*

The *dba_alert_history* table has the same structure as the *dba_outstanding_alerts*, except for the last field. Table 4.4 describes the additional column in the *dba_alert_history* view.

Column	Description
RESOLUTION	Resolution -Cleared or N/A

Table 4.4 – *Additional column in dba_alert_history*

There are 161 metrics with definable threshold values such as physical reads per second, user commits per second, etc. For example, threshold values can be set so that an alert is sent to the DBA when the SALES tablespace exceeds 90% threshold warning level or the 96% critical level.

Alerts can also be stateless or not based on threshold levels. These stateless alerts are written directly to the history table and might include "snapshot too old" or "resumable session has been suspended." Since OEM stores stateless alerts in its own repository, clearing the stateless alerts make sense only in OEM environment.

When Oracle crashes, the DBA is blamed first!

An alert message will be sent to the SYS owned predefined persistence queue called *alert_que.* Oracle Enterprise Manager (OEM) reads this queue to provide notifications about outstanding alerts, and may suggest corrective actions. The alerts are displayed on the Enterprise Manager console. OEM can be customized to send these messages to pager or email addresses. If the alert cannot be written to the queue, a message about the alert will be written to the Oracle Database alert log.

For sending alerts pushed to a third party tool or paging software, subscribe to *alert_que* with the *dbms_aqadm.add_subscriber* procedure. Use the *enable_db_access* procedure to associate a database user with the subscribing agent. Optionally, an asynchronous notification can be received by enqueing alerts using *alert_que.* Subscribers will have to de-enqueue the message metadata to get the content. For enqueue notifications through email or HTTP posts, configure the database server through *dbms_aqelm* with information on mail server or proxy server.

How are Alerts Recorded by AWR?

Background processes periodically flush the data to the Automatic Workload Repository. Thus the AWR captures a history of metric values. The alert history table and *alert_que* are automatically purged periodically by the system.

"I think it might be a network problem."

The tablespace alert feature is currently coded to wake up every 10 minutes and check for tablespace related alerts. Currently there is no way to change this behavior without changing the code. The 10-minute interval is only specific to the tablespace alerts, other alerts can have different values. For example, if the alert is matrix based, then the interval can be set to every one minute since MMON collects metrics every minute and will compare them to their thresholds.

In order to set and view the threshold values using Enterprise Manager, do the following steps:

1. Invoke OEM and connect to the database.
2. On the Home page, click on the Manage Metrics link at the bottom of the page.

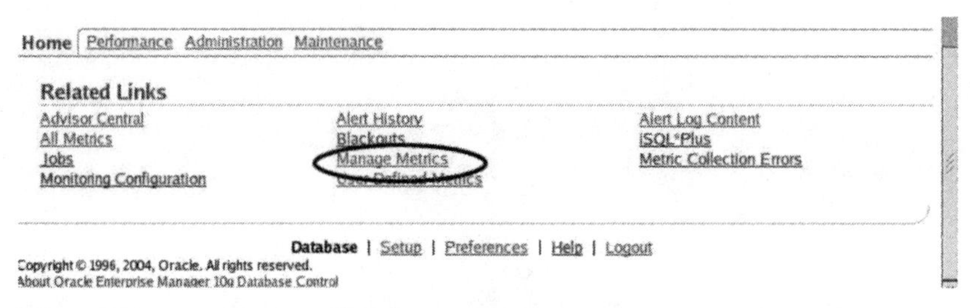

Figure 4.1 - *Manage Metrics*

3. This will call the Thresholds page. On the Thresholds page, click on Edit Thresholds.

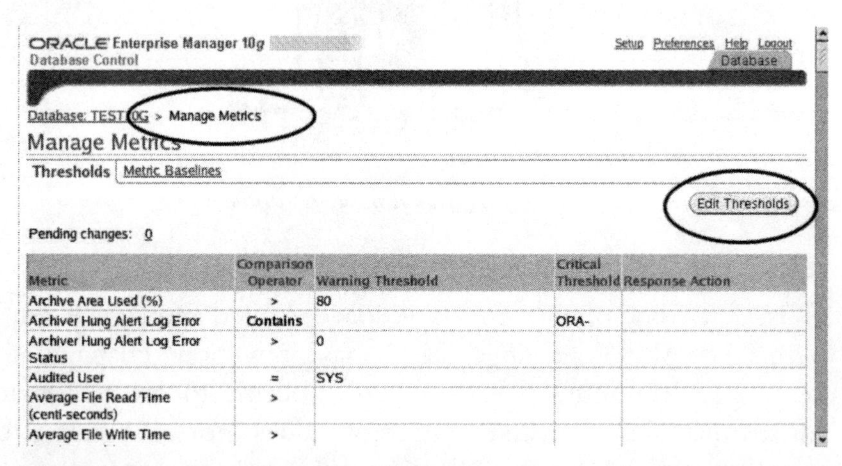

Figure 4.2 - *Manage Metrics – Edit Thresholds*

4. On the Edit Thresholds page, Select the Metric and edit the values.

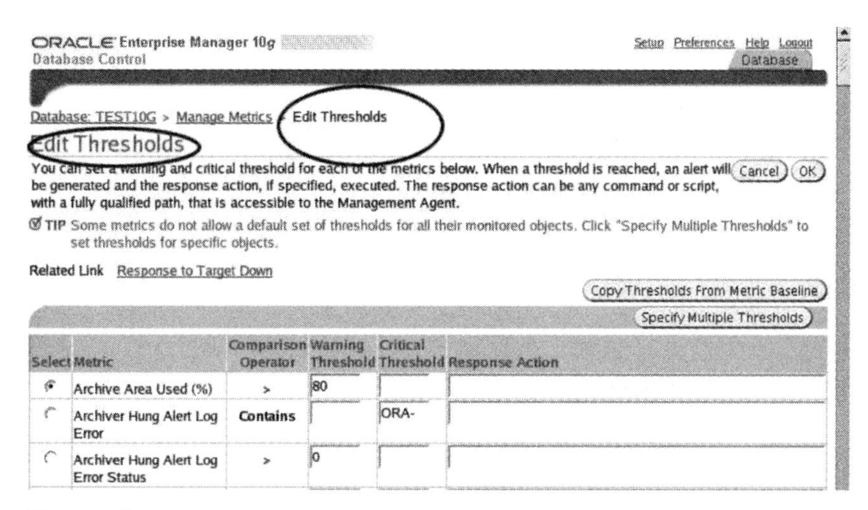

Figure 4.3 - *Manage Metrics – Edit Threshold values*

Using PL/SQL Packages for Sever Generated Alerts

An alert is generated with advice to correct the problem. The *dbms_aq* and *dbms_aqadm* packages supply the procedures for accessing and reading alert messages in the alert queue. The *dbms_server_alert* package is used to set up thresholds for all metrics. If the warning threshold is reached, this package generates a Severity Level 5 Alert. On reaching the critical threshold, a Severity Level 1 Alert is generated. *set_threshold* defines threshold settings, and *get_threshold* reads or retrieves current settings for any given metric.

The basic usage model for server generated alerts is either DBMS_SERVER_ALERT.SET_THRESHOLD or DBMS_SERVER_ALERT.GET_THRESHOLD. The parameters are the same for both procedures:

```
DBMS_SERVER_ALERT.SET_THRESHOLD(
   metrics_id                IN   NUMBER,
   warning_operator          IN   NUMBER,
   warning_value             IN  VARCHAR2,
   critical_operator         IN  NUMBER,
   critical_value            IN  VARCHAR2,
   observation_period        IN  NUMBER,
   consecutive_occurrences   IN  NUMBER,
   instance_name             IN   VARCHAR2,
   object_type               IN   NUMBER,
   object_name               IN   VARCHAR2);
```

- *metrics_id* - internal name of the metrics.
- *warning_operator* - operator for comparing the actual value with the warning threshold.
- *warning_value* - warning threshold value. NULL if no warning threshold is set.
- *critical_operator* - operator for the comparing the actual value with the critical threshold.
- *critical_value* - critical threshold value. NULL if not set.
- *observation_period* - period for which the metrics values are calculated and verified against the thresholds. Usually 1 to 60 minutes.
- *consecutive_occurrences* - number of observation periods the metrics value violate the threshold value before issuing the alert.
- *instance_name* - instance name for which the threshold is set. NULL for database-wide alerts.
- *object_type* - Object Types.
- *object_name* - name of the object. NULL for SYSTEM

The threshold settings can be changed as needed using the above referenced PL/SQL procedures or OEM. OEM functionalities can also be used to set up notification rules. OEM will display the alert in its console and will notify the administrators registered to receive alerts. There is no PL/SQL procedure provided to set thresholds based on baselines. DB Control has a screen that shows the metric values based on baselines.

The amount that thresholds are to be higher or lower than the baseline values can be specified by percentage. DB Control then sets the thresholds using the derived values for each metric using the DBMS_SERVER_ALERT.SET_THRESHOLD procedure. All thresholds except for space related alerts should be explicitly defined. Set the *statistical_level* initialization parameter to TYPICAL or ALL.

The metric values are regularly calculated by MMON and kept in memory for an hour. These in-memory values can be queried from the *v$sysmetric* and *v$sysmetric_history* views. By enabling the automatic snapshot mechanism of AWR, these metrics can be collected on disk. The on-disk values can be viewed from *dba_hist_** views. Remember that the metric history is purged periodically like other snapshots.

v$alert_types, dba_outstanding_alerts, dba_alert_history, and *dba_thresholds* are some of the dictionary views used to view alert information. Note the following:

- *v$alert_types* provides information about group and type of each alert.
- *dba_outstanding_alerts* has the list of outstanding alerts in the database.
- *dba_alert_history* has a history of alerts that have been cleared.
- *dba_thresholds* lists the various threshold settings for the instance. The table shown below describes the columns in this view.

COLUMN	DESCRIPTION
METRICS_NAME	Metrics name

COLUMN	DESCRIPTION
WARNING_OPERATOR	Relational operator for warning threshold - GT, EQ, LT, LE, GE, CONTAINS, NE, DO NOT CHECK
WARNING_VALUE	Warning threshold value
CRITICAL_OPERATOR	Relational operator for critical threshold - GT, EQ, LT, LE, GE, CONTAINS, NE, DO NOT CHECK
CRITICAL_VALUE	Critical threshold value
OBSERVATION_PERIOD	Duration of observation period in minutes
CONSECUTIVE_OCCURRENCES	Number of occurrences before issuing an alert
INSTANCE_NAME	Instance name - NULL for database wide alerts
OBJECT_TYPE	Object type -SYSTEM, SERVICE, EVENT_CLASS, TABLESPACE, FILE
OBJECT_NAME	Object's name for which the threshold is set
STATUS	Status of threshold on a valid object (VALID or INVALID)

Table 4.5 – *dba_thresholds*

Server generated alerts will greatly help in automating the DBA tasks. The next topic to review is the advisory framework in Oracle10g.

Advisory Framework

Oracle Database 10g has server components called advisors to provide feedback about resource utilization and performance. The important advisors are listed below:

- **Automatic Database Diagnostic Monitor (ADDM)** - ADDM does a top-down analysis of the database, identifies problems and potential issues, and gives recommendations for fixing these problems. ADDM can invoke other advisors.
- **SQL Tuning Advisor** - provides tuning advice for SQL statements.
- **SQL Access Advisor** - provides advice on database schema issues and determines optimal data access paths.
- **SGA Advisor** – is responsible for tuning SGA size depending on the pattern of access for various SGA components.
- **PGA Advisor** - gives detailed statistics for the work areas and provides recommendations on optimal PGA usage based on workload characteristics.
- **Buffer Cache Advisor** - predicts buffer cache hit rates for different buffer cache sizes.
- **Library Cache Advisor** - predicts the cursor cache hit rate for different library cache sizes.
- **Segment Advisor** - tracks object space issues and analyzes growth trends.
- **Undo Advisor** - recommends parameter values and amount of additional space needed for flashback support for a specified time.

All of the database advisors listed above have certain attributes in common. An advisor can be launched in one of two modes, either Limited Mode or Comprehensive Mode, depending on how much time is available for completing the advisory task. Some advisors support both modes. When an advisor is launched to look at a problem; the more statistics it looks at, the more in-depth analysis it performs and the better the quality of advice it generates. For a long running analysis, the DBA may want to limit running time of the advisor to get a smaller time frame or

Limited period. Limited means a relatively shallow analysis; while Comprehensive means a thorough, in-depth analysis taking a much longer time to complete.

The *btime_limit* specifies the maximum amount of time that the advisor should run. The *interruptible* parameter specifies whether and advisor provides partial results if interrupted during its run. *User directive* specifies if the user can provide directives to the advisor influencing the recommendations generated.

A typical tuning session consists of the following tasks:

- **Create an Advisor Task** (DBMS_ADVISOR.CREATE_TASK) - An advisor task is an executable data area in the advisor repository that manages the tuning efforts.
- **Adjust the Appropriate Task Parameters** (DBMS_ADVISOR.SET_TASK_PARAMETER) - Parameters are set in the main advisor task, which controls its behavior. Typical parameters are *target_objects*, *time_window*, and *time_limit*.
- **Perform Analysis** (DBMS_ADVISOR.EXECUTE_TASK) - Task execution is a synchronous process. Until the execution is completed or interrupted by a user, the control is retained by the database. The DBA can interrupt the process at any time and review the results up to that point in the analysis process. If the results are not satisfactory, the execution can be resumed or restarted with new task data.
- **Review the Results** (DBMS_ADVISOR.CREATE_TASK_REPORT) - The results of the analysis can be reviewed using the above procedure or built-in views. The DBA can accept, reject or ignore the recommendations. If the recommendation is

rejected, it is advisable to re-run the analysis using the rejected recommendation as advice for the next analysis operation.

The next topic to focus on is ADDM performance monitoring.

"I know RAC, TAF, FGAC and three other Oracle acronyms."

ADDM Performance Monitoring

The ADDM component in Oracle Database 10g provides proactive and reactive features for monitoring instead of the tedious tuning process in earlier versions. Proactive monitoring is done by ADDM and Server Generated Alerts. Reactive monitoring is used by the DBA to do manual tuning through OEM or SQL scripts.

ADDM is the ultimate resource for database tuning. It automatically detects bottlenecks within Oracle Database 10g. It also makes recommendations for fixing these bottlenecks in conjunction with other manageability components. Oracle Database 10g also has new data sources and performance reporting capabilities coupled with Enterprise Manager to provide an integrated performance management console that uses all relevant data sources. The new data sources include in-memory statistics for real time diagnosis as well as statistical history stored in AWR.

Statistical information is automatically captured from the SGA and stored inside the workload repository in the form of snapshots in sixty (60) minute intervals. These snapshots are then written to disk and are similar to STATSPACK snapshots, except that they are more detailed.

The ADDM also initiates the MMON process to run automatically on every database instance to detect problems proactively. Every time a snapshot is taken, the ADDM triggers an analysis of the period corresponding to the last two snapshots. This helps the ADDM to proactively monitor the instance and detect bottlenecks before they become catastrophic. The analysis results are stored inside the workload repository. These results are accessible through the OEM console. The ADDM can also be invoked manually from the OEM - Advisory Central page to perform analysis across any two snapshots.

In earlier releases of Oracle, STATSPACK was unable to identify some problems because of lack of granularity in the statistics. In Oracle Database 10g, the new wait and time model statistics help the ADDM identify the top performance issues. ADDM concentrates its analysis on top problems.

ADDM uses an internal tree structure to represent all possible tuning issues. This tree is based on the new wait and time statistics used by the Oracle database. The root of the tree represents the symptoms and going down to the leaves helps the ADDM to identify root causes. ADDM navigates the tree using a time-based threshold for each node. If the time-based threshold is not exceeded for a particular node, ADDM looks at the corresponding sub-tree to identify non-problem areas. This tree structure enables ADDM to efficiently go over the search space to identify the problems quickly.

ADDM can be invoked from the OEM screen or manually invoked using the *runad* PL/SQL procedure and by the $ORACLE_HOME/rdbms/admin/*addmrpt.sql* procedure. This procedure has four arguments: *db_id*, *snap1*, *snap2*, and *task_nm*. The *db_id* is the database identifier, *snap1* and *snap2* are the beginning and ending snapshot identifiers, and *task_nm* is the name of the task used to invoke the advisor.

Using OEM to Track Problems Detected by ADDM

ADDM proactively examines the data periodically captured in the AWR and performs analysis to determine any issues. ADDM also recommends solutions and expected benefits from implementing those solutions. The Oracle Enterprise Manager (OEM) homepage enables monitoring of the general health of the database and all functions performed by ADDM.

The General section provides a quick overview of the database. This section gives information on whether the database is up or down, the time the database was last started, instance name, host name, and the time of the most recent entry in the alert log.

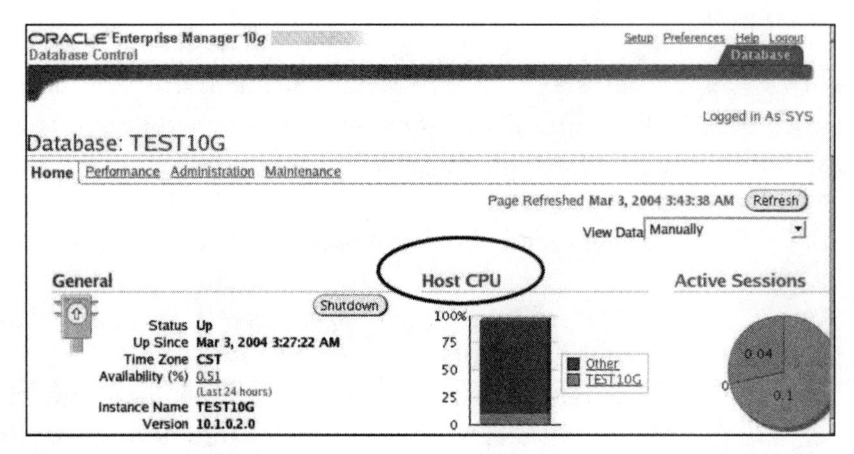

Figure 4.4 *OEM - General*

On the OEM home page, the Diagnostic Summary link provides the latest ADDM findings including any critical or warning alerts in the Alerts section. See the Figure 4.5.

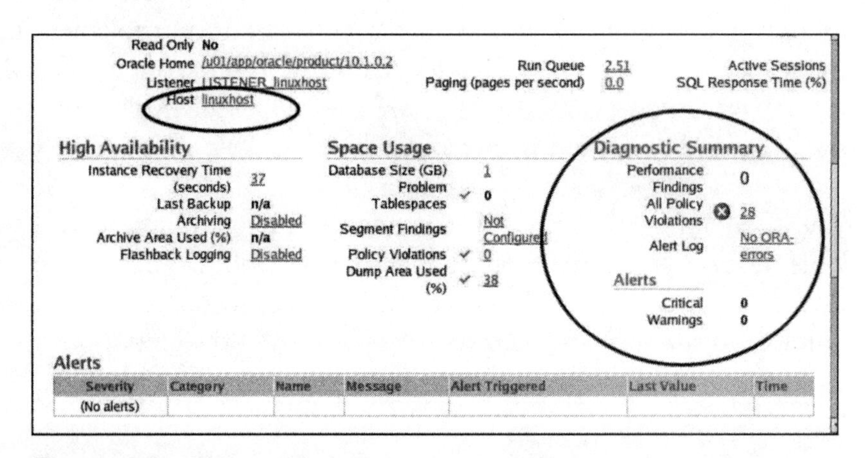

Figure 4.5 *OEM – Host (General)*

The Host CPU section shows the percentage of CPU used in the over-all system. The Active Sessions summary can be used to identify the database processes using CPU, waiting on I/O, etc. Additional information can be obtained by clicking on links. The

Host link under the General section gives information about the machine such as operating system, how long the machine has been up, and any potential machine problems.

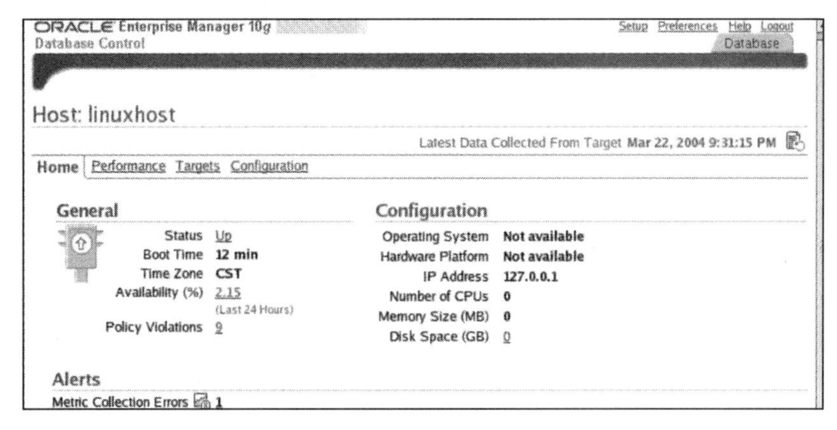

Figure 4.6 *OEM – Host Information*

To view the server performance summary, click on the Performance link. Here the CPU and memory utilization, disk utilization, etc. over a time period can be viewed. The top ten sessions using the CPU can also be viewed.

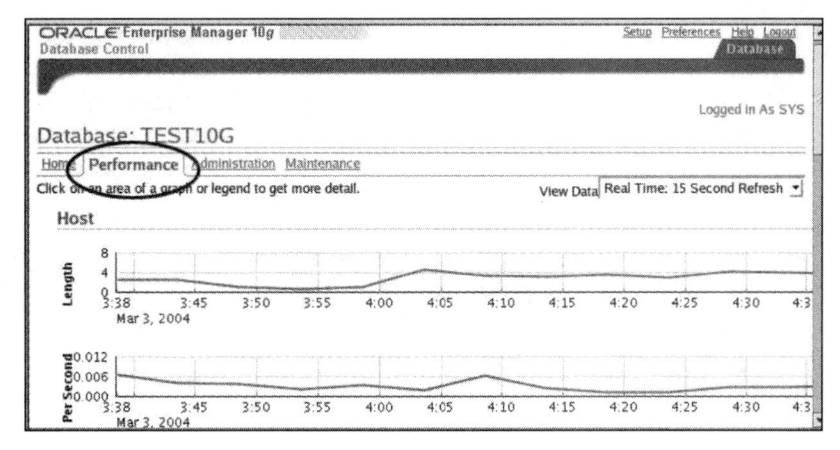

Figure 4.7 *OEM – Server Performance*

The Alerts table has information on alerts that have been generated along with severity ratings for each alert. Managing alerts will be examined in more detail in Chapter 8.

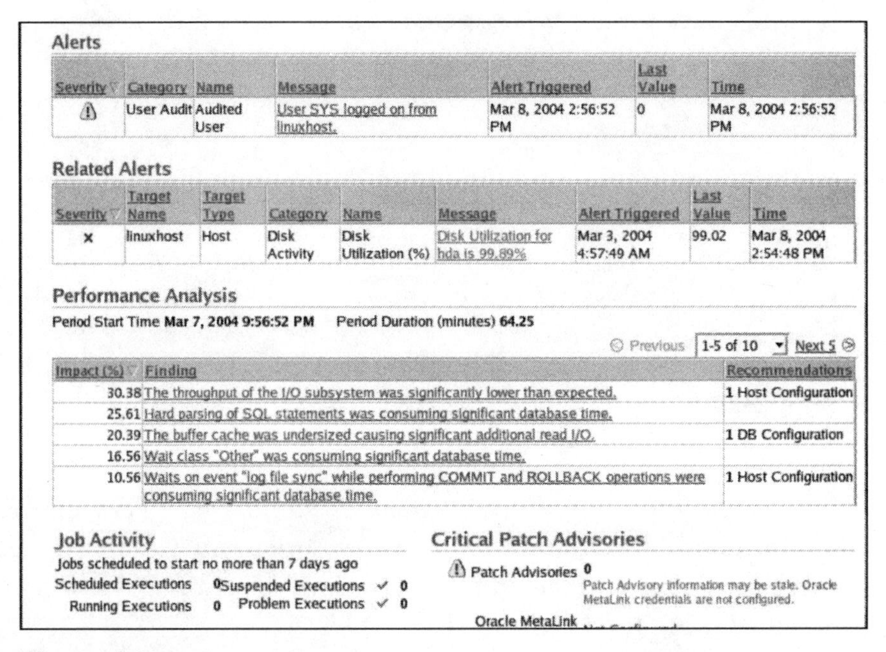

Figure 4.8 *OEM – Alerts*

The Performance Analysis section provides a summary of the latest ADDM findings including the issues that are causing significant performance impact, which includes SQL statements.

The data generated by the system monitors can be voluminous and sometimes difficult to decipher. The following section will include a more detailed view into the architecture of the system monitors and how to interpret the results.

Guru Conversation for the Senior DBA

The following figure displays the architecture of the Automatic Workload Repository. The MMON process scans the *v$* views from the SGA region and stores them in the AWR tables. From the AWR tables, the performance data is instantly available through the Oracle Enterprise Manager, through ADDM for automated tuning analysis, and from SQL*Plus to run customized tuning reports.

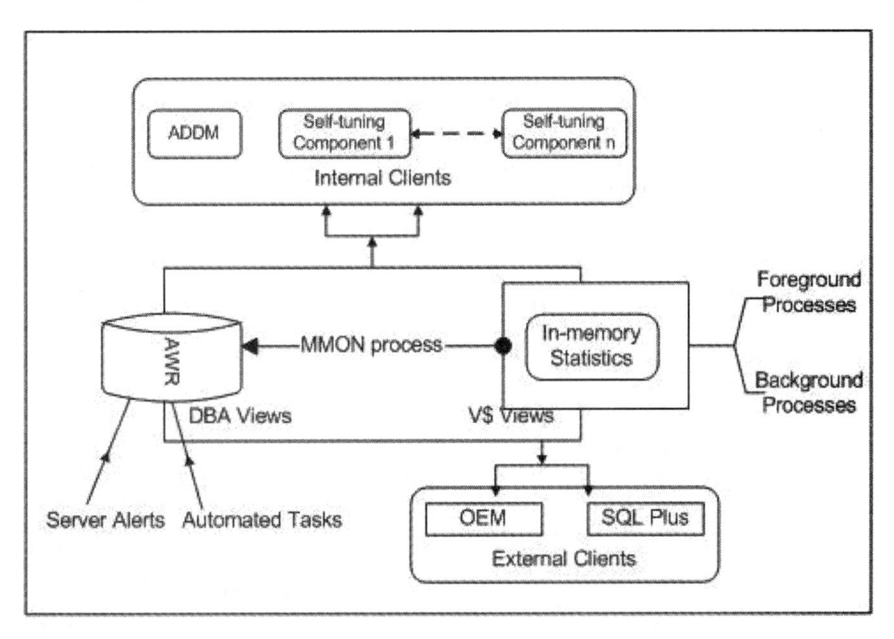

Figure 4.9 - *AWR and relation with components*

There are literally thousands of distinct metrics captured by the AWR, enough to keep even the most experienced Oracle tuning professional busy for months. For example, the *dba_hist_systat* view now collects over 300 individual performance metrics. Refer to the following listing:

STAT #	STATISTIC_NAME	STAT #	STATISTIC_NAME
0	logons cumulative	161	global cache blocks lost
1	logons current	162	global cache claim blocks lost
2	opened cursors cumulative	163	global cache blocks corrupt
3	opened cursors current	164	global cache CPU used by this session
4	user commits	165	global cache prefetch made stale
5	user rollbacks	166	total number of slots
6	user calls	167	instance recovery database freeze count
7	recursive calls	168	background checkpoints started
8	recursive cpu usage	169	background checkpoints completed
9	session logical reads	170	number of map operations
10	session stored procedure space	171	number of map misses
11	CPU used when call started	172	flashback log writes
12	CPU used by this session	173	serializable aborts
13	DB time	174	transaction lock foreground requests
14	Cluster wait time	175	transaction lock foreground wait time
15	concurrency wait time	176	transaction lock background gets
16	application wait time	177	transaction lock background get time
17	user I/O wait time	178	undo change vector size
18	session connect time	179	transaction tables consistent reads - undo records applied
19	process last non-idle time	180	transaction tables consistent read rollbacks

STAT #	STATISTIC_NAME	STAT #	STATISTIC_NAME
20	session uga memory	181	data blocks consistent reads - undo records applied
21	session uga memory max	182	no work - consistent read gets
22	messages sent	183	cleanouts only - consistent read gets
23	messages received	184	rollbacks only - consistent read gets
24	background timeouts	185	cleanouts and rollbacks - consistent read gets
25	session pga memory	186	RowCR attempts
26	session pga memory max	187	RowCR hits
27	enqueue timeouts	188	RowCR - row contention
28	enqueue waits	189	rollback changes - undo records applied
29	enqueue deadlocks	190	transaction rollbacks
30	enqueue requests	191	immediate (CURRENT) block cleanout applications
31	enqueue conversions	192	immediate (CR) block cleanout applications
32	enqueue releases	193	deferred (CURRENT) block cleanout applications
33	global enqueue gets sync	194	commit txn count during cleanout
34	global enqueue gets async	195	active txn count during cleanout
35	global enqueue get time	196	cleanout - number of ktugct calls
36	global enqueue releases	197	immediate CR cleanouts (index blocks)
37	IPC CPU used by this session	198	deferred CUR cleanouts (index blocks)
38	gcs messages sent	199	Commit SCN cached
39	ges messages sent	200	Cached Commit SCN referenced

STAT #	STATISTIC_NAME	STAT #	STATISTIC_NAME
40	global enqueue CPU used by this session	201	number of auto extends on undo tablespace
41	Db block gets	202	number of drop segment calls under space pressure
42	Db block gets from cache	203	total number of undo segments dropped
43	Db block gets direct	204	doubling up with imu segment
44	consistent gets	205	number of tune down retentions under space pressure
45	consistent gets from cache	206	number of steps of tune down retentions in space pressure
46	consistent gets - examination	207	number of times space was found by tune down
47	consistent gets direct	208	number of times space was not found by tune down
48	physical reads	209	IMU commits
49	physical reads cache	210	IMU Flushes
50	physical reads direct	211	IMU contention
51	physical read IO requests	212	IMU recursive-transaction flush
52	Db block changes	213	IMU undo retention flush
53	consistent changes	214	IMU ktichg flush
54	recovery blocks read	215	IMU bind flushes
55	physical writes	216	IMU mbu flush
56	physical writes direct	217	IMU pool not allocated
57	physical writes from cache	218	IMU CR rollbacks
58	physical write IO requests	219	IMU undo allocation size
59	physical writes non checkpoint	220	IMU Redo allocation size
60	summed dirty queue length	221	IMU- failed to get a private strand

STAT #	STATISTIC_NAME	STAT #	STATISTIC_NAME
61	DBWR checkpoint buffers written	222	Misses for writing mapping
62	DBWR thread checkpoint buffers written	223	table scans (short tables)
63	DBWR tablespace checkpoint buffers written	224	table scans (long tables)
64	DBWR parallel query checkpoint buffers written	225	table scans (rowid ranges)
65	DBWR object drop buffers written	226	table scans (cache partitions)
66	DBWR transaction table writes	227	table scans (direct read)
67	DBWR undo block writes	228	table scan rows gotten
68	DBWR revisited being-written buffer	229	table scan blocks gotten
69	DBWR make free requests	230	table fetch by rowid
70	DBWR free buffers found	231	table fetch continued row
71	DBWR lru scans	232	cluster key scans
72	DBWR summed scan depth	233	cluster key scan block gets
73	DBWR buffers scanned	234	rows fetched via callback
74	DBWR checkpoints	235	queue update without cp update
75	DBWR fusion writes	236	leaf node splits
76	prefetch clients - keep	237	leaf node 90-10
77	prefetch clients - recycle	238	branch node splits
78	prefetch clients - default	239	native hash arithmetic execute
79	prefetch clients - 2k	240	native hash arithmetic fail
80	prefetch clients - 4k	241	index fast full scans (full)
81	prefetch clients - 8k	242	index fast full scans (rowid ranges)
82	prefetch clients – 16k	243	index fast full scans (direct read)
83	prefetch clients – 32k	244	index fetch by key

STAT #	STATISTIC_NAME	STAT #	STATISTIC_NAME
84	change write time	245	index scans kdiixs1
85	redo synch writes	246	queue splits
86	redo synch time	247	queue flush
87	exchange deadlocks	248	queue position update
88	free buffer requested	249	queue single row
89	dirty buffers inspected	250	queue ocp pages
90	pinned buffers inspected	251	queue qno pages
91	hot buffers moved to head of LRU	252	heap block compress
92	free buffer inspected	253	session cursor cache hits
93	commit cleanout failures: write disabled	254	session cursor cache count
94	commit cleanout failures: block lost	255	java call heap total size
95	commit cleanout failures: cannot pin	256	java call heap total size max
96	commit cleanout failures: hot backup in progress	257	java call heap used size
97	commit cleanout failures: buffer being written	258	java call heap used size max
98	commit cleanout failures: callback failure	259	java call heap live size
99	commit cleanouts	260	java call heap live size max
100	commit cleanouts successfully completed	261	java call heap object count
101	recovery array reads	262	java call heap object count max
102	recovery array read time	263	java call heap live object count
103	CR blocks created	264	java call heap live object count max
104	current blocks converted for CR	265	java call heap gc count
105	switch current to new buffer	266	java call heap collected count

STAT #	STATISTIC_NAME	STAT #	STATISTIC_NAME
106	write clones created in foreground	267	java call heap collected bytes
107	write clones created in background	268	java session heap used size
108	write clones created for recovery	269	java session heap used size max
109	physical reads cache prefetch	270	java session heap live size
110	physical reads prefetch warmup	271	java session heap live size max
111	prefetched blocks aged out before use	272	java session heap object count
112	prefetch warmup blocks aged out before use	273	java session heap object count max
113	prefetch warmup blocks flushed out before use	274	java session heap live object count
114	physical reads retry corrupt	275	java session heap live object count max
115	physical reads direct (lob)	276	java session heap gc count
116	physical reads direct temporary tablespace	277	java session heap collected count
117	physical writes direct (lob)	278	java session heap collected bytes
118	physical writes direct temporary tablespace	279	cursor authentications
119	cold recycle reads	280	queries parallelized
120	shared hash latch upgrades - no wait	281	DML statements parallelized
121	shared hash latch upgrades - wait	282	DDL statements parallelized
122	physical reads for flashback new	283	DFO trees parallelized
123	calls to kcmgcs	284	Parallel operations not downgraded

STAT #	STATISTIC_NAME	STAT #	STATISTIC_NAME
124	calls to kcmgrs	285	Parallel operations downgraded to serial
125	calls to kcmgas	286	Parallel operations downgraded 75
126	next scns gotten without going to GES	287	Parallel operations downgraded 50
127	Unnecessary process cleanup for SCN batching	288	Parallel operations downgraded 25
128	calls to get snapshot scn: kcmgss	289	Parallel operations downgraded 1
129	kcmgss waited for batching	290	PX local messages sent
130	kcmgss read scn without going to GES	291	PX local messages recv'd
131	kcmccs called get current scn	292	PX remote messages sent
132	redo entries	293	PX remote messages recv'd
133	redo size	294	buffer is pinned count
134	redo buffer allocation retries	295	buffer is not pinned count
135	redo wastage	296	no buffer to keep pinned count
136	redo writer latching time	297	table lookup prefetch client count
137	redo writes	298	workarea memory allocated
138	redo blocks written	299	workarea executions - optimal
139	redo write time	300	workarea executions - onepass
140	redo log space requests	301	workarea executions - multipass
141	redo log space wait time	302	parse time cpu
142	redo log switch interrupts	303	parse time elapsed
143	redo ordering marks	304	parse count (total)
144	redo subscn max counts	305	parse count (hard)
145	global cache gets	306	parse count (failures)

STAT #	STATISTIC_NAME	STAT #	STATISTIC_NAME
146	global cache get time	307	execute count
147	global cache converts	308	bytes sent via SQL*Net to client
148	global cache convert time	309	bytes received via SQL*Net from client
149	global cache cr blocks served	310	SQL*Net roundtrips to/from client
150	global cache cr block build time	311	bytes sent via SQL*Net to dblink
151	global cache cr block flush time	312	bytes received via SQL*Net from dblink
152	global cache cr block send time	313	SQL*Net roundtrips to/from dblink
153	global cache current blocks served	314	sorts (memory)
154	global cache current block pin time	315	sorts (disk)
155	global cache current block flush time	316	sorts (rows)
156	global cache current block send time	317	OTC commit optimization attempts
157	global cache cr blocks received	318	OTC commit optimization hits
158	global cache cr block receive time	319	OTC commit optimization failure - setup
159	global cache current blocks received		
160	global cache current block receive time		

Table 4.6 - *dba_hist_systat view*

This section provided a quick glimpse into the type of metrics collected. The next section will examine how the data is collected.

How Does AWR Collect Data?

Oracle Database 10g uses an automated polling mechanism to collect a huge amount of performance data from Oracle on a periodic basis and stores it for time-based analysis. This data collection process is run every 60 minutes by default, and the data is retained for seven days in the Automatic Workload Repository.

The data collection process involves the capture of in-memory statistics from the *v$* views and their transfer to the *wrh$* tables. Flushing all ASH data to disk is unacceptable because of its volume. The recommended approach is to filter the data while flushing it to disk. This is done automatically by MMON every 60 seconds and by MMNL (Manageability Monitor Light) whenever the buffer is full.

ASH memory comes from the SGA and is fixed for the lifetime of the instance. It represents 2MB of memory per CPU. However, ASH size cannot exceed 5% of the shared pool size.

Recall that the default retention of AWR data is for seven days. If data needs to be retained for a few months, the storage time needs to be increased by using the dbms package called *dbms_workload_repository.modify_snapshot_settings.* This package will alter the retention period and collection frequency to provide for a longer history:

```
execute dbms_workload_repository.modify_snapshot_settings (
   interval => 60,
   retention => 1296000);
```

In this example the retention period has been modified to 90 days (1,296,000 min), and the interval between each snapshot is altered to 60 minutes. After executing the above procedure, query the *dba_hist_wr_control* view to verify the changes.

The next section will briefly review the list of AWR tables and proceed to creating customized reports from the AWR views.

Review of AWR Dynamic Performance Tables

Oracle Database 10g has dynamic performance tables that serve as the basis for the sophisticated automation and advisory tools. The Automatic Workload Repository (AWR) is a core feature of the Oracle Database 10g kernel. It automatically collects and stores important run-time performance information for historical analysis.

These *wrh$* tables are very similar in function to the STATSPACK tables. The Oracle Enterprise Manager (OEM) automatically displays and interprets this valuable time-series performance data where STATSPACK operations required use of complex query scripts.

The AWR tables store historical statistical information about the database in the form of snapshots. Each snapshot is a capture of the in–memory database statistics data at a certain point in time. All of the names of the AWR tables are prefixed with *wrm$* for metadata tables, *wrh$* for history tables, or *wri$* for advisory tables.

wrm$* tables - *wrm$ tables store the metadata information for the Workload Repository. Here is the complete list of *wrm$* tables.

- *wrm$_baseline*
- *wrm$_database_instance*
- *wrm$_snapshot*
- *wrm$_snap_error*
- *wrm$_wr_control*

wrh$* tables - *wrh$ tables store historical data or snapshots. The following is the complete list of *wrh$* tables:

wrh$_active_session_history	*wrh$_rowcache_summary*
wrh$_active_session_history_bl	*wrh$_rowcache_summary_bl*
wrh$_bg_event_summary	*wrh$_seg_stat*
wrh$_buffer_pool_statistics	*wrh$_seg_stat_bl*
wrh$_class_cache_transfer	*wrh$_seg_stat_obj*
wrh$_class_cache_transfer_bl	*wrh$_service_name*
wrh$_cr_block_sender	*wrh$_service_stat*
wrh$_current_block_server	*wrh$_service_stat_bl*
wrh$_datafile	*wrh$_service_wait_class*
wrh$_db_cache_advice	*wrh$_service_wait_class_bl*
wrh$_db_cache_advice_bl	*wrh$_sessmetric_history*
wrh$_dlm_misc	*wrh$_sga*
wrh$_dlm_misc_bl	*wrh$_sgastat*
wrh$_enqueue_stat	*wrh$_sgastat_bl*
wrh$_event_name	*wrh$_shared_pool_advice*
wrh$_filemetric_history	*wrh$_sqlbind*
wrh$_filestatxs	*wrh$_sqlbind_bl*
wrh$_filestatxs_bl	*wrh$_sqlstat*
wrh$_instance_recovery	*wrh$_sqlstat_bl*
wrh$_java_pool_advice	*wrh$_sqltext*
wrh$_latch	*wrh$_sql_plan*
wrh$_latch_bl	*wrh$_sql_summary*
wrh$_latch_children	*wrh$_sql_workarea_histogram*
wrh$_latch_children_bl	*wrh$_stat_name*
wrh$_latch_misses_summary	*wrh$_sysmetric_history*
wrh$_latch_misses_summary_bl	*wrh$_sysmetric_summary*
wrh$_latch_name	*wrh$_sysstat*
wrh$_latch_parent	*wrh$_sysstat_bl*
wrh$_latch_parent_bl	*wrh$_system_event*
wrh$_librarycache	*wrh$_system_event_bl*

wrh$_log	*wrh$_sys_time_model*
wrh$_metric_name	*wrh$_sys_time_model_bl*
wrh$_mttr_target_advice	*wrh$_tablespace_space_usage*
wrh$_optimizer_env	*wrh$_tablespace_stat*
wrh$_osstat	*wrh$_tablespace_stat_bl*
wrh$_osstat_bl	*wrh$_tempfile*
wrh$_osstat_name	*wrh$_tempstatxs*
wrh$_parameter	*wrh$_thread*
wrh$_parameter_bl	*wrh$_undostat*
wrh$_parameter_name	*wrh$_waitclassmetric_history*
wrh$_pgastat	*wrh$_waitstat*
wrh$_pga_target_advice	*wrh$_waitstat_bl*
wrh$_resource_limit	

Table 4.7 - *wrh$ views*

wri$* tables - These 49 tables store data related to advisory functions. The following is the complete list of *wri$ tables:

wri$_adv_actions	*wri$_adv_tasks*
wri$_adv_definitions	*wri$_adv_usage*
wri$_adv_def_parameters	*wri$_aggregation_enabled*
wri$_adv_directives	*wri$_alert_history*
wri$_adv_findings	*wri$_alert_outstanding*
wri$_adv_journal	*wri$_alert_threshold*
wri$_adv_message_groups	*wri$_alert_threshold_log*
wri$_adv_objects	*wri$_dbu_feature_metadata*
wri$_adv_parameters	*wri$_dbu_feature_usage*
wri$_adv_rationale	*wri$_dbu_high_water_mark*
wri$_adv_recommendations	*wri$_dbu_hwm_metadata*
wri$_adv_rec_actions	*wri$_dbu_usage_sample*
wri$_adv_sqla_fake_reg	*wri$_optstat_aux_history*

wri$_adv_sqla_map	*wri$_optstat_histgrm_history*
wri$_adv_sqla_stmts	*wri$_optstat_histhead_history*
wri$_adv_sqla_tmp	*wri$_optstat_ind_history*
wri$_adv_sqlt_binds	*wri$_optstat_opr*
wri$_adv_sqlt_plans	*wri$_optstat_tab_history*
wri$_adv_sqlt_rtn_plan	*wri$_sch_control*
wri$_adv_sqlt_statistics	*wri$_sch_votes*
wri$_adv_sqlw_colvol	*wri$_sqlset_binds*
wri$_adv_sqlw_stmts	*wri$_sqlset_definitions*
wri$_adv_sqlw_sum	*wri$_sqlset_references*
wri$_adv_sqlw_tables	*wri$_sqlset_statements*
wri$_adv_sqlw_tabvol	*wri$_tracing_enabled*

Table 4.8 - *wri$ views*

The next section examines the underlying data structures to help explain how these tables store time-series performance data.

How Does AWR Compare Against STATSPACK?

The first effective time-series tool for Oracle performance started with the Oracle8i STATSPACK tables. While many important time-series reports are now instantly charted within OEM, the senior Oracle DBA may want to go beyond the recommendations of ADDM and the SQL. Complex time series analysis such as hypothesis testing, correlation analysis etc. still require that custom queries be written against the *wrh$* tables.

The table below shows a comparison of the STATSPACK tables to their AWR equivalents. The names of many of the *wrh$* tables are identical to their *stats$* equivalents in the following table:

STATSPACK Tables	*dba_hist* Views	*wrh$* Table
stats$bg_event_ summary	*dba_hist_event_summary*	*wrh$_bg_event_ summary*

STATSPACK Tables	*dba_hist* Views	*wrh$* Table
stats$buffer_pool_ statistics	*dba_hist_buffer_pool_ statistics*	*wrh$_buffer_pool_ statistics*
stats$filestatxs	*dba_hist_filestatxs*	*wrh$_filestatxs*
stats$latch	*dba_hist_latch*	*wrh$_latch*
stats$latch_children	*dba_hist_latch_children*	*wrh$_latch_children*
stats$librarycache	*dba_hist_librarycache*	*wrh$_librarycache*
stats$rowcache_ summary	*dba_hist_rowcache_summary*	*wrh$_rowcache_ summary*
stats$sgastat	*dba_hist_sgastat*	*wrh$_sgastat*
stats$sql_summary	*dba_hist_sql_summary*	*wrh$_sql_summary*
stats$sysstat	*dba_hist_sysstat*	*wrh$_sysstat*
stats$system_event	*dba_hist_system_event*	*wrh$_system_event*
stats$waitstat	*dba_hist_waitstat*	*wrh$_waitstat*

Table 4.9 - *STATSPACK, dba_hist and wrh$ equivalents*

Note that the contents of the *wrh$* tables are almost identical to STATSPACK tables. Several of the STATSPACK time-series scripts can be run against the *wrh$* tables with minimal modifications. The *reads.sql* script gathers physical reads from the *phyrds* column of *dba_hist_filestatxs*, and then joins the *dba_hist_snapshot* view to get the BEGIN_INTERVAL_TIME column.

reads.sql

```
-- ************************************************
-- Copyright © 2004 by Rampant TechPress
-- This script is free for non-commercial purposes
-- with no warranties.  Use at your own risk.
--
-- To license this script for a commercial purpose,
-- contact info@rampant.cc
-- ************************************************

break on begin_interval_time skip 2

column phyrds  format 999,999,999
column begin_interval_time format a25

select
   begin_interval_time,
   filename,
```

```
   phyrds
from
   dba_hist_filestatxs
  natural join
   dba_hist_snapshot ;
```

The output of the script is shown below. It shows a list total of physical reads by datafile. Note that the snapshots are collected every half-hour. Starting with this script, where clause criteria could easily be added to create a unique time-series exception report.

```
SQL> @reads

BEGIN_INTERVAL_TIME        FILENAME                                    PHYRDS
-------------------------  ----------------------------------------
24-FEB-04 11.00.32.000 PM E:\ORACLE\ORA92\FSDEV10G\SYSTEM01.DBF         164,700
                          E:\ORACLE\ORA92\FSDEV10G\UNDOTBS01.DBF         26,082
                          E:\ORACLE\ORA92\FSDEV10G\SYSAUX01.DBF         472,008
                          E:\ORACLE\ORA92\FSDEV10G\USERS01.DBF            1,794
                          E:\ORACLE\ORA92\FSDEV10G\T_FS_LSQ.ORA           2,123

24-FEB-04 11.30.18.296 PM E:\ORACLE\ORA92\FSDEV10G\SYSTEM01.DBF         167,809
                          E:\ORACLE\ORA92\FSDEV10G\UNDOTBS01.DBF         26,248
                          E:\ORACLE\ORA92\FSDEV10G\SYSAUX01.DBF         476,616
                          E:\ORACLE\ORA92\FSDEV10G\USERS01.DBF            1,795
                          E:\ORACLE\ORA92\FSDEV10G\T_FS_LSQ.ORA           2,244

25-FEB-04 12.01.06.562 AM E:\ORACLE\ORA92\FSDEV10G\SYSTEM01.DBF         169,940
                          E:\ORACLE\ORA92\FSDEV10G\UNDOTBS01.DBF         26,946
                          E:\ORACLE\ORA92\FSDEV10G\SYSAUX01.DBF         483,550
                          E:\ORACLE\ORA92\FSDEV10G\USERS01.DBF            1,799
                          E:\ORACLE\ORA92\FSDEV10G\T_FS_LSQ.ORA           2,248
```

With a little tweaking to the *reads.sql* script, reports could be generated on physical writes, read time, write time, single block reads, and a host of other metrics from the *dba_hist_filestatxs* view.

The following section explores the AWR table contents more deeply.

Inside the Automatic Workload Repository Tables

All of the information collected by the AWR is taken from the *x$* structures in the Oracle heap. In Oracle Database 10g, major changes have been made to the *x$* structures as well as many new and modified *v$* views, which are built from the *x$* structures.

The overview presented here will start by taking a quick look at the 10g *v$* views relating to database events.

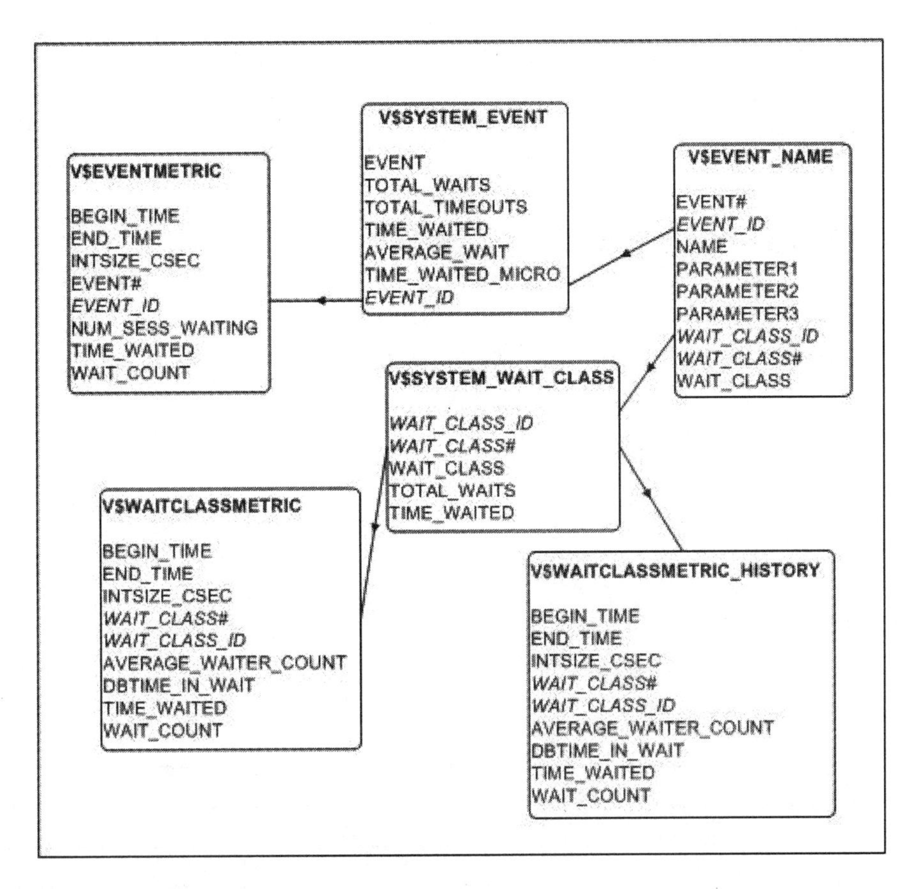

Figure 4.10 - *The new 10g v$ system event structure*

In all versions prior to Oracle Database10g, the *v$* views never captured time-series data. Administrators were forced to take snapshots using BSTAT-ESTAT or STATSPACK to see the changes over time. Oracle Database10g introduces new *v$* metric tables, *v$eventmetric, v$waitclassmetric* and *v$waitclassmetric_history*, which keep elapsed-time data.

In 10g, all *v$* views that contain the BEGIN_TIME and END_TIME columns are used to store performance information. Because of the transient nature of the *v$* views, this information needed to be persistent. This was accomplished by the introduction of the *wrh$* tables in Oracle Database 10g. The next section will provide a more detailed examination of the *wrh$* wait event structure.

The AWR and ASH Wait Event Tables

Oracle Database 10g has radically changed the way it captures wait event information. There are a host of new *v$* and *wrh$* views related to Oracle wait events. The list of wait events has been expanded and Oracle Database 10g now captures statistics on over 800 specific wait events. The new wait events are a result of separating latch waits into their individual components and separating enqueue waits or locks into a finer level of granularity.

The foundation of the new wait event architecture is called the time model. Oracle has introduced several important new wait event *v$* views in 10g.

v$ View	*dba_hist* View
v$active_sess_hist	*dba_hist_active_sess_history*
v$sys_time_model	*dba_hist_sys_time_model*
v$active_session_history	*dba_hist_active_sess_history*
v$event_histogram	No equivalent DBA view

Table 4.10 – *New v$ views and their dba_hist alternative*

The ASH collects very detailed system-event information for immediate access to every detail on Oracle execution. Oracle Database 10g collects the event information at the system and session level. AWR and ASH together make the foundation of the Oracle tuning framework and passes on this information to the DBA through scripts or OEM.

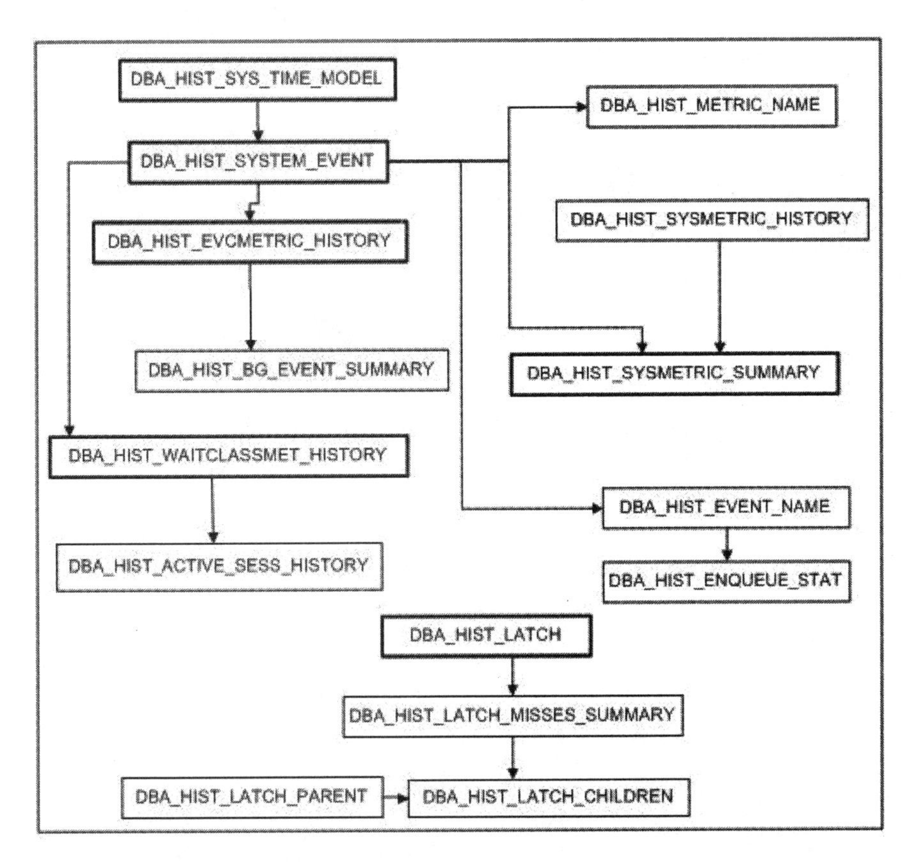

Figure 4.11 – *dba_hist views*

With the traditional *v$session* and *v$session_wait* views, waits could only be seen during the instance they occurred. But with the new *v$session_wait_history* and v*$sys_time_model* views, Oracle Database 10g captures system waits details in a cumulative fashion.

Another important area of wait event statistics is the Oracle Database 10g Active Session History (ASH) component using the *v$active_sess_hist* view and the *wrh$active_session_history* table. The

ASH stores the history of a recent session's activity, and facilitates the analysis of system performance at the current time. ASH is designed as a rolling buffer in memory, and earlier information is overwritten when needed. ASH uses the memory of the SGA.

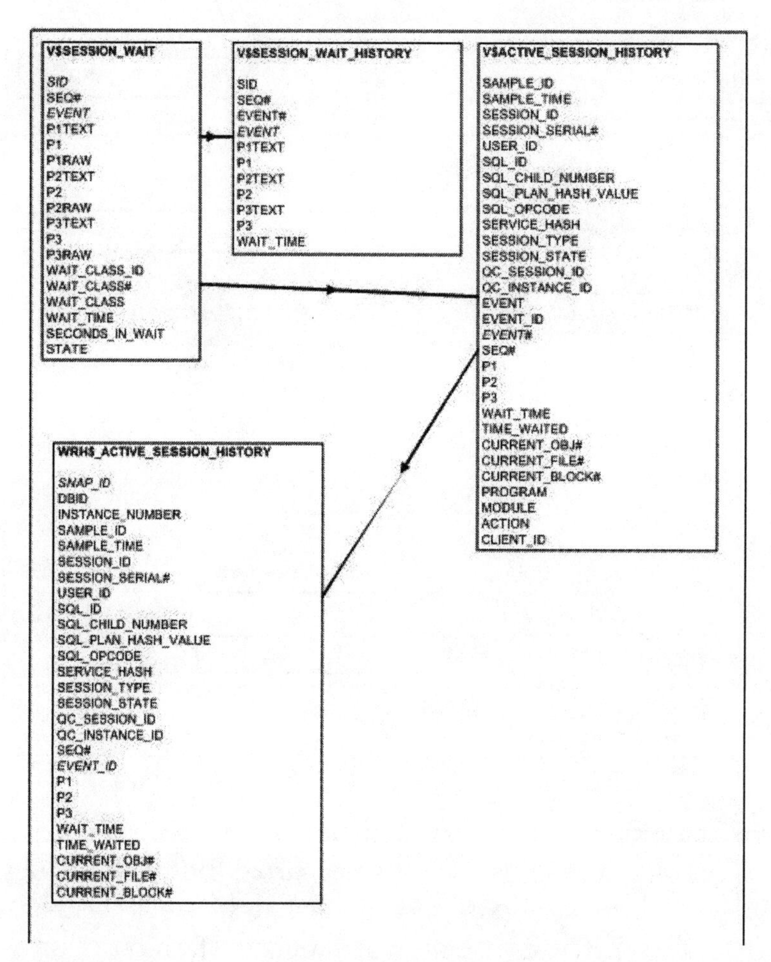

Figure 4.12 - *Relationship between v$ views and wrh$ event tables*

Another innovation is the hash key for tracking session identification. This hash key tracks common session processes and allows session tracking in cases like OCI session bouncing where each call to Oracle has a different session ID.

The ASH samples wait events every second and tracks the waits in the new *v$active_sess_hist* view. This view is flushed to the *wrh$* tables every hour, or when a new AWR snapshot is taken. The following list shows the Oracle Database 10g *wrh$* wait event tables.

- *wrh$_active_session_history*
- *wrh$_active_session_history_bl*
- *wrh$_bg_event_summary*
- *wrh$_event_name*
- *wrh$_metric_name*
- *wrh$_sessmetric_history*
- *wrh$_sys_time_model*
- *wrh$_sys_time_model_bl*
- *wrh$_sysmetric_history*
- *wrh$_sysmetric_summary*
- *wrh$_sysstat*
- *wrh$_sysstat_bl*
- *wrh$_system_event*
- *wrh$_system_event_bl*
- *wrh$_waitclassmetric_history*
- *wrh$_waitstat*
- *wrh$_waitstat_bl*

The *dba_hist* views will be examined next as they are used to create time-series performance reports. The next section will begin with an overview of the *dba_hist* views, as they are used to create time-series performance reports. Examples of custom Oracle Database 10g performance exception reports will be given that can be generated from these views.

Inside the DBA_HIST Views

Oracle Database 10g has 64 *dba_hist* views, each mapping to their underlying *x$* and *wrh$* components. For example, the following shows the internal creation syntax for the *dba_hist_sysstat* view. Note that *dba_hist_sysstat* is built from several workload repository tables, *wrm$_snapshot, wrh$_sysstat,* and *dba_hist_stat_name.*

dba_hist_sysstat view creation syntax

```
-- *************************************************
-- Copyright © 2004 by Rampant TechPress
-- This script is free for non-commercial purposes
-- with no warranties.  Use at your own risk.
--
-- To license this script for a commercial purpose,
-- contact info@rampant.cc
-- *************************************************
select
    s.snap_id, s.dbid, s.instance_number, s.statistic#,
    s.statistic_hash, nm.statistic_name, value
from
    WRM$_SNAPSHOT sn, WRH$_SYSSTAT s, DBA_HIST_STAT_NAME nm
where
    s.statistic_hash = nm.statistic_hash
    and s.statistic# = nm.statistic#
    and s.dbid = nm.dbid
    and s.snap_id = sn.snap_id
    and s.dbid = sn.dbid
    and s.instance_number = sn.instance_number
    and sn.status = 0
    and sn.bl_moved = 0
    union all
select
    s.snap_id, s.dbid, s.instance_number, s.statistic#,
    s.statistic_hash, nm.statistic_name, value
from
    WRM$_SNAPSHOT sn, WRH$_SYSSTAT_BL s, DBA_HIST_STAT_NAME nm
where
    s.statistic_hash = nm.statistic_hash
    and s.statistic# = nm.statistic#
    and s.dbid = nm.dbid
```

```
and s.snap_id = sn.snap_id
and s.dbid = sn.dbid
and s.instance_number = sn.instance_number
and sn.status = 0
and sn.bl_moved = 1;
```

Because of the overwhelming amount of data, the focus here will be on the *dba_hist* views that may be familiar from STATSPACK. The column names are different from the STATSPACK tables, but the types of performance data collected by these STATSPACK tables are essentially the same as that found inside the *dba_hist* views.

dba_hist View	STATSPACK Table
dba_hist_bg_event_summary	*stats$bg_event_summary*
dba_hist_buffer_pool_statistics	*stats$buffer_pool_statistics*
dba_hist_filestatxs	*stats$filestatxs*
dba_hist_latch	*stats$latch*
dba_hist_latch_children	*stats$latch_children*
dba_hist_librarycache	*stats$librarycache*
dba_hist_rowcache_summary	*stats$rowcache_summary*
dba_hist_sgastat	*stats$sgastat*
dba_hist_sql_summary	*stats$sql_summary*
dba_hist_sysstat	*stats$sysstat*
dba_hist_system_event	*stats$system_event*
dba_hist_waitstat	*stats$waitstat*

Table 4.11 *STATSPACK and dba_hist name equivalencies*

The complete list of *dba_hist* views is shown below:

dba_hist_database_instance	*dba_hist_sql_workarea_hstgrm*
dba_hist_snapshot	*dba_hist_pga_target_advice*
dba_hist_snap_error	*dba_hist_instance_recovery*
dba_hist_baseline	*dba_hist_java_pool_advice*
dba_hist_wr_control	*dba_hist_thread*
dba_hist_datafile	*dba_hist_stat_name*

dba_hist_filestatxs	dba_hist_sysstat
dba_hist_tempfile	dba_hist_sys_time_model
dba_hist_tempstatxs	dba_hist_osstat_name
dba_hist_sqlstat	dba_hist_osstat
dba_hist_sqltext	dba_hist_parameter_name
dba_hist_sql_summary	dba_hist_parameter
dba_hist_sql_plan	dba_hist_undostat
dba_hist_sqlbind	dba_hist_seg_stat
dba_hist_optimizer_env	dba_hist_seg_stat_obj
dba_hist_event_name	dba_hist_metric_name
dba_hist_system_event	dba_hist_sysmetric_history
dba_hist_bg_event_summary	dba_hist_sysmetric_summary
dba_hist_waitstat	dba_hist_sessmetric_history
dba_hist_enqueue_stat	dba_hist_filemetric_history
dba_hist_latch_name	dba_hist_waitclassmet_history
dba_hist_latch	dba_hist_dlm_misc
dba_hist_latch_children	dba_hist_cr_block_server
dba_hist_latch_parent	dba_hist_current_block_server
dba_hist_latch_misses_summary	dba_hist_class_cache_transfer
dba_hist_librarycache	dba_hist_active_sess_history
dba_hist_db_cache_advice	dba_hist_tablespace_stat
dba_hist_buffer_pool_stat	dba_hist_log
dba_hist_rowcache_summary	dba_hist_mttr_target_advice
dba_hist_sga	dba_hist_tbspc_space_usage
dba_hist_sgastat	dba_hist_service_name
dba_hist_pgastat	dba_hist_service_stat
dba_hist_resource_limit	dba_hist_service_wait_class
dba_hist_shared_pool_advice	dba_high_water_mark_statistics

Table 4.12 - *dba_hist views*

These views are fully documented in the *Oracle Database 10g Reference Manual*. The following sections will focus more on the *dba_hist* views for time-series and exception reporting and related reports.

AWR Reporting

Recall that the *dba_hist* views are built from their *wrh$* equivalents. These views provide the data source for a wealth of customizable reports for identification of trends and time-series performance optimization. This type of reporting identifies signatures or regularly repeating patterns that are unique to the database instance.

Once the DBA understands the patterns for the important metrics, he or she can use the Oracle Database 10g scheduler to re-allocate system resources just-in-time for the repeating event.

All queries against the *dba_hist* views require a join into the *dba_hist_snapshot* view, which is the main anchor for the AWR history views. In the following figure, the anchor view and samples of summary and detail *dba_hist* views are shown:

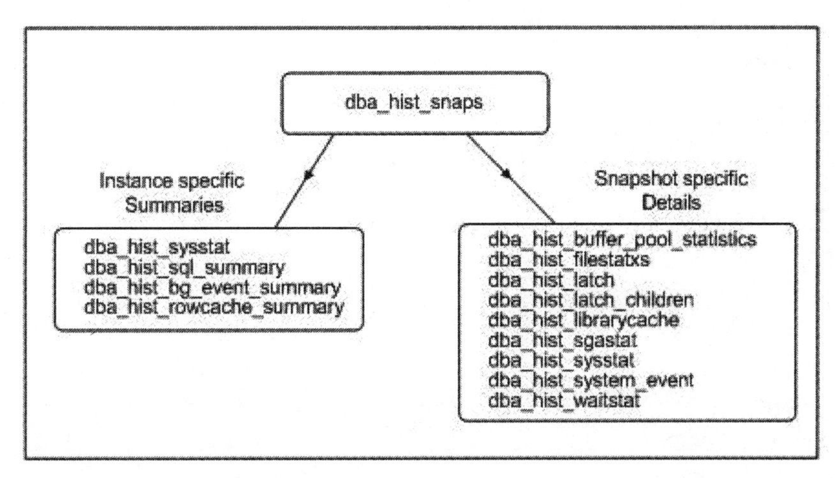

Figure 4.13 - *A sample of the dba_hist views for the AWR*

With 64 *dba_hist* views and thousands of possible statistics to examine, the focus needs to be narrowed to some commonly used tuning approaches. The following is a list of AWR *dba_hist* views:

- *dba_hist_sysstat*
- *dba_hist_filestatxs*
- *dba_hist_waitstat*

These will be examined more closely during the progression through simple AWR reports to more sophisticated reports such as exception reporting, trend identification, correlation analysis and hypothesis testing.

Creating Custom AWR Reports

The first example will use the most popular *dba_hist* view, *dba_hist_sysstat.* This is one of the most valuable AWR history tables because it contains instance-wide summaries on important metrics. The full list of all 320 system statistics was shown previously, but these are the most commonly used statistics for exception reporting:

STATISTIC_NAME
cluster wait time
concurrency wait time
application wait time
user I/O wait time
enqueue waits
enqueue deadlocks
db block gets
consistent gets
physical reads
physical read IO requests
db block changes
physical writes
DBWR buffers scanned
DBWR checkpoints

hot buffers moved to head of LRU
shared hash latch upgrades - wait
redo log space requests
redo log space wait time
table scans (short tables)
table scans (long tables)
table fetch continued row
leaf node splits
leaf node 90-10 splits
index fast full scans (full)
session cursor cache hits
buffer is not pinned count
workarea executions - multipass
parse time cpu
parse time elapsed
parse count (total)
SQL*Net roundtrips to/from client
sorts (memory)
sorts (disk)
sorts (rows)

A simple query to plot the user I/O wait time statistic for each AWR snapshot will be shown first. From *physical_reads.sql* the physical read counts from the AWR can be easily extracted.

physical_reads.sql

```
-- *************************************************
-- Copyright © 2004 by Rampant TechPress
-- This script is free for non-commercial purposes
-- with no warranties.  Use at your own risk.
--
-- To license this script for a commercial purpose,
-- contact info@rampant.cc
-- *************************************************

break on begin_interval_time skip 2

column phyrds              format 999,999,999
column begin_interval_time format a25
```

```
select
   begin_interval_time,
   filename,
   phyrds
from
   dba_hist_filestatxs
natural join
   dba_hist_snapshot
;
```

Below is the result. Note that the snapshots are collected every half-hour. Using this script and adding *where* clause criteria could create a unique time-series exception report.

```
SQL> @physical_reads

BEGIN_INTERVAL_TIME       FILENAME                                     PHYRDS
------------------------- ----------------------------------------
24-FEB-04 11.00.32.000 PM E:\ORACLE\ORA92\FSDEV10G\SYSTEM01.DBF       164,700
                          E:\ORACLE\ORA92\FSDEV10G\UNDOTBS01.DBF       26,082
                          E:\ORACLE\ORA92\FSDEV10G\SYSAUX01.DBF       472,008
                          E:\ORACLE\ORA92\FSDEV10G\USERS01.DBF          1,794
                          E:\ORACLE\ORA92\FSDEV10G\T_FS_LSQ.ORA         2,123
```

The next section will explore how to enhance these simple scripts to produce powerful exception reports.

Exception Reporting with Enterprise Manager

Oracle Enterprise Manager (OEM) has a fantastic interface for creating exception alerts and mailing them directly to the Oracle professional. However, the OEM has limitations. Until OEM evolves into a true Decision Support System (DSS) for the Oracle DBA, the DBA will still need to use the workload information in the AWR for:

- Complex exception reporting
- Correlation analysis
- Developing metric signatures
- Hypothesis testing
- Data Mining

There are more sophisticated exception reports that cannot be provided by OEM. The data inside the AWR *dba_hist* views can be used by the Oracle DBA to perform complex analysis as mentioned below.

Signature Analysis – The AWR data can be used to plot values of important metrics, averaged by hour-of-the-day and day-of-the-week. For example, plotting physical read and write signatures will give the DBA excellent insight into the regular variations in database stress. Knowing this information is critical to scheduling just-in-time changes to SGA resources; the foundation of creating a self-tuning database. For more information on signature analysis for Oracle, refer to the book *Creating a Self-Tuning Oracle Database* published by Rampant TechPress.

Hypothesis Testing – The senior Oracle DBA can easily run correlation analysis to detect correlations between important performance metrics. Queries can be developed to show the correlation between buffer busy waits and DML per second for specific tables, averaged over long periods of time.

Comparing a Single Value to a System-wide Value – For example, issue an alert when the physical writes for any data files exceeds 25% of total physical writes.

The next section will be an examination of how an Oracle professional can obtain valuable information from the AWR.

Exception Reporting with the AWR

At the highest level, exception reporting involved adding a *where* clause to a query to eliminate any values that fall beneath the pre-defined threshold. Below is a simple script called *report_sysstat.sql* which displays a time-series exception report for any statistic in *dba_hist_sysstat*. Note that the script accepts the statistics number and the value threshold for the exception report.

report_sysstat.sql

```
-- ************************************************
-- Copyright © 2004 by Rampant TechPress
-- This script is free for non-commercial purposes
-- with no warranties.  Use at your own risk.
--
-- To license this script for a commercial purpose,
-- contact info@rampant.cc
-- ************************************************

prompt
prompt  This will query the dba_hist_sysstat view to display all
values
prompt  that exceed the value specified in
prompt  the "where" clause of the query.
prompt

set pages 999

break on snap_time skip 2

accept stat_name   char   prompt 'Enter Statistic Name:  ';
accept stat_value  number prompt 'Enter Statistics Threshold value:
';


col snap_time    format a19
col value        format 999,999,999

select
   to_char(begin_interval_time,'yyyy-mm-dd hh24:mi') snap_time,
   value
from
   dba_hist_sysstat
  natural join
   dba_hist_snapshot
where
   stat_name = '&stat_name'
and
  value > &stat_value
order by
   to_char(begin_interval_time,'yyyy-mm-dd hh24:mi')
;
```

When this script is run, it prompts for the statistic name and threshold value.

```
SQL> @report_sysatst

Copyright 2004 by Donald K. Burleson -used with permission

This will query the dba_hist_sysstat view to display all values
that exceed the value specified in
the "where" clause of the query.

Enter Statistic Name:  physical writes
Enter Statistics Threshold value:  200000

SNAP_TIME                   VALUE
-------------------- ------------
2004-02-21 08:00          200,395
2004-02-27 08:00          342,231
2004-02-29 08:00          476,386
2004-03-01 08:00          277,282
2004-03-02 08:00          252,396
2004-03-04 09:00          203,407
```

The listing above indicates a repeating trend, where physical writes seem to be high at 8:00 AM on certain days. This powerful script permits quick extraction of exception conditions from any instance-wide Oracle metric to review over time. A more powerful exception report will be examined next that compares system-wide values to individual snapshots.

Exception reporting with *dba_hist_filestatxs*

The *dba_hist_filestatxs* view contains important file-level information about Oracle I/O activities. Because most Oracle databases perform a high amount of reading and writing from disk, the *dba_hist_filestatxs* view can be very useful for identifying high-use data files.

For an Oracle Database 10g customer using the SAME (Stripe and Mirror Everywhere) approach, this view is indispensable for locating and isolating hot data files. Many Oracle shops will isolate hot data files onto high-speed solid-state disk (SSD), or relocate the hot files to another physical disk spindle.

A describe of *dba_hist_filestatxs* is shown below. The important information relates to physical reads and writes, the actual time spent performing reads and writes, and the wait count associated with each data file for each snapshot.

COLUMN	DESCRIPTION
SNAP_ID	Unique snapshot ID
FILENAME	Name of the datafile
PHYRDS	Number of physical reads done
PHYWRTS	Number of times DBWR is required to write
SINGLEBLKRDS	Number of single block reads
READTIM	Time (in hundredths of a second) spent doing reads if the *timed_statistics* parameter is true; 0 if *timed_statistics* is false
WRITETIM	Time (in hundredths of a second) spent doing writes if the *timed_statistics* parameter is true; 0 if *timed_statistics* is false
SINGLEBLKRDTIM	Cumulative single block read time (in hundredths of a second)
PHYBLKRD	Number of physical blocks read
PHYBLKWRT	Number of blocks written to disk, which may be the same as PHYWRTS if all writes are single blocks
WAIT_COUNT	Wait Count

Table 4.13 - *Important metrics on file-level I/O in dba_hist_filestatxs*

Next, a customized exception report will be examined. In this simple report called *hot_write_files.sql*, the *dba_hist_filestatxs* will be queried to identify hot write datafiles where the file consumed more than 25% of the total physical writes for the instance. The query compares the physical writes or the *phywrts* column of *dba_hist_filestatxs,* with the instance-wide physical writes or *statistic#* = 55 from *dba_hist_sysstat.*

This simple yet powerful script allows the Oracle professional to track hot-write datafiles over time, thereby, gaining important insight into the status of the I/O sub-system over time.

hot_write_files.sql

```
-- ************************************************
-- Copyright © 2004 by Rampant TechPress
-- This script is free for non-commercial purposes
-- with no warranties.  Use at your own risk.
--
-- To license this script for a commercial purpose,
-- contact info@rampant.cc
-- ************************************************

prompt
prompt  This will identify any single file whose write I/O
prompt  is more than 25% of the total write I/O of the database.
prompt

set pages 999

break on snap_time skip 2

col filename       format a40
col phywrts        format 999,999,999
col snap_time      format a20

select
   to_char(begin_interval_time,'yyyy-mm-dd hh24:mi') snap_time,
   filename,
   phywrts
from
   dba_hist_filestatxs
natural join
   dba_hist_snapshot
where
   phywrts > 0
and
   phywrts * 4 >
(
select
   avg(value)                all_physical_writes
from
   dba_hist_sysstat
  natural join
   dba_hist_snapshot
where
   stat_name = 'physical writes'
and
  value > 0
)
order by
```

```
    to_char(begin_interval_time,'yyyy-mm-dd hh24:mi'),
    phywrts desc
;
```

Below is the sample output. This is a very useful report because it shows the high-write datafiles and the times when they are hot.

```
SQL> @hot_write_files

This will identify any single file whose write I/O
is more than 25% of the total write I/O of the database.


SNAP_TIME            FILENAME
PHYWRTS
----------------- ---------------------------------------- --------
2004-02-20 23:30  E:\ORACLE\ORA92\FSDEV10G\SYSAUX01.DBF       85,540

2004-02-21 01:00  E:\ORACLE\ORA92\FSDEV10G\SYSAUX01.DBF       88,843

2004-02-21 08:31  E:\ORACLE\ORA92\FSDEV10G\SYSAUX01.DBF       89,463

2004-02-22 02:00  E:\ORACLE\ORA92\FSDEV10G\SYSAUX01.DBF       90,168

2004-02-22 16:30  E:\ORACLE\ORA92\FSDEV10G\SYSAUX01.DBF      143,974
                  E:\ORACLE\ORA92\FSDEV10G\UNDOTBS01.DBF      88,973
```

Time-series exception reporting is extremely useful for detecting those times when Oracle Database 10g is experiencing stress. Many Oracle professionals will schedule these types of exception reports for automatic e-mailing every day.

This completes the review of trend identification. The next section will examine a more sophisticated type of report wherein it is possible to identify repeating trends within data.

Trend Identification with the AWR

With the examination of *dba_hist* queries complete, the next topic to explore is trend identification with the AWR views. The senior Oracle professional knows that aggregating important Oracle performance metrics over time (day-of-the-week and hour-of-the-day) allows them to see hidden "signatures." These signatures are extremely important for proactive tuning because they show regularly occurring changes in processing demands. This knowledge allows the DBA to anticipate upcoming changes and reconfigure Oracle just in time to meet the changes.

For example, listed below is a report called *report_sysstat_hour.sql* that will show the "signature" for any Oracle system statistic, averaged by hour of the day.

report_sysstat_hour.sql

```
-- ************************************************
-- Copyright © 2004 by Rampant TechPress
-- This script is free for non-commercial purposes
-- with no warranties.  Use at your own risk.
--
-- To license this script for a commercial purpose,
-- contact info@rampant.cc
-- ************************************************

prompt
prompt  This will query the dba_hist_sysstat view to
prompt  display average values by hour of the day
prompt

set pages 999

break on snap_time skip 2

accept stat_name char prompt 'Enter Statistics Name:  ';


col snap_time   format a19
col avg_value   format 999,999,999

select
   to_char(begin_interval_time,'hh24') snap_time,
   avg(value)                          avg_value
from
   dba_hist_sysstat
  natural join
   dba_hist_snapshot
where
   stat_name = '&stat_name'
group by
   to_char(begin_interval_time,'hh24')
order by
   to_char(begin_interval_time,'hh24')
;
```

The report below displays data averaged for every hour of the day. This information can then be easily pasted into an MS-Excel spreadsheet and plotted with the chart wizard. See Figure 4.14 for an example chart.

```
SQL> @report_sysstat_hour

This will query the dba_hist_sysstat view to
display average values by hour of the day

Enter Statistics Name:  physical reads

SNAP_TIME               AVG_VALUE
------------------- ------------
00                       120,861
01                       132,492
02                       134,136
03                       137,460
04                       138,944
05                       140,496
06                       141,937
07                       143,191
08                       145,313
09                       135,881
10                       137,031
11                       138,331
12                       139,388
13                       140,753
14                       128,621
15                       101,683
16                       116,985
17                       118,386
18                       119,463
19                       120,868
20                       121,976
21                       112,906
22                       114,708
23                       116,340
```

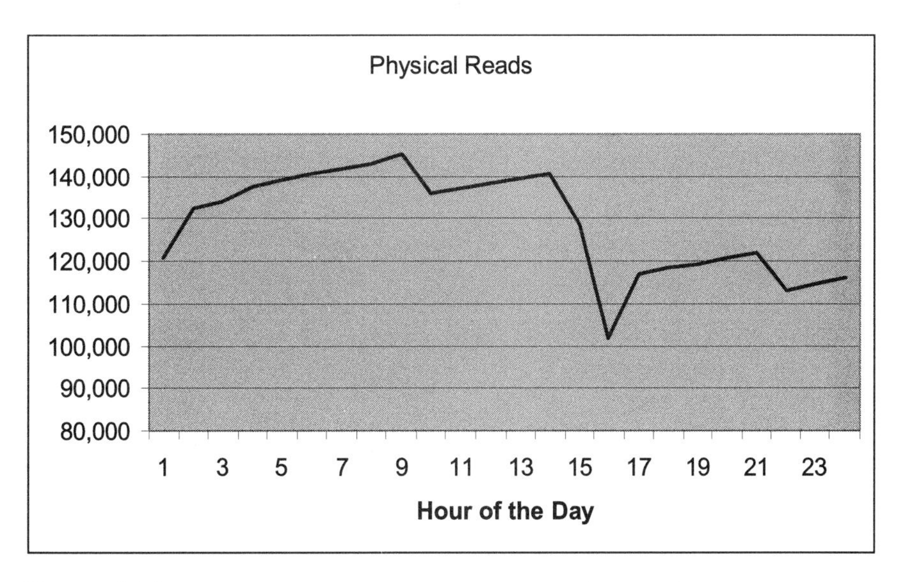

Figure 4.14 - *An hourly Signature can show hidden trends*

For more details on the procedures for plotting Oracle performance data, see the OTN article *Perfect Pitch* at http://otn.oracle.com/oramag/webcolumns/2003/techarticles/burleson_wait.html. Open source products such as RRDtool (http://people.ee.ethz.ch/~oetiker/webtools/rrdtool/) can be used to automate the plotting of data from the AWR and ASH.

The same types of reports aggregated by day-of-the week can also be created. Over long periods of time, almost all Oracle databases will develop distinct signatures that reflect the regular daily processing patterns of the end-user community.

The *report_sysstat_day.sql* will accept any of the values from *dba_hist_sysstat* and will plot the average values for physical reads by hour-of-the-day.

report_sysstat_day.sql

```
-- ***********************************************
-- Copyright © 2004 by Rampant TechPress
-- This script is free for non-commercial purposes
-- with no warranties.  Use at your own risk.
--
-- To license this script for a commercial purpose,
-- contact info@rampant.cc
-- ***********************************************

prompt  This will query the dba_hist_sysstat view to display
prompt  average values for physical reads by day-of-the-week
prompt

set pages 999

accept stat_name char prompt 'Enter Statistic Name:  ';


col snap_time   format a19
col avg_value   format 999,999,999

select
   to_char(begin_interval_time,'day')   snap_time,
   avg(value)                           avg_value
from
   dba_hist_sysstat
natural join
   dba_hist_snapshot
where
   stat_name = '&stat_name'
group by
   to_char(begin_interval_time,'day')
order by
   decode(
   to_char(begin_interval_time,'day'),
    'sunday',1,
    'monday',2,
    'tuesday',3,
    'wednesday',4,
    'thursday',5,
    'friday',6,
    'saturday',7
   )
;
```

The listing below displays the output.

```
SQL> @report_sysstat_day

This will query the dba_hist_sysstat view to display
average values by day-of-the-week

Enter Statistics Name:  physical reads


SNAP_TIME              AVG_VALUE
------------------- ------------
sunday                   190,185
monday                   135,749
tuesday                   83,313
wednesday                139,627
thursday                 105,815
friday                   107,250
saturday                 154,279
```

This report shows an average for every day of the week. These types of signatures will become very stable for most Oracle databases, and they can be used to develop a predictive model for proactive tuning activities.

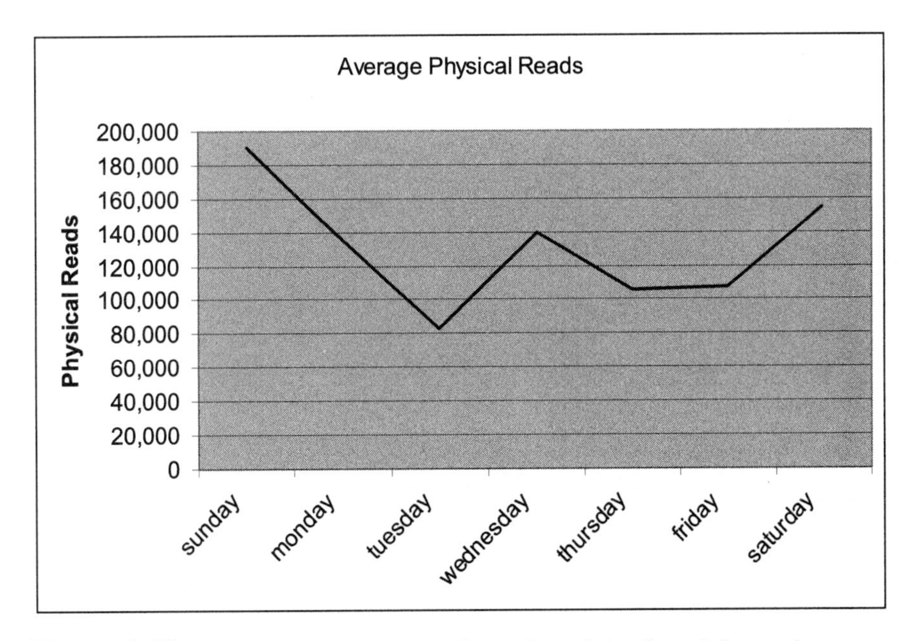

Figure 4.15 - *Signature for average physical reads by day of the week*

Correlation Analysis Reports with AWR and ASH Views

For those tuning with the Oracle Wait Interface, there are interesting statistics that relate to system-wide wait events from *dba_hist_waitstat* with detailed wait event information from *dba_hist_active_sess_history.*

COLUMN	DESCRIPTION
SNAP_ID	Unique snapshot ID
DBID	Database ID for the snapshot
INSTANCE_NUMBER	Instance number for the snapshot
CLASS	Class of the block
WAIT_COUNT	Number of waits by the OPERATION for this CLASS of block
TIME	Sum of all wait times for all the waits by the OPERATION for this CLASS of block

Table 4.14 - *dba_hist_waitstat statistics used to wait event analysis*

For advanced correlation analysis, the DBA would seek to identify correlations between instance-wide wait events and block-level waits. This is a critical way of using human insight and of using the AWR and ASH information to isolate the exact file and object where the wait contention is occurring.

Remember, the ASH stores the history of a recent session's activity in *dba_hist_active_sess_history* and this data is designed as a rolling buffer in memory where earlier information is overwritten when needed. To do this, the *dba_hist_active_sess_history* view is needed as it contains historical block-level contention statistics.

COLUMN	DESCRIPTION
SNAP_ID	Unique snapshot ID

COLUMN	DESCRIPTION
SAMPLE_TIME	Time of the sample
SESSION_ID	Session identifier
SESSION_SERIAL#	Session serial number (used to uniquely identify a session's objects)
USER_ID	Oracle user identifier
CURRENT_OBJ#	Object ID of the object that the session is currently referencing
CURRENT_FILE#	File number of the file containing the block that the session is currently referencing
CURRENT_BLOCK#	ID of the block that the session is currently referencing
WAIT_TIME	Total wait time for the event for which the session last waited (0 if currently waiting)
TIME_WAITED	Time that the current session actually spent waiting for the event. This column is set for waits that were in progress at the time the sample was taken.

Table 4.15 - *Selected columns from the dba_hist_active_sess_history view*

The listing below displays the *wait_time_detail.sql* script that compares the wait event values from *dba_hist_waitstat* and *dba_hist_active_sess_history*. This allows for identification of the exact objects that are experiencing wait events.

wait_time_detail.sql

```
-- ***********************************************
-- Copyright © 2004 by Rampant TechPress
-- This script is free for non-commercial purposes
-- with no warranties.  Use at your own risk.
--
-- To license this script for a commercial purpose,
-- contact info@rampant.cc
-- ***********************************************

prompt  This will compare values from dba_hist_waitstat with
```

```
prompt  detail information from dba_hist_active_sess_historyError!
Bookmark not defined..
prompt

set pages 999
set lines 80

break on snap_time skip 2

col snap_time     heading 'Snap|Time'    format a20
col file_name     heading 'File|Name'    format a40
col object_type   heading 'Object|Type'  format a10
col object_name   heading 'Object|Name'  format a20
col wait_count    heading 'Wait|Count'   format 999,999
col time          heading 'Time'         format 999,999

select
   to_char(begin_interval_time,'yyyy-mm-dd hh24:mi') snap_time,
--   file_name,
   object_type,
   object_name,
   wait_count,
   time
from
   dba_hist_waitstat             wait,
   dba_hist_snapshot             snap,
   dba_hist_active_sess_history ash,
   dba_data_files                df,
   dba_objects                   obj
where
   wait.snap_id = snap.snap_id
and
   wait.snap_id = ash.snap_id
and
   df.file_id = ash.current_file#
and
   obj.object_id = ash.current_obj#
and
   wait_count > 50
order by
   to_char(begin_interval_time,'yyyy-mm-dd hh24:mi'),
   file_name
;
```

Note that this script is enabled to join into the *dba_data_files* view to get the file names associated with the wait event. This is a very powerful script that can be used to quickly drill-in to find the cause of specific waits. The sample output is listed below.

```
SQL> @wait_time_detail

Copyright 2004 by Donald K. Burleson -used with permission

This will compare values from dba_hist_waitstat with
detail information from dba_hist_active_sess_hist.

Snap                 Object     Object              Wait
Time                 Type       Name               Count     Time
-------------------- ---------- -------------- -------- --------
2004-02-28 01:00     TABLE      ORDOR             4,273       67
                     INDEX      PK_CUST_ID       12,373      324
                     INDEX      FK_CUST_NAME      3,883       17
                     INDEX      PK_ITEM_ID        1,256      967


2004-02-29 03:00     TABLE      ITEM_DETAIL          83       69


2004-03-01 04:00     TABLE      ITEM_DETAIL       1,246       45


2004-03-01 21:00     TABLE      CUSTOMER_DET      4,381      354
                     TABLE      IND_PART            117       15


2004-03-04 01:00     TABLE      MARVIN           41,273       16
                     TABLE      FACTOTUM          2,827       43
                     TABLE      DOW_KNOB            853        6
                     TABLE      ITEM_DETAIL          57      331
                     TABLE      HIST_ORD          4,337      176
                     TABLE      TAB_HIST            127       66
```

This example should demonstrate how the AWR and ASH data can be used to create an almost infinite number of sophisticated custom performance reports.

Poor Oracle response time has huge productivity costs.

AWR and ADDM in a Nutshell

Using the wealth of metrics within the AWR can be greatly useful for the senior DBA who wants to obtain detailed correlation information between any of the 500+ performance metrics captured by the AWR.

The AWR repository can also be used for Oracle Data Mining. Using The Oracle Database 10g Data Mining (ODM) option, the Oracle DBA can automatically scan the AWR seeking statistically significant correlations between metrics using multivariate Chi-Square techniques to reveal hidden patterns within the performance information. The Oracle Database 10g ODM uses sophisticated Support Vector Machines (SVM) algorithms for binary, multi-class classification models, and has built-in linear regression functionality.

As Oracle Database 10g continues to evolve, Oracle will continue to enhance the mechanisms for analyzing the valuable performance information in AWR. At the present rate, future releases of Oracle may have true artificial intelligence built-in to detect and correct even the most challenging Oracle optimization issues.

The creation of AWR and ASH provides a complete repository for diagnosing and fixing any Oracle performance issue.

The AWR *dba_hist* views are similar to the well-known STATSPACK tables, making it easy to migrate existing performance reports to Oracle Database 10g. The *dba_hist* views are fully-documented and easy to use for writing custom scripts.

The AWR provides the foundation for sophisticated performance analysis including exception reporting, trend analysis, correlation analysis, hypothesis testing, and data mining.

The AWR and ASH are valuable performance optimization tools and provide the foundation for the use of artificial intelligence techniques to be applied to Oracle performance monitoring and optimization. As Oracle evolves it is expected that the AWR and ASH will largely automate the tedious and time-consuming task of Oracle tuning.

Oracle has invested millions of dollars to make the AWR and self-tuning features, and an important licensing issue needs to be recognized. As of February 2004, Oracle is requiring extra licensing to access AWR and ADDM table information.

The *Database Diagnostic Pack* covers access to the following:

- AWR- Automatic Workload Repository

- *dbms_workload_repository* package
- *awrrpt.sql* and *awrrpti.sql* reports
- *dba_hist_** and *v$active_session_history* views
- ADDM - Automatic Database Diagnostic Monitor
- All *dbms_advisor* package with ADDM as the value to the *advisor_name* parameter.
- The *addmrpt.sql* and *addmrpti.sql* reports.
- Views starting with *dba_advisor_** of all tasks generated by ADDM (i.e. tasks with ADDM as the *advisor_name* column in *dba_advisor_tasks* view).

The *Database Tuning Pack* is required to access the SQL Tuning Advisor PL/SQL packages located in $ORACLE_HOME/rdbms/admin. These packages include: *dbms_advisor* package with SQL Tuning Advisor as the value to the *advisor_name* parameter and *dbms_sqltune* package.

Conclusion

This chapter discussed the Automatic Workload Repository and Automatic Diagnostic Monitor. The AWR architecture, Active Session History (ASH), server Generated Alerts, and ADDM performance monitoring were explored. The following information was covered:

- AWR provides services to the database to access, collect, process, and maintain performance statistics on various database functionalities.
- AWR snapshots are taken every hour and kept in the repository for seven days by default.

- Oracle Database 10g invokes server generated alerts automatically to inform about performance or resource issues and when an alert situation is cleared.
- *dba_alert_history* table and *alert_que* retain the alert information which is periodically purged.
- ADDM does a top-down analysis of the database, identifies problems and potential issues, and gives recommendations for fixing these problems.
- OEM can be used to keep a visual track of all database health and functionality issues.

This concludes the initial review and analysis of AWR and ADDM and the Oracle Database 10g manageability infrastructure. The next topic to explore is storage enhancements. Information about Automatic Storage Management (ASM) concepts will be presented in the following chapter.

Automatic Storage Management

CHAPTER 5

Monitoring Oracle storage used to requires constant vigilance

Automatic Storage Management (ASM)

Most Oracle database installations have undergone explosive growth lately with increased storage and data retention requirements, resulting in the DBAs and System Administrators struggling to manage hundreds of disks. The sheer volume of disks and disk management issues have led to longer delays in identifying and rectifying database I/O bottlenecks and performance issues.

Fortunately, Oracle Database 10g offers the new Automatic Storage Management (ASM) feature for the efficient management of disk drives with 24x7 availability.

It does so by creating disk groups, which are comprised of disks and the files that reside on them. With it, the DBA only need to manage a smaller number of disk groups. With the use of ASM, all that is required is to allocate disks to Oracle with the preferences for striping and mirroring using templates and let it handle the rest of the storage management chaos.

ASM Concepts

When the DBA creates database structures like tablespaces, archive logs, redo logs, and control files, he or she needs to specify the file location for the structure in terms of disk groups. The Automatic Storage Management (ASM) process will create and manage the underlying files for the structures.

Adding ASM will not eliminate any existing database functionality. ASM maintains the existing database functionalities with file systems or raw devices, and Oracle Managed Files (OMF) as in previous versions. In an environment with different database versions, older versions or existing databases can use storage with file systems or with storage on raw devices, as they always have done in the past.

New files can be created as ASM files, while old files are administered the traditional way. In a nutshell, it is possible to have a mixture of ASM files, Oracle managed files, and manually managed files all at the same time. Existing files can be migrated to ASM if needed.

ASM is responsible for file management and prevents accidental file deletion by eliminating the file system interface. It provides raw disk I/O performance for all files, striping them across multiple storage arrays. It reduces the cost of managing storage with a clustered volume manager and integrated file system functionality.

ASM adds the reliability features found in LVM (Logical Volume Managers) such as mirroring protection and eliminating the purchase of third party products. Similarly in a RAC environment, ASM eliminates the need for a Cluster LVM or Cluster File System (CFS).

ASM also offers the benefits of mirroring and striping. An advantage of ASM over the conventional methods is the file based storage reliability policy. Hence, the same disk group can have a combination of files protected by mirroring or no protection. ASM does not manage binaries, alert logs, trace files, or password files.

"It might be a hot disk."

ASM Architecture

For the ASM architecture, Oracle Database 10g utilizes a separate smaller database instance, which is installed in a separate oracle home and created during database set up. An ASM instance manages the metadata that is needed to make ASM files available to regular database instances. ASM instance and database instances have access to a common set of disks called disk groups.

Database instances communicate with an ASM instance only to get information about the layout of these files and access the contents of ASM files directly. To create a database that uses storage managed by ASM, the ASM instance needs to be started.

An ASM instance has two new background process types, one for coordinating the disk group rebalance activity and one for data extent movements (ORB0, ORB1, etc.) Each database instance using ASM has two new background processes called OSMB and RBAL. In database instances, OSMB connects to foreground processes. In ASM instances, RBAL performs global calls to open the disks in disk groups. Using these connections, periodic messages are exchanged to update statistics and to verify that both instances are running healthy.

For certain database operations like file creation, ASM intervention is required and the database foreground connects directly to the ASM instance. Whenever a connection is made to the ASM instance, the OSMB process is started dynamically. Database instances are only allowed to connect to one ASM instance at a time, so they have at most one OSMB background process.

Like RAC, the ASM instances themselves may be clustered using the existing Global Cache Services (GCS) infrastructure. There is usually one ASM instance per node on a cluster. As with existing RAC configurations, ASM requires that the Operating System make the disks globally visible to all of the ASM instances, irrespective of node. Database instances only communicate with ASM instances on the same node. If there are several database instances for different databases on the same node, they are likely to share the same ASM instance on that node.

A basic component of Automatic Storage Management is the disk group. ASM is configured by creating disk groups, which in database instances can be used as the default location for files created in the database. Oracle provides SQL statements to create and manage disk groups, their contents, and their metadata.

Group services are used to register the connection information needed by the database instances to find ASM instances. Group Services are a part of Oracle's portable clusterware, which gets automatically installed on every node that runs Oracle10g. ASM eliminates the need for manual disk tuning.

The ASM hierarchy can be explained using a diagram. Compare it with previous versions of Oracle databases.

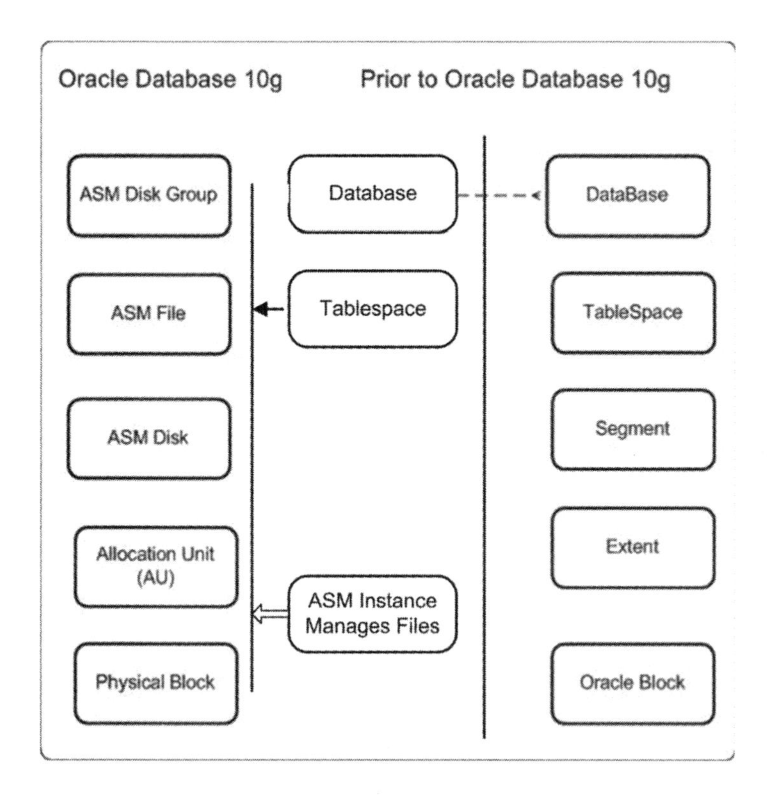

Figure 5.1 *Automatic Storage Management Hierarchy*

A datafile can be stored as an ASM file, a file system file, or a raw device. Each ASM file belongs to a single disk group. A disk group may contain files belonging to several databases, and a single database may form multiple disk groups. ASM files are always spread across all the disks in the disk group. ASM files can be created for redo log files, temporary files, RMAN files, parameter files, and data pump dump files.

ASM introduces the concept of an allocation unit (AU), the smallest contiguous disk space allocated by the ASM. The typical value for an AU is 1MB and is not user configurable. ASM does not allow physical blocks to be split across allocation units.

A disk group is a collection of disks managed as a logical unit. Within a disk group, I/Os are balanced across all the disks. Each disk group has its own file directory, disk directory, and other directories.

For better database performance, dissimilar disks should be partitioned in to separate disk groups. The redundancy characteristics are set up while defining a disk group. Please note the following:

- EXTERNAL REDUNDANCY indicates that ASM does not provide any redundancy for the disk group.
- NORMAL REDUNDANCY (default) enables the disk group to tolerate the loss of a single failure without data loss.
- HIGH REDUNDANCY provides a greater degree of protection using three-way mirroring. ASM provides near-optimal I/O balancing without any manual tuning.

A failure group is a set of disks within a particular disk group that share a common resource whose failure needs to be tolerated. For example, a failure of the SCSI controller leads to all its associated disks becoming unavailable, though each of the disks is functional. Failure groups are used to identify which disks are used to store redundant data. If two-way mirroring is specified for a file, then redundant copies of file extents must be stored in separate failure groups.

Storage is added or removed from disk groups in units of ASM disks. ASM files are Oracle database files stored in ASM disk groups. When a file is created, certain file attributes such as a protection policy or a striping policy are set. These files are visible to RMAN and other Oracle supplied tools, but are invisible from the operating system and its utilities.

Templates are provided to simplify file creation by mapping complex file attribute specifications about ASM files in ASM disk groups to a single name. For example, a template named ARCHIVELOG provides the file redundancy and the striping attributes for all archive log files written to ASM disks. A list of templates is given later in this chapter.

ASM file operations are specified in terms of database objects. The names of the file are exposed through data dictionary views or the ALTER DATABASE BACKUP CONTROLFILE TO TRACE command. The DBA is never required to know filenames for database administration.

The use of ASM filename formats depends on the context of file usage such as referencing an existing file, creating a single file, or creating multiple files.

Fully qualified filenames specify a disk group name, a database name, a file type, a type-specific tag, a file number, and an incarnation number. The fully qualified name is generated on every ASM file on its creation. More information will be provided regarding fully qualified names later in this chapter.

Numeric names are derived from the fully qualified name. The DBA can specify user-friendly alias names for ASM files. Alias names are used for existing as well as new ASM files. But, a hierarchical directory structure for these alias names must be created. Incomplete filenames with disk group names are used only for ASM file creation operations.

ASM Instance Management

Automatic Storage Management is installed by default with Oracle Universal Installer. The Database Configuration Assistance (DBCA) looks for an existing ASM instance and if it does not find one, there is the option of creating and configuring one during the installation process. It is available in both the Enterprise Edition and Standard Edition installations.

An ASM instance is started like any other database instance, except that the initialization parameter file contains the parameter *instance_type*=ASM. For ASM instances, the mount option does not try to mount a database, but tries to mount the disk groups that are specified by the *asm_diskgroups* initialization parameter. ASM instances require a much smaller SGA (typically 64 MB) and should be brought up automatically on sever reboots and kept running at all times. Similarly, the ASM instance can be shutdown like any other database instance using similar commands.

The Oracle Enterprise Manager (OEM) or the database Configuration Assistant (DBCA) can be used for a GUI interface to connect to ASM to configure and alter disk groups and their metadata. OEM provides an integrated approach for managing the ASM instance as well as database instances while DBCA is for database instances only. The footprint for an ASM instance is around 100MB.

An ASM instance does not have a data dictionary. Therefore, SYSDBA and SYSOPER have to be used to connect to an ASM instance. For connecting remotely to an ASM instance, use the password file. No other user administration is maintained by the ASM instance. Those who connect to the ASM instance with SYSDBA privilege have complete administrative access to all disk groups in the system.

The SYSOPER privilege is limited to the following SQL commands:

- STARTUP AND SHUTDOWN

- ALTER DISKGROUP MOUNT/DISMOUNT/REPAIR
- ALTER DISKGROUP ONLINE/OFFLINE DISK
- ALTER DISKGROUP REBALANCE/CHECK

Access to all *v$asm_** views will be discussed later in this chapter.

An ASM instance should always be up and running on the host. It should be brought up automatically whenever the host is rebooted. It should also use the auto startup mechanism supported by the underlying operating system. For example, it should run as a service under Windows. It is also expected to run under Oracle Cluster Ready Services (CRS) framework for high availability.

Initialization Parameters for ASM Instance

While there are a lot of initialization parameters meant for the database instance, only a handful are relevant for the ASM instance. The following is a list of ASM initialization parameters:

- *instance_type* - Must be set to *ASM*. This is the only required parameter. All other parameters assume defaults suited for most environments.
- *db_unique_name* - Unique name for ASM or group of instances within the cluster or on node. Default is +ASM.
- *asm_diskstring* - Limits the set of disks that ASM considers for recovery. Default is NULL.
- *asm_diskgroups* - List of names of disk groups mounted by the ASM instance at startup or when ALTER DISKGROUP ALL MOUNT is used. Default is NULL. If using SPFILE, this dynamic value may rarely need to be altered.

- *asm_power_limit* - The maximum power on an ASM instance for disk rebalancing. Possible values range from 1 to 11, with 11 being the fastest. Default is 1.
- *large_pool_size* - The internal packages used by ASM utilize the Large Pool. The value of *large_pool_size* should be set to a value greater than 8MB. For other buffer parameters, use the default values.

Parameters that start with ASM can be set only for ASM instances. If a database initialization parameter is set in an ASM initialization parameter file, it will cause one of the following scenarios:

- For an invalid parameter, the ASM instance will produce an ORA-15021 error.
- For parameters related to buffer cache and dump destinations valid for ASM instance, the values will be accepted.
- If an ASM specific parameter is specified in a database instance, it will produce an ORA-15021 error.

Disk Recovery Time

The *asm_diskstring* initialization parameter, used to limit the set of disks considered for recovery, is dependent on the operating system. When a new disk is added to the disk group, every ASM instance that has this disk group mounted will be able to see the new disk using its *asm_diskstring* parameter.

The default value of NULL is sufficient for most cases. NULL will cause ASM to find all disks in platform specific locations with read/write access. With a more restrictive value, the ASM can reduce the time required for discovery, and thus, improve time to add disk to the disk group or disk group mount time.

Rebalance Operation

Oracle database can perform one rebalance operation of disks at a given time on an instance. This is set by the value of *asm_power_limit*. This parameter can be changed dynamically. With a higher value, a faster rebalance operation will take place, and vice versa for a lower value.

The *v$asm_operation* view provides information that can be used for adjusting the power of *asm_power_limit* and the rebalance operations. If the DESIRED_POWER_COLUMN is less than the ACTUAL_POWER_COLUMN for a rebalance operation, then the *asm_power_limit* will impact the operation. This view also gives an estimate of the amount of time remaining to complete the operation through the EST_MINUTES column.

The *asm_power_limit* value has an impact on the resource consumption of the server. A lower value of *asm_power_limit* frees up CPU and I/O bandwidth needed for rebalance operation by the ASM. This will leave the resources available for other applications. The default value is meant to minimize any disruptions to other applications.

ASM Instance Operations

As explained in previous sections of this chapter, an ASM instance is similar to any other Oracle instance except that its initialization parameter file contains *instance_type* = ASM. ASM instances do not have a data dictionary, so the only way to connect to one is by using OS authentication, which is SYSDBA or SYSOPER.

To connect remotely, a password file must be used. This parameter differentiates it as an ASM instance to the Oracle executable. Oracle recommends the use of the SPFILE server parameter file, as a SPFILE will eliminate any chances of errors with manual editing. When using an ASM instance, make sure that it is created with sufficient SGA as in a small database instance. Around 32MB to 64MB SGA is sufficient for small to medium sized ASM instance installations.

Starting Up and Shutting Down of an ASM Instance

The STARTUP command in SQL*Plus tries to mount the disk groups specified in *asm_diskgroups* instead of the database. ASM interprets other extensions to the STARTUP command as given below:

- MOUNT - mounts the disk groups specified by *asm_diskgroups.*
- NOMOUNT - does not mount any disk groups, but starts up the instance.
- OPEN - not valid for an ASM instance.
- FORCE - issues the command SHUTDOWN ABORT to the ASM instance and restarts it.

Shutting down an ASM instance is like any other database instance. Just issue the command SHUTDOWN NORMAL and the instance goes down. The following extensions to the SHUTDOWN command can also be added:

- NORMAL - ASM waits for the connected ASM instances and other active ASM SQL sessions to exit before shutting down.
- IMMEDIATE - ASM waits for SQL sessions in progress to finish before shutting down. Database instances need not be disconnected to shutdown the instance.
- ABORT - ASM immediately shuts down.
- TRANSACTIONAL - Similar to IMMEDIATE.

Discovering the Disks and Disk Groups

As previously reviewed, the ASM instance reads the *asm_diskstring* initialization parameter while initializing. This parameter has information on all disks in the disk groups. It eliminates the need for adding paths for all disks in disk groups to the initialization parameter file.

To mount a disk group, ASM has to find all the disks in that particular group. Therefore, all disk configuration errors have to be resolved before mounting a disk group. This feature also helps in recovery of ASM instances.

An ASM instance updates ASM metadata and writes to the disk group log during its operation. After it fails and reinitializes, it reads the disk group log and recovers all transient changes.

ASM Instance Configuration

In Chapter 3, installing an Oracle database instance with or without using ASM disk groups was reviewed. For novice users and those who are not comfortable with the ASM technology, a standard database installation is preferred. ASM managed files can be added to the database later.

Regardless of how the database is setup, if ASM component management is needed, there are certain rules and steps to be considered throughout the process. The limits of ASM and the rules will be reviewed next.

Automatic Storage Management has the following operational limits:

- A maximum of 63 disk groups for every storage system.
- A maximum of 10,000 ASM disks for every storage system.

- A maximum storage of 4 petabytes for each ASM disk.
- A maximum storage of 40 exabytes for each storage system.
- A maximum of 1 million files for each disk group.
- A maximum of 2.4 terabyte storage for each file.

To get an idea of the storage in terms of kilobytes, use the following table:

PREFIX	SYMBOL	X BYTES
Mega	M	1000 kilobytes
Giga	G	1000 megabytes
Tera	T	1000 gigabytes
Peta	P	1000 terabytes
Exa	E	10,00,000 terabytes

Table 5.1 - *Storage Limits*

Rules and Guidelines for ASM Instance Configuration

When there is more than one disk in a disk group, they should have similar size and performance characteristics. It is better to group disks according to their size and performance. Keep disks with dissimilar characteristics for maintenance purposes only, if absolutely needed. Also keep separate disk groups for database files, control files, and flash recovery areas.

If using storage array disks, do not divide the physical volumes into logical volumes, as it will interfere with ASM operation. To the ASM instance, any such disk division will hide the physical disk boundaries and hinder its performance.

ASM requires a minimum of two failure groups for normal redundancy disk groups and three failure groups for high redundancy disk groups. If a lesser number is provided in either case, reliability of the system is affected.

ASM allows dynamically adding and removing disks in a disk group without data loss. ASM will reallocate files in a manner that rebalancing of data will not cause the database instance to shutdown nor block any database operations.

A disk cannot be removed from a disk group until the data is offloaded to another disk. Similarly, a new disk cannot support any I/O operations until the data is re-balanced. Adding and removing disks will temporarily cause a performance impact on I/O operations. So judiciously scheduling these operations will be beneficial to a production environment.

Creating a Disk Group

A disk group is created using the CREATE DISK GROUP command. The DBA can specify the disks that are to be formatted as ASM disks under the disk group, failure groups, and redundancy level for each disk group. The redundancy level can be NORMAL REDUNDANCY, HIGH REDUNDANCY, or EXTERNAL REDUNDANCY. The NORMAL and HIGH options are defined by disk group templates, while EXTERNAL is for external disk groups like storage arrays.

ASM calculates the size of each disk. To limit the size of a disk, use the SIZE clause for each disk. The DBA can name the disks or allow ASM to create operating system independent names for the disks as default.

The ASM instance verifies that a disk in a disk group is addressable and usable. It reads the first block of the disk to determine if it belongs to a group and writes a header to disks not in any group.

A disk can belong to only one disk group. A disk in a disk group can be forced to become a member of another disk group by using the FORCE clause in the command. For this, the original disk group should not be mounted and the disk must have a disk group header. NOFORCE is the default, and it will read only disks that are not part of other disk groups.

When the CREATE DISKGROUP command is issued, it mounts the disk group for the first time and adds the disk group name to the *asm_diskgroups* initialization parameter in the SPFILE. If using the *init.ora* file and needing the disk group to be automatically mounted at startup, manually add the disk group name to the *asm_diskgroups* entry.

Consider this example, which will be used throughout this chapter. The *asm_diskstring* is set to /dev/*. The following disks in /dev: /dska01, /dska02, /dskb01, /dskb02. /dska01 and /dska02 are on a separate SCSI controller from other disks.

```
CREATE DISKGROUP dskgrp01 NORMAL REDUNDANCY
FAILGROUP fgcontrol01 DISK '/dev/dska01', '/dev/dska02',
FAILGROUP fgcontrol02 DISK '/dev/dskb01', '/dev/dskb02' ;
```

Here the dskgrp01 is made up of four disks belonging to the failure group, fgcontrol01 or fgcontrol02. With the NORMAL REDUNDANCY option, ASM provides redundancy for all files in dskgrp01 and dskgrp02 subject to the attributes given in the disk group templates.

Since no names were specified to the disks using the NAME clause, they will be named as dskgrp01_0001, dskgrp01_0002, dskgrp01_0003, and dskgrp01_0004.

Altering a Disk Group (add, drop, undrop, resize, rebalance)

After creating a disk group, use the ALTER DISKGROUP command to add, drop or resize any disk(s). This command can be used for multiple disks in one statement. After issuing an ALTER DISKGROUP statement, ASM rebalances the file extents automatically to suit the new disk group configuration. The rebalancing operation continues as a long running operation, even after the ALTER DISKGROUP command completes successfully. The progress of this rebalancing task can be viewed from *v$asm_operation.*

To add a disk /dska03 to the dskgrp01 disk group, use the ADD DISK clause as in the following command:

```
ALTER DISKGROUP dskgrp01 ADD DISK '/dev/dska03' ;
```

This command adds the disk and assigns dska03 to its own FAILGROUP since none was specified in the command.

To add a handful of disks (/dskc01, /dskc02, /dskc03) under a different failure group (fgcontrol03), issue the following command:

```
ALTER DISKGROUP dskgrp01 NORMAL REDUNDANCY
FAILGROUP fgcontrol03 DISK '/dev/dskc*' ;
```

To drop a disk from a disk group, use the DROP DISK clause of the ALTER DISKGROUP command. For dropping all disks in a failure group, use the DROP DISKS IN FAILUREGROUP clause of the ALTER DISKGROUP command.

When a disk is dropped, the files in the dropped disk are moved to other disks in the disk groups, and the header entry on dropped disk is cleared.

With the FORCE clause of the DROP operation, the disk is dropped without waiting for ASM to read or write to the disk. The FORCE clause is possible only for disk groups made under NORMAL or HIGH REDUNDANCY options.

To drop the disk /dska03 from the dskgrp01 disk group, use the DROP DISK clause as in the following command:

```
ALTER DISKGROUP dskgrp01 DROP DISK '/dev/dska03' ;
```

A disk can be dropped and another one added at the same time in a single command as follows:

```
ALTER DISKGROUP dskgrp01 DROP DISK '/dev/dska03'
ADD FAILGROUP fgcontrol04 DISK '/dev/dskd01', '/dev/dskd02' ;
```

To cancel a drop operation of all disks in a diskgroup, use the UNDROP DISKS clause of the ALTER DISKGROUP command. This statement will cancel all pending drop disk operations within a disk group. If the statement has completely finished, this statement will not work. Also, UNDROP DISKS will restore disks that are being dropped as part of the DROP DISKGROUP or FORCE statements.

```
ALTER DISKGROUP dskgrp01 UNDROP DISKS;
```

To resize a disk or all disks in a disk group or a failure group, use the RESIZE clause of ALTER DISKGROUP command. The RESIZE option needs a *size* parameter otherwise it will resize the disks to the size of the disk as returned by the operating system. The new size after the RESIZE operation is written to the ASM disk header record. If the new size is higher, it is immediately available for utilization, while a lower size will require the completion of the rebalance operation.

After the RESIZE command is issued to reduce the size of a disk, the rebalance operation tries to reallocate the files among other disks. The RESIZE command will fail if the extents cannot be successfully transferred and rebalanced. Similarly, the RESIZE command fails if a disk is resized to values higher than disk capacity.

Assume that the disks in above examples were of 168 GB size. To reduce the size of /dska01 to 120 GB, use the following command:

```
ALTER DISKGROUP dskgrp01
RESIZE DISK '/dev/dska01' SIZE 120G;
```

To reduce the size of all disks under the failgroup, fgcontrol01; modify the command as follows:

```
ALTER DISKGROUP dskgrp01
RESIZE DISKS IN FAILGROUP fgcontrol01 SIZE 120G;
```

Manual rebalancing of a disk group is possible with the REBALANCE clause of the ALTER DISKGROUP command. A manual rebalance is seldom needed, but if the DBA feels that the speed of the rebalance operation is not enough, this command is deployed.

Recall what was reviewed regarding *asm_power_limit* in ASM architecture. This parameter has a profound effect on the rebalance operation as follows. The POWER clause used along with the REBALANCE option specifies the degree of parallelism and speed of the rebalance operation. The POWER value can be from 0 to 11 where 0 stops rebalancing and 11 is the fastest. The speed of an ongoing operation can be changed by altering the POWER with a new level. With a zero value for POWER, the rebalance is stopped until the value is revoked.

The *asm_power_limit* controls the degree of parallelization for rebalance operations. Even with a value of POWER at eleven (11), the degree of parallelization will not exceed the value specified in *asm_power_limit* (default = 1). So the rebalance operation is limited by this initialization parameter.

The *asm_power_limit* can be found in the *v$asm_operation* view. If the value of the DESIRED_POWER column is less than the ACTUAL_POWER column for a rebalance operation, then *asm_power_limit* is limiting the speed. The time remaining to finish the operation is found in the EST_MINUTES column of the view.

An example for a rebalance operation with *asm_power_limit* of 10 is as follows:

```
ALTER DISKGROUP dskgroup01 REBALANCE POWER 6;
```

The next topic to review in disk group operations is how to mount and use them.

Mounting Disk Groups

We have learned that disk groups specified in the *asm_diskgroups* initialization parameter are automatically mounted at the ASM instance startup. These are also unmounted when ASM instance is shutdown. ASM will mount a new disk group when you initially create it, and unmount it when you drop it.

The *ALTER DISKGROUP.MOUNT (UNMOUNT)* command is used whenever you want to do manual operations on a disk group. These operations can be performed by calling the disk groups by name or using ALL. To dismount a disk group with open files, use the FORCE clause of the DISMOUNT option.

To dismount an individual disk group, use the following command:

```
ALTER DISKGROUP dskgrp01 dismount;
```

To mount dskgrp01 back to normal, issue the following command:

```
ALTER DISKGROUP dskgrp01 mount;
```

For dismounting all disk groups in the above examples, use the ALL clause as follows:

```
ALTER DISKGROUP ALL DISMOUNT;
```

The next section reviews disk group templates.

Disk Group Templates

Database templates were reviewed in Chapter 3. What exactly is a disk group template? A disk group template is a collection of attributes that are applied to all files created within the disk group. Oracle provides an initial set of default templates for use by ASM. The *v$asm_template* view gives a list of all templates identifiable by the ASM instance.

New templates can be added to a disk group, existing ones can be modified, and they can even be dropped using the *ALTER DISKGROUP* statement. Oracle strongly advocates against the use of unprotected files.

Here is a table listing all commonly used ASM system default templates.

Name of Template	Type of File	Normal Redundancy	High	External Redundancy	Striping
ARCHIVELOG	Archive logs	2-Way Mirroring	3-Way Mirroring	Unprotected	Coarse
AUTOBACKUP	Automatic backup files	2-Way Mirroring	3-Way Mirroring	Unprotected	Coarse
BACKUPSET	Datafile, datafile incremental, archive log – backups	2-Way Mirroring	3-Way Mirroring	Unprotected	Coarse
CONTROL	Control files	2-Way Mirroring	3-Way Mirroring	Unprotected	Fine
DATAFILE	Datafiles	2-Way Mirroring	3-Way Mirroring	Unprotected	Coarse
DATAGUARDCONFIG	Disaster recovery configurations	2-Way Mirroring	3-Way Mirroring	Unprotected	Coarse
DUMPSET	Data Pump dump	2-Way Mirroring	3-Way Mirroring	Unprotected	Coarse
FLASHBACK	Flashback log	2-Way Mirroring	3-Way Mirroring	Unprotected	Fine
ONLINELOG	Online log	2-Way Mirroring	3-Way Mirroring	Unprotected	Fine
PARAMETERFILE	SPFILE	2-Way Mirroring	3-Way Mirroring	Unprotected	Coarse
TEMPFILE	Tempfile	2-Way Mirroring	3-Way Mirroring	Unprotected	Coarse

Table 5.2 - *ASM Default Templates*

To add a template for a disk group, use the ADD TEMPLATE clause of the ALTER DISKGROUP command along with its attributes. Assume that the DBA wants to create several templates for use in different projects and that DBAHELPER1 is the required template for dskgrp01.

```
ALTER DISKGROUP dskgrp01 ADD TEMPLATE DBAHELPER1 ATTRIBUTES (MIRROR
FINE);
```

The above statement will create a template with the following attributes to files:

Name of Template	Normal Redundancy	High Redundancy	External Redundancy	Striping
DBAHELPER1	2-Way Mirroring	3-Way Mirroring	Cannot be specified	64 KB

To modify an existing template, use the ALTER TEMPLATE clause. When using the ALTER TEMPLATE command on an existing template whether it is system defined or user defined, only specified attributes are changed. Attributes that are not specified are left untouched. Also, when an existing template is modified, new files created using that template are affected. Existing files continue to retain their attributes.

To change the striping for the DBAHELPER1 template, use the following command:

```
ALTER DISKGROUP dskgrp01 ALTER TEMPLATE DBAHELPER1 ATTRIBUTES
(COARSE);
```

To drop an existing template, use the DROP TEMPLATE clause. This can be applied to one or more templates from a disk group. System defined templates supplied by Oracle cannot be dropped. Only user defined templates can be dropped.

To drop the DBAHELPER1 template, issue the following command:

```
ALTER DISKGROUP dskgrp01 DROP TEMPLATE DBAHELPER1;
```

The next topic that will be explored involves disk group directories.

Disk Group Directories

A disk group contains a hierarchical directory structure with fully qualified file names along with alias filenames. On a new file creation, the system alias is automatically created by ASM. To create more friendly aliases for filenames, a directory structure has to be created to support the new naming conventions.

To create a new directory, use the ADD DIRECTORY clause of the ALTER DISKGROUP command. The directory path should begin with a plus (+) sign, followed by subdirectory names separated by forward slash (/) characters.

An example using the dskgrp01 disk group would be as follows:

```
ALTER DISKGROUP dskgrp01 ADD DIRECTORY '+dskgrp01/new10gdb';
```

To add a new directory called newuser under new10gdb, use the following command.

```
ALTER DISKGROUP dskgrp01 ADD DIRECTORY '+dskgrp01/new10gdb/newuser';
```

Care should be taken to see that relative paths are accurate, and that no subdirectory is left out in this process.

To rename a directory, use the RENAME DIRECTORY clause as follows:

```
ALTER DISKGROUP dskgrp01 RENAME DIRECTORY
'+dskgrp01/new10gdb/newuser' to '+dskgrp01/new10gdb/createuser';
```

Similar to disk group templates, a directory can be dropped. To drop a directory, use the DROP DIRECTORY clause. System created directories cannot be dropped. Use the FORCE clause to drop a directory with contents.

In our above example, the new10gdb directory has createuser underneath it in the tree structure. To drop the new10gdb directory, use the following command:

```
ALTER DISKGROUP dskgrp01 DROP DIRECTORY '+dskgrp01/new10gdb' FORCE;
```

In the next section, creating alias names for ASM files will be explored.

Alias Filenames

Once the directory structure is in place, alias names can be added to provide more meaningful names to ASM files. Use the ADD ALIAS, RENAME ALIAS, or DELETE ALIAS clauses of the ALTER DISKGROUP command to add, rename or delete alias names, except for system alias. The *v$asm_alias* view has information on every alias known to the ASM instance. If the alias is system generated, it will be specified under the SYSTEM_CREATED column.

Column	Data type	Description
NAME	VARCHAR2(48)	ASM Alias or alias directory name
GROUP_NUMBER	NUMBER	Owning disk group number of the alias
FILE_NUMBER	NUMBER	ASM file number of the alias
FILE_INCARNATION	NUMBER	ASM file incarnation number for the alias
ALIAS_INDEX	NUMBER	Alias entry number for the alias
ALIAS_INCARNATION	NUMBER	Incarnation number for the parent of the alias
PARENT_INDEX	NUMBER	Number of the directory containing the alias
REFERENCE_INDEX	NUMBER	Number of the directory describing the current entry. REFERENCE_INDEX = 0, for alias entries.

Column	Data type	Description
ALIAS_DIRECTORY	VARCHAR2(1)	Alias is to a directory (Y) or to ASM (N)
SYSTEM_CREATED	VARCHAR2(1)	Alias is system created (Y) or user created (N)

Table 5.3 - *ASM Default Templates*

To add an alias name for an ASM filename, use the ADD ALIAS clause with full directory path and the alias.

```
ALTER DISKGROUP dskgrp01 ADD ALIAS
'+dskgrp01/new10gdb/SALES_TBL01.dbf' FOR
''+dgroup1/qadata/testdb1/sales.325.1' ;
```

The same command can be specified with the numeric form of the ASM filename as follows:

```
ALTER DISKGROUP dskgrp01 ADD ALIAS
'+dgroup01/new10gdb/SALES_TBL01.dbf' FOR ''+dskgrp1.325.1' ;
```

To rename an alias name, use the RENAME ALIAS clause with full directory path and the alias.

```
ALTER DISKGROUP dskgrp01 RENAME ALIAS
'+dskgrp01/SALESDB/salesdata_1.dbf' FOR
''+dgroup1/qadata/testdb2/sales.325.3' ;
```

To drop an alias name, use the DELETE ALIAS clause with the full directory path and the alias. It is very important to note that dropping an alias will not remove the underlying file on the file system.

```
ALTER DISKGROUP dskgrp01 DELETE ALIAS
'+dskgrp01/SALESDB/salesdata_1.dbf';
```

To drop files and associated alias names from a disk group, use the DROP FILE clause of the ALTER DISKGROUP command. In the example given above, the alias

+dskgrp01/SALESDB/salesdata_1.dbf was dropped, but the file still remains on the system.

To remove the file along with its alias name, issue the following command:

```
ALTER DISKGROUP dskgrp01 DROP FILE
'+dskgrp01/SALESDB/salesdata_1.dbf';
```

The system generated alias in the DROP FILE command can also be used.

```
ALTER DISKGROUP dskgrp01 DROP FILE
''+dgroup1/qadata/testdb2/sales.325.3';
```

The next section will review the process of dropping an ASM disk group.

Dropping a Disk Group

An ASM disk group can be dropped with the DROP DISKGROUP command and, optionally, its files using the INCLUDING CONTENTS clause. The default option for DROP DISKGROUP is EXCLUDING CONTENTS, which prevents dropping a disk group with contents.

To drop a disk group, the ASM instance has to be up and running, the disk group has to be mounted, and no files in the disk group should be open. The DROP DISKGROUP command does not return until the action is completed. This command will remove the disk group name from the *asm_diskgroups* parameter when the server parameter file is used. With *init.ora* files, the diskgroup has to be manually removed from the *asm_diskgroups* parameter after the DROP operation and before the next shutdown of the ASM instance.

To drop dskgrp01 with its contents, use the following command:

```
DROP DISKGROUP dskgrp01 INCLUDING CONTENTS
```

Internal Consistency of Disk Groups

After doing any of these operations to disk groups, the DBA may want to verify the internal consistency of the disk group metadata. For this purpose use the ALTER DISKGROUP …. CHECK command. Specific files can be checked, some disks or all disks in a disk group can be checked, or specific failure groups in a disk group can be checked. The disc group has to be in the mounted state for these checks to occur.

ASM will attempt to correct any errors during this operation. If there are any errors, it will be displayed and written to an alert log. Unless the user specifies a NOREPAIR clause, ASM will fix any error situation.

To check the consistency in the metadata for all disks in the dskgrp01 disk group, use the following command:

```
ALTER DISKGROUP dskgrp01 CHECK ALL;
```

File Types Supported by ASM

ASM supports most file types in a database. But some administrative file types such as audit files, alert log, backup files, binaries, export file, and trace files cannot be supported on an ASM disk group. The following table lists the different file types, whether ASM supports it, and system default templates for their file creation.

File Type	ASM Supported	Default Templates
Archive Log Backup	YES	BACKUPSET

File Type	ASM Supported	Default Templates
Archive Log	YES	ARCHIVELOG
Change Tacking File	YES	CHANGETRACKING
Control File	YES	CONTROLFILE
Data Pump Dump	YES	DUMPSET
Data File Backup	YES	BACKUPSET
Data File Copy	YES	DATAFILE
Data file	YES	DATAFILE
Disaster Recovery Configurations	YES	DATAGUARDCONFIG
Flashback Log	YES	FLASHBACK
Operating System File	NO	NOT APPLICABLE
SPFILE	YES	PARAMETERFILE
Redo Log	YES	ONLINELOG
Temporary File	YES	TEMPFILE
Trace File	NO	NOT APPLICABLE

Table 5.4 - *File types, ASM support, and system default templates*

Now that the basics have been reviewed, the next topics to explore are the *v$* and *dba_hist* views that help monitor ASM.

Dynamic Performance Views on ASM

The following views are useful to get more information on Automatic Storage Management. These views are available in the ASM instance as well as database instances. The views in ASM instances will be introduced and compared with database instances.

v$asm_diskgroup – has information about disk groups in an ASM instance. In a database instance, it has one row for every mounted ASM disk group.

Column	Description
GROUP_NUMBER	Cluster-wide number for the disk group
NAME	disk group's name
SECTOR_SIZE	Physical block size in bytes
BLOCK_SIZE	ASM metadata block size in bytes
ALLOCATION_UNIT_SIZE	Allocation unit size in bytes
STATE	State of the disk group relative to the database instance - CONNECTED, BROKEN, UNKNOWN, MOUNTED, DISMOUNTED
TYPE	Redundancy type - NORMAL, HIGH, EXTERN
TOTAL_MB	Total disk group capacity in megabytes
FREE_MB	Unused capacity in megabytes

v$asm_disk - has information about all disks in an ASM instance which are independent or part of disk groups. In a database instance, it has one row for every mounted disk.

Column	Description
GROUP_NUMBER	Cluster-wide number for the disk group containing the disk (foreign key to *v$asm_diskgroup*)
DISK_NUMBER	Disk number within its disk group
COMPOUND_INDEX	32-bit number with disk group number and disk number
INCARNATION	Incarnation number for the disk
MOUNT_STATUS	Per-instance status of the disk relative to group mounts -OPENED, CLOSED, MISSING,CACHED

Column	Description
HEADER_STATUS	Status of the disk per instance -MEMBER, FORMER, CANDIDATE, UNKNOWN, INCOMPATIBLE, PROVISIONED,CONFLICT
MODE_STATUS	Global status about kinds of I/O requests allowed to the disk - ONLINE, OFFLINE, UNKNOWN
STATE	Global state of the disk with respect to its disk group -NORMAL, HUNG, ADDING, DROPPING, FORCING, DROPPED, UNKNOWN
REDUNDANCY	External redundancy of the disk - MIRROR, PARITY, UNPROT, UNKNOWN
LIBRARY	Library name that discovered the disk
TOTAL_MB	Total disk capacity in megabytes
FREE_MB	Unused disk capacity in megabytes
NAME	Disk name
FAILGROUP	Failure group name containing the disk
LABEL	Disk label name
PATH	Operating system pathname
UDID	Universal Device ID
CREATE_DATE	Date and time of adding the disk to the disk group
MOUNT_DATE	Date and time when the disk was mounted by the first instance
REPAIR_TIMER	Seconds remaining until the disk is automatically dropped (0 if not failed)
READS	Total number of I/O read requests to the disk
WRITES	Total number of I/O write requests to the disk
READ_ERRS	Total number of failed I/O read requests to the disk
WRITE_ERRS	Total number of failed I/O write requests to the disk

Column	Description
READ_TIME	Total I/O time for read requests for the disk in hundredths of a second (if *timed_statistics* =TRUE, or 0 if FALSE)
WRITE_TIME	Total I/O time for write requests for the disk in hundredths of a second (if *timed_statistics*=TRUE, or 0 if FALSE)
BYTES_READ	Bytes read from the disk
BYTES_WRITTEN	Bytes written to the disk

v$asm_client - identifies databases using ASM managed disk groups. In a database instance, *v$asm_client* will display one row for the ASM instance if the database has open ASM files.

Column	Description
GROUP_NUMBER	Disk group number used by the client database instance (foreign key to *v$asm_diskgroup*)
INSTANCE_NAME	Database client instance identifier
DB_NAME	Unique database instance name
STATUS	Status of the client connection - CONNECTED, DISCONNECTED, BROKEN

v$asm_file - has information on every ADM file in every disk group mounted by the ASM instance. In a database instance, it has no information.

Column	Description
GROUP_NUMBER	Number of the disk group containing the file
FILE_NUMBER	Number of the file within the disk group
COMPOUND_INDEX	32-bit number consisting of disk group number and file number

Column	Description
INCARNATION	Incarnation number for the file
BLOCK_SIZE	File block size in bytes
BLOCKS	Number of blocks in the file
BYTES	Number of bytes in the file
SPACE	Space in bytes allocated to the file
TYPE	File type
REDUNDANCY	Redundancy of the file - MIRROR, PARITY, UNPROT
STRIPED	Type of file striping - FINE, COARSE
CREATION_DATE	File creation date
MODIFICATION_DATE	Last open/close date for writing

v$asm_template - has information on every template present in every disk group mounted by the ASM instance. In a database instance, it has no information.

Column	Description
GROUP_NUMBER	Disk group number (foreign key to *v$asm_diskgroup*)
ENTRY_NUMBER	Template entry number (Primary key)
REDUNDANCY	Redundancy of the template - MIRROR, PARITY, UNPROT
STRIPE	Striping type for template - FINE, COARSE
SYSTEM	System template or not (Y/N)
NAME	Template name

v$asm_alias - has information on every alias present in every disk group mounted by the ASM instance. In a database instance, it has no information. The structure of *v$asm_alias* has been described earlier under alias names.

v$asm_operation - has information on every active long running ASM operation in the ASM instance. In a database instance, it has no information.

Column	Description
GROUP_NUMBER	Disk group number - Primary key
OPERATION	Operation type – REBAL
STATE	State of the operation - RUNNING, QUEUED
POWER	Power requested for the operation
ACTUAL	Power allocated to the operation
SOFAR	Number of allocation units moved so far by the operation
EST_WORK	Estimated number of allocation units to be moved by the operation
EST_RATE	Estimated number of allocation units being moved per minute by the operation
EST_MINUTES	Estimated amount of time expected for the remainder of the operation to complete in minutes

The next section goes into ASM deployment in a database.

How Are ASM Files Used in the Database?

ASM files are Oracle managed files. Unless the ASM files are created using an alias name, they are treated as Oracle managed files and deleted when no longer in use.

Default disk groups can be created for use when creating data files, control files, temp files, redo log files, etc. The name of the default disk group will be stored in an initialization parameter file and is not specified during file creation using ASM files.

The following initialization parameters take the ASM filenames or ASM directory names as destinations: *log_archive_dest*, *log_archive_dest_n*, and *standby_archive_dest*. These initialization parameters take the ASM filenames as destinations: *control_files*, *db_create_file_dest*, *db_create_online_log_dest_n*, and *db_recovery_file_dest*.

Here is an example of how to create a datafile using a default disk group specified by an initialization parameter setting. The initialization parameter file is set as follows and then a tablespace is created:

```
DB_CREATE_FILE_DEST = '+dskgrp01'

CREATE TABLESPACE SALESDATA;
```

These commands will create the SALESDATA tablespace and all data files underneath it on dskgrp01.

A template can also be used to specify the redundancy and striping of datafiles in a disk group. Using the example given above, issue the following commands.

```
ALTER SYSTEM SET DB_CREATE_FILE_DEST = '+dskgrp01 (DBAHELPER1) ';

CREATE TABLESPACE SALESDATA;
```

When ASM creates a datafile, the default size is 100MB with the auto-extensible feature turned on to allow unlimited size. The SIZE clause can be used to override the default.

To create the index tablespace for the SALESDATA with just one datafile of 800 MB, use the following command:

```
CREATE TABLESPACE SALESIDX DATAFILE '+dskgrp02' SIZE 800 MB
AUTOEXTEND ON;
```

To create redo log files using ASM files by the same method given above, specify them in the initialization parameter file and use the ADD LOGFILE command. The following example creates a log file with a member in each of the two disk groups, dskgrp03 and dskgrp04.

```
DB_CREATE_ONLINE_LOG_DEST_1 = '+dskgrp03'
DB_CREATE_ONLINE_LOG_DEST_2 = '+dskgrp04'
ALTER DATABASE ADD LOGFILE;
```

The next topic to explore is how to create a database using ASM files.

Using ASM to Create a Database

Oracle recommends the use of the Database Configuration Assistant (DBCA) to create a new database. However, one can be created manually with minimal user intervention using ASM files as the following example shows. Use the following initialization parameter settings in *init.ora* file:

```
DB_CREATE_FILE_DEST = '+dskgrp01'
DB_RECOVERY_FILE_DEST = '+dskgrp02'
CONTROL_FILES = '+dskgrp03'
DB_CREATE_ONLINE_LOG_DEST_1 = '+dskgrp04'
DB_CREATE_ONLINE_LOG_DEST_2 = '+dskgrp05'
LOG_ARCHIVE_DEST = '+dskgrp02'
```

Issue the following command at the SQL prompt to create a new database:

```
CREATE DATABASE QASALES ;
```

This command will create a database with SYSTEM and SYSAUX tablespaces in the disk group dskgrp01. It will create a multiplexed online redo with two log groups with one member of each group in dskgrp04 and dskgrp05. The control files will be created in dskgrp03 and dskgrp01. An undo tablespace will be created in dskgrp01, if automatic undo is enabled. Since *log_archive_format* is set to a disk group, *log_archive_format* is ignored and unique filenames for archive logs in dskgrp02 are generated.

It would be worthwhile to look at the new storage structures in Oracle Database 10g.

Now that ASM files have been explored in more detail, it would be appropriate to examine more information regarding temporary tablespace groups and BigFile Tablespaces. These topics are presented next.

New Tablespace Types

There are new storage structures in Oracle Database 10g. They are Temporary Tablespace Groups (TTG) and BigFile Tablespaces (BFT).

Temporary Tablespace Groups

A Temporary Tablespace Group (TTG) can be described as a group of temporary tablespaces. The *dba_tablespace_groups* view provides all the temporary tablespace group information.

TTGs have the following characteristics:

- A TTG contains at least one temporary tablespace.
- A TTG cannot have the same name as tablespace.
- A TTG name can be used instead of a temporary tablespace name. It is created implicitly when the first TEMPORARY tablespace is assigned. It is deleted when the last TEMPORARY tablespace is removed from the TTG.

The benefits of having TTG s are as follows:

- Multiple temporary tablespaces can be used in different sessions at the same time. Slave processes in a single parallel operation can use multiple temporary tablespaces. Multiple default temporary tablespaces can be specified at the database level.

- More than one default temporary tablespace can be defined for a database. A single database operation can use multiple temporary tablespaces in sorting operations. This prevents large tablespace operations from running out of space. If a TTG is specified as the default temporary tablespace for the database, no tablespaces in that group can be dropped.

In Oracle Database 10g, the DBA can simply rename any tablespace excluding the SYSTEM or SYSAUX tablespaces. This helps in situations like transporting a tablespace to a target database which has a similar tablespace with the same name.

Each database user has a permanent tablespace for storing permanent data and a temporary tablespace for storing temporary data. In previous versions of Oracle, if a user is created without specifying a default tablespace, SYSTEM tablespace will be allotted as default. For 10g, a default permanent tablespace can be defined to be used for all new users without a specific permanent tablespace.

By creating a default permanent tablespace, non-system user objects can be prevented from being created in the SYSTEM tablespace.

BigFile Tablespaces (BFT)

A BFT is a tablespace containing a single very large data file. With the new addressing scheme in 10g, up to four billion blocks are permitted in a single data file and file sizes can be from 8 Tera Bytes to 128 Tera Bytes. To distinguish a regular tablespace from BFT, a regular tablespace is called a small file tablespace. Oracle

Database 10g can be a mixture of small file tablespaces and bigfile tablespaces.

BFTs are supported only for locally managed tablespaces with ASM segments and locally managed UNDO and TEMPORARY tablespaces. When BFTs are used with Oracle Managed Files, data files become completely transparent to the DBA and no reference is needed for them. BFT makes a tablespace logically equivalent to a data file allowing operations in earlier releases to be performed on tablespaces.

BFTs should be used only with the logical volume manager, with ASM supporting dynamically extensible logical volumes, and with systems that support striping to prevent negative consequences on RMAN backup parallelization and parallel query execution. BFT should not be used when there is a limited free disk space available.

ROWIDs of rows that belong to BFTs do not contain a relative file number but the block number. A bigfile tablespace has only one datafile, and always has a relative file number of 1024. There is no need to include this filenumber in the ROWID. The block numbers are relative to their tablespace and are unique with in tablespace. The only supported ways to retrieve the ROWID component is to use the *dbms_rowid* package.

The default tablespace type is a persistent database parameter in the data dictionary. If this parameter is not set by either the CREATE DATABASE or ALTER DATABASE command, the default will be SMALLFILE. Two new keywords, BIGFILE and SMALLFILE, are added to override the default tablespace type when creating tablespaces. The *v$tablespace* and *dba/user_tablespaces* data dictionary views have a new column to indicate the tablespace type.

Prior to Oracle Database 10g, K and M were used to specify data file sizes. Since 10g introduces larger file sizes up to 128 Tera bytes using BFTs, the sizes can be specified using G and T for Gigabytes and Terabytes.

In Oracle Database 10g, transportable tablespaces can be moved across different supported platforms like Solaris, Windows, Linux, HP-UX, AIX and HP Tru 64. The benefits include easy distribution of data from data warehouses to data marts on smaller and different platforms.

Read-only tablespaces can be shared across heterogeneous clusters, and databases can be migrated between different platforms by rebuilding the catalog and transporting other tablespaces. For transporting tablespaces between different platforms, endian ordering has to be the same on both platforms. *v$transportable_platform* determines if endian formatting is the same on both platforms. Refer to Chapter 2 for a brief introduction. Use RMAN if they are different.

```
SQL> desc v$transportable_platform
Name                                      Null?           Type
----------------------------------- -------- ----------------------
PLATFORM_ID                                             NUMBER
PLATFORM_NAME                                           VARCHAR2(101)
ENDIAN_FORMAT                                           VARCHAR2(14)
```

The *db_file_name_convert* clause can be used to convert a file to a different format and place it in a different location. The converted files are placed in the new flash recovery area introduced in Oracle Database 10g.

Oracle 10g Automated Space Management features will be examined next.

Automated Space Management in Oracle10g

Oracle Database 10g proactively manages the disk space used by tablespaces. This is done by the use of database alerts as well as by growth trend analysis using AWR. When a database runs low on diskspace, the server sends an alert, and the DBA can intervene with more disk space. By utilizing the information in AWR, growth-trend analysis and capacity planning can be done for the database.

Proactive tablespace monitoring is beneficial because it provides tablespaces with more disk space before it runs out of space and does efficient monitoring of space usage. Proactive tablespace management does not support dictionary managed tablespaces.

Every tablespace has two thresholds, critical and warning. They are defined in terms of the fullness of the tablespace. The threshold is expressed in terms of bytes or as a percentage of the tablespace size. The *dbms_server_alert* package contains procedures to set and get threshold values. When the space usage exceeds either of the two thresholds, an appropriate alert is issued. If the thresholds are not specified, the defaults are 85% for warning and 97% for critical thresholds.

When a database is migrated, the alert is disabled by default and set to NULL. The database wide default can be reset as desired. An ideal setting for warning threshold will result in an alert early enough to ensure enough time to resolve the problem before it becomes critical, and late enough to be not bothered when the space is adequate.

The MMON background process checks for tablespace threshold violations every 10 minutes. An alert is triggered when the threshold has been reached. This alert is cleared when a subsequent MMON finds that the space consumption has gone below the threshold often by appropriate DBA actions.

For temporary tablespaces, the threshold value has to be set up as a limit on the used space in the tablespace. In read-only mode tablespaces or offline tablespaces, alerts should not be flagged as nothing more can be done to those tablespaces.

Undo tablespaces are very similar to temporary tablespaces as other segments can reuse the free space in undo segments. Any extent is reusable if it does not contain any active or unexpired undo. The sum of active and unexpired extents is considered as used space for calculating threshold violations. For tablespaces with autoextensible files, the thresholds are calculated according to the maximum file size specified or to the maximum OS file size.

Space thresholds for tablespaces can also be set through Oracle Enterprise Manager on the Edit Metric Thresholds page. This page is launched from the database home page by selecting Edit Metric Thresholds from Related Links. Besides setting the threshold values, OEM can be used to enable or disable the values when creating or editing a tablespace.

Each database instance has an internal memory structure that keeps track of the space usage in every file in the database. This table has one row for each database file, and each row contains the filesize, the allocated space, and a Change SCN number.

Although RAC is not being reviewed extensively in this book, space management will be briefly introduced. An excellent source for RAC information, besides the Oracle documentation, is Rampant's *Oracle 10g Grid & Real Application Clusters*. With Real Application clusters, each database instance has its own MMON process. But each MMON process reads the aggregated data from the *gv$* views to avoid conflicts. When a tablespace goes over the thresholds, the first MMON process that discovers the exceeded threshold raises the alert.

When segments have unused space above and below the high water mark (HWM), the database may suffer poor performance during scans and DML operations. Since data is spread across many data blocks, more I/Os are needed for data retrieval. Row migration occurs and unused space becomes unavailable to other database objects. In previous versions of Oracle database, space allocated below HWM could be freed only by moving or redefining the segment. In Oracle Database 10g, the segments can be shrunk. When a segment is shrunk, the data is compacted and the HWM is pushed down to release unused space. Sparsely populated segments get improved scan performance and faster DML operations by shrinking.

A shrink operation is an online operation that does not take extra database space to run. As a result of the shrink operation, row migration may or may not be reduced as shrinking may not touch all segment blocks. The segments must reside on Automatic Segment Space Managed (ASSM) tablespaces for the shrink operation to be successful. It will not work on segments managed by free lists. Similarly, the following objects cannot be shrunk:

- Tables with on-commit or ROWID based materialized views.
- Tables in clusters or tables with LONG columns.
- LOB indexes and shared LOB segments.
- IOT mapping tables and IOT overflow segments.
- Temporary segments.
- Undo segments.

During the segment shrink operation, index dependency is not affected. The shrink operation does not affect any indexes, though rebuilding secondary indices on an IOT is often recommended. DML triggers are not fired, as the data is not changed by this internal INSERT/DELETE operation.

A shrink operation may cause ROWIDs to change in heap-organized segments. So row movement has to be enabled to circumvent this issue before a shrink operation. To enable row movement, use the {CREATE|ALTER} TABLE ..ENABLE ROW movement command.

A shrink operation consists of two phases, compaction and adjusting the HWM to release the unused space. If the COMPACT option is used, only the first phase is executed. The shrink results are saved in bitmap blocks of the corresponding segment. The next time a shrink operation is performed on the same segment, Oracle Database 10g will remember what has been done. If CASCADE is specified, the shrinking cascades to all dependent segments that support a shrink operation.

During the COMPACT phase, individual rowlocks are held. Concurrent DML operations serialize on these rowlocks and DML operations can block the compaction progress. When the HWM is adjusted in the second phase, the object is locked in exclusive mode for a short duration.

More details on the shrink operation are given in the next section.

Oracle Segment Advisor

The segment advisor determines whether an object is a good candidate for a shrink operation. It makes recommendations based on the amount of space that can be released and future space requirements from growth-trend information. The DBA can choose whether to implement these recommendations. The shrinks can be invoked at the segment or tablespace level.

OEM is the interface to invoke online segment shrinking. OEM offers the option of selecting various inputs and scheduling a job to call the Segment Advisor to get shrink advice. The OEM wizard can be invoked with no context, in the context of a tablespace, in the context of a schema object, or in the context of a database user.

Without context involves areas like alert table and tablespace alerts recommendations page, detected storage problems page, ADDM results page involving Segment Advisor recommendations, and maintenance page of database home page. In the context of tablespace and object involves selecting the appropriate entity and selecting a Segment Advisor menu item in OEM.

Segment Advisor collects growth trend data from segments and makes it available to advisories and reporting tools such as AWR or OEM. The AWR collects the persistent space usage statistics and stores it in the WR schema.

Space usage recording and reporting data is provided to the AWR when snapshots are created and alerts are triggered. The snapshot based statistics are created every 30 minutes. The current space usage details of the tablespace are registered in the AWR. MMON checks the tablespace thresholds every ten minutes and passes the data to AWR on detecting any violations.

The new segment resource estimation feature available through OEM, estimates the amount of resources required for creating a new segment. Oracle Database 10g estimates the amount of disk space likely to be consumed by the object based on the structure of a table or index and the estimated rows per table. This feature also predicts the amount of CPU and I/O resources for the creation process.

Automatic Undo Management

The automatic undo management feature introduced in Oracle 9i has been improved with the following capabilities. Some of the undo management related initialization parameters are eliminated in Oracle Database 10g as they are automatically calculated. They include *max_rollback_segment, row_locking, undo_suppress_errors, serializable,* and *transaction_auditing.* Undo Tablespace Sizing Advisor helps to size the undo tablespace based on the workload history. Automatic undo retention tuning is enabled by default and determines the optimal undo retention time depending on the undo tablespace size. There is no need to manually set the undo retention period. Proactive monitoring and notification warns of any current or impending problems such as snapshot too old.

Oracle Database 10g remembers optimal undo settings to avoid repeated ramp ups and performance problems during instance restart, database migration, and switching the undo tablespace. After a system restart or an undo tablespace switch, Oracle Database 10g decides how many undo segments to place online based on existing data stored in the AWR.

The Undo Advisor analyzes the undo usage. In AUM mode, the advisor suggests optimal undo tablespace size to support the longest running queries. If AUM is not used, it suggests undo tablespace size for a given retention period and the retention period for a given undo tablespace size.

Resumable space allocation, introduced in Oracle 9i, is for all tablespaces at the session level. Database operations are suspended when an out-of-space condition is encountered. These suspended operations automatically resume when the error condition disappears. In Oracle Database 10g, this can be enabled at the instance level. Besides this improvement, automatic alert notification is sent when an operation is suspended.

This feature can be enabled by the SQL command.

```
ALTER SYSTEM SET RESUMABLE_TIMEOUT = <value in seconds>;
(Substitute 3600 for 1 hour)
```

The next topic presented will involve the Redo logfile Advisor.

Redo Logfile Advisor

Oracle Database 10g introduces the Redo Logfile Advisor which determines the optimal smallest online redo log file size based on the current *fast_start_mttr_target* setting and *mttr* statistics. Therefore, setting up the *fast_start_mttr_target* parameter is necessary for enabling the advisor. It suggests an optimal value for the online redo log file and eliminates the need to determine optimal logfile sizes manually. An online redo logfile is considered to be of optimal size when it does not drive incremental checkpointing more than *fast_start_mttr_target.* The *v$instance_recovery* view has a new column for this value called OPTIMAL_LOGFILE_SIZE. Table 5.5 shows all the columns available in the *v$instance_recovery* view. The OPTIMAL_LOGFILE_SIZE column shows the redo logfile size in megabytes based on the current *fast_start_mttr_target* setting. All online redo log files should be set to this value or higher.

Column	Data type
RECOVERY_ESTIMATED_IOS	NUMBER
ACTUAL_REDO_BLKS	NUMBER
TARGET_REDO_BLKS	NUMBER
LOG_FILE_SIZE_REDO_BLKS	NUMBER
LOG_CHKPT_TIMEOUT_REDO_BLKS	NUMBER
LOG_CHKPT_INTERVAL_REDO_BLKS	NUMBER
FAST_START_IO_TARGET_REDO_BLKS	NUMBER

Column	Data type
TARGET_MTTR	NUMBER
ESTIMATED_MTTR	NUMBER
CKPT_BLOCK_WRITES	NUMBER
OPTIMAL_LOGFILE_SIZE	NUMBER
ESTD_CLUSTER_AVAILABLE_TIME	NUMBER
WRITES_MTTR	NUMBER
WRITES_LOGFILE_SIZE	NUMBER
WRITES_LOG_CHECKPOINT_SETTINGS	NUMBER
WRITES_OTHER_SETTINGS	NUMBER
WRITES_AUTOTUNE	NUMBER
WRITES_FULL_THREAD_CKPT	NUMBER

Table 5.5 – *v$instance_recovery view*

The next section provides some practical tips on ASM implementation.

Guru Conversation for the Senior DBA

In this chapter, the topics of ASM, ASM files, ASM instance, etc. have been explored. There will be some databases in any company using traditional files as well as ASM managed files. When the author tested the scenario of using multiple types of files in a database on Redhat Linux, there were some DBCA issues with Oracle recognizing these devices. There is also documentation on Oracle Metalink (#266028.1) for this problem. Here is a review of how a new disk that is added and configured in a Linux server can be used by ASM.

Refer to Linux documentation on adding a new disk using *fdisk*, and adding entries in the /etc/fstab file as *root*. The server will have to be rebooted for the new disk to be visible in the operating system. Once the disk is added to Linux and used for ASM files with DBCA, the following errors may be encountered:

ORA-15018, diskgroup cannot be created; ORA-15059, invalid device type for ASM disk. These errors have been reported only on Linux platforms, and can be rectified by creating files instead of real devices.

Assuming an 80 GB disk is added to a Linux server. Also assume that when it was used one of the previously mentioned ORA errors was generated. The solution is to create new files to be used by ASM as free devices instead of real disks. The following steps could be attempted as an *oracle* user or as a *root* user. If using *root*, permissions may have to be changed on the files to be seen by ASM. Veteran DBAs with Linux experience may know how to run many of these individual commands in a single step.

Step 1 - Create new files using dd command. If the complete space out of the last disk is not achieved, reduce the count to 8000000.)

```
$dd if=/dev/zero of=file_dsk1 bs=1k count=10000000
$dd if=/dev/zero of=file_dsk2 bs=1k count=10000000
$dd if=/dev/zero of=file_dsk3 bs=1k count=10000000
$dd if=/dev/zero of=file_dsk4 bs=1k count=10000000
$dd if=/dev/zero of=file_dsk5 bs=1k count=10000000
$dd if=/dev/zero of=file_dsk6 bs=1k count=10000000
$dd if=/dev/zero of=file_dsk7 bs=1k count=10000000
$dd if=/dev/zero of=file_dsk8 bs=1k count=10000000
```

The above commands will create virtual disk files of 10 gigabytes each.

Step 2 - Using the *losetup* command, associate a loop (block) device with each of these files. Use *man losetup* to learn more about this command. The *losetup* command has to be run as *root.*

```
#losetup /dev/loop1 file_dsk1
#losetup /dev/loop2 file_dsk2
#losetup /dev/loop3 file_dsk3
#losetup /dev/loop4 file_dsk4
#losetup /dev/loop5 file_dsk5
#losetup /dev/loop6 file_dsk6
#losetup /dev/loop7 file_dsk7
#losetup /dev/loop8 file_dsk8
```

Step 3 – Use the *raw* utility to bind a raw device to the newly created block devises from Step 2. Use *man raw* to learn more about this command.

```
# raw /dev/raw/raw1 /dev/loop1
# raw /dev/raw/raw2 /dev/loop2
# raw /dev/raw/raw3 /dev/loop3
# raw /dev/raw/raw4 /dev/loop4
# raw /dev/raw/raw5 /dev/loop5
# raw /dev/raw/raw6 /dev/loop6
# raw /dev/raw/raw7 /dev/loop7
# raw /dev/raw/raw8 /dev/loop8
```

Step 4 - Since the above commands were run as *root*, change the ownership of these new raw devices to *oracle*.

```
# chown oracle:dba /dev/raw/raw1
# chown oracle:dba /dev/raw/raw2
# chown oracle:dba /dev/raw/raw3
# chown oracle:dba /dev/raw/raw4
# chown oracle:dba /dev/raw/raw5
# chown oracle:dba /dev/raw/raw6
# chown oracle:dba /dev/raw/raw7
# chown oracle:dba /dev/raw/raw8
```

Step 5 - Now change the permissions on these devices.

```
# chmod 660 /dev/raw/raw1
# chmod 660 /dev/raw/raw2
# chmod 660 /dev/raw/raw3
# chmod 660 /dev/raw/raw4
# chmod 660 /dev/raw/raw5
# chmod 660 /dev/raw/raw6
# chmod 660 /dev/raw/raw7
# chmod 660 /dev/raw/raw8
```

Congratulations, now there are 8 disks of 10 Giga bytes each. These are free devices available for use by the ASM setup.

The DBCA can be used for these files in the new database or add them using SQL*Plus commands.

```
CREATE DISKGROUP dskgrp01 NORMAL REDUNDANCY
FAILGROUP fgcontrol01 DISK '/dev/raw/raw1',
FAILGROUP fgcontrol02 DISK '/dev/raw/raw2' ;
```

These files will show up in the *init.ora* file of the ASM instance as ASM_DISKSTRING='/dev/raw/raw*'.

Conclusion

This chapter explored the Automatic Storage Management (ASM) features of Oracle Database 10g. The salient points are as follows.

- Automatic Storage Mechanism (ASM) will create and manage the underlying files for database structures.
- For the ASM architecture, Oracle Database 10g utilizes a separate smaller database instances installed in a separate oracle home, created during database set up.
- ASM instance manages the metadata that is needed to make ASM files available to regular database instances.
- ASM instance and database instances have access to a common set of disks called disk groups.
- ASM instance is expected to always be up and running on the host.
- A Bigfile tablespace (BFT) is a tablespace containing a single very large data file with sizes from the 8 Tera Bytes to 128 Tera Bytes range.
- To distinguish a regular tablespace from BFT, a regular tablespace is called a small file tablespace.
- Automatic undo management feature has been improved to provide proactive monitoring and notification of undo issues.

A more detailed examination of the automatic system resource management will be presented in the next chapter.

Automatic System Resource Management

CHAPTER 6

Management judges a DBA's performance on Oracle's performance!

Automatic Shared Memory Management (ASMM)

The commonly tuned System Global Area (SGA) components are the database buffer cache, the shared pool, the large pool, and the Java pool. The ASMM enables Oracle Database 10g to automatically determine the appropriate values of these components within the limits of the total SGA.

In previous versions of Oracle Database, the Oracle server allotted the memory for the fixed SGA and other internal allocations. Under-sizing can lead to poor performance and out-of-memory errors (ORA-4031), while over-sizing can waste memory. In Oracle Database 10g, the DBA can set the total amount of SGA memory available to an instance using the *sga_target* initialization parameter. Oracle database will automatically distribute this memory among various sub-components to ensure the most effective memory utilization.

The *sga_target* parameter includes all SGA memory, including automatically sized components, manually sized components, and internal allocations during the database startup. The default value is 0, and ASMM is disabled for this value.

The initialization parameters for the SGA components, *db_cache_size (default pool only)*, *shared_pool_size*, *large_pool_size*, and *java_pool_size,* are still valid in the Oracle Database 10g and are referred to as auto-tuned SGA parameters. When the automatic SGA memory management feature is enabled in the database, the sizes of different components are flexible to resize to adapt to the needs of the workload without additional intervention. The database automatically distributes the SGA among the various components as required, allowing the system to maximize the consumption of all available memory. Whenever an application needs more shared pool memory, it will obtain the extra memory from free memory in the buffer cache. Consequently, no out of memory errors are generated until the system has completely run out of memory.

When *sga_target* is not set or set to zero, the parameters listed above, except for *shared_pool_size,* behave as in previous releases of Oracle Database. The *shared_pool_size* will add internal overhead for metadata including data structures for processes and sessions to its value and adjust accordingly. The *statistical_level* has to be set to TYPICAL or ALL to use ASMM.

The following buffers are considered as manually sized components in Oracle Database 10g: Log Buffer, Streams Pool which is new in Oracle Database 10g, other buffer caches such as RECYCLE and KEEP), fixed SGA, and internal allocations.

With manual configuration, it is possible for compiled SQL statements to frequently age out of the shared pool due to inadequate size. With automatic SGA management, the internal tuning algorithm monitors the workload performance and increases the shared pool as needed to reduce the number of parses.

The ASMM feature uses a new Memory Manager (MMAN) background process. MMAN coordinates the sizing of the memory components and acts as a memory broker. The MMAN keeps track of all memory components and pending resize operations.

Based on workload information from AWR, the ASMM can capture statistics periodically, every 60 minutes for example, in the background, use different memory advisories, and move memory to where it is most needed whether that be the large pool or buffer cache. For example in a long running OLTP day job, a larger buffer cache is needed; while for a data warehousing (DSS) batch job at night, more memory is needed for the large pool. The ASMM moves the memory to buffer cache or large pool as needed.

When *sga_target* is set to a non-zero value to enable ASMM, the auto tuned SGA parameters are set to zero values. These components are then automatically sized by ASMM. If the four parameters are set to non-zero values along with ASMM, the specified values are considered as a lower limit by the auto-tuning algorithm. Whenever an auto tuned component is resized to a larger value, the memory is taken from another auto-tuned component to supplement the change, while the manually tuned components are left untouched.

The *sga_target* is a dynamic parameter and is set from OEM or with the ALTER SYSTEM command. The *sga_target* can be raised up to *sga_max_size*. It can be reduced until the auto-tuned components are reduced to their minimums. Any change in *sga_target* only affects the size of the auto-tuned components.

Manually sized SGA components are tuned by the user. The total size of manual SGA parameters is subtracted from the *sga_target* to be allotted to auto tuned components.

Some of the manually sized SGA components are: Keep/Recycle buffer caches which are controlled by *db_keep_size* and *db_recycle_cache_size*; multiple block size caches such as *db_nk_cache_size* where n=2, 4, 8, 16, 32; Streams Pool which is controlled by *streams_pool_size*; *log_buffer*, and etc. The memory consumed by these manually sized components reduces the amount of memory available for the automatic tuning of automatically sized components.

For example if *sga_target* is set to 8g and *db_16k_cache_size* is set to 1g, then the total size for the four auto-tuned components is limited to 7g. The 7g size includes the fixed SGA and log buffer, and only after those have been allocated is the rest of the memory divided between the auto-tuned components. A list of parameters and their values can be accessed using the *v$parameter* view.

More about using memory advisor through OEM will be presented in the next section.

Using Memory Advisor through OEM

The Memory Advisor can be used only when the automatic memory tuning is disabled. This will help to tune the size of memory structures. The Memory Advisor has three advisors that give recommendations: Shared pool in SGA; Buffer Cache in SGA; and PGA.

To use Memory Advisor and tune its underlying structures, do the following steps:

1. Click on Memory Advisor in the Advisor Central Page.

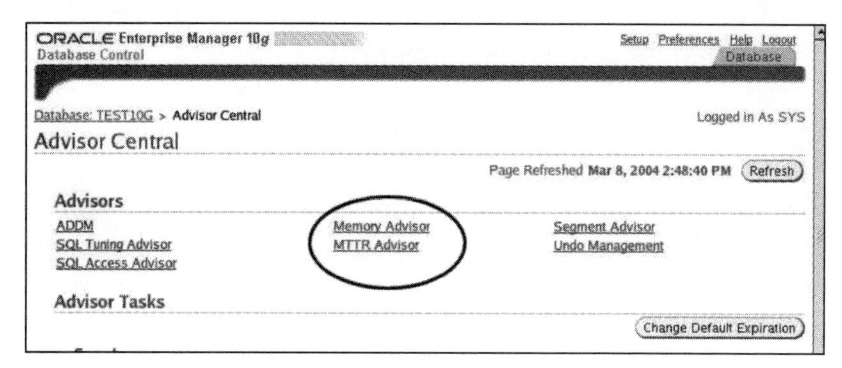

Figure 6.1 - *Memory Advisor*

The Memory Parameters page: The SGA page appears. This page has all the details on memory usage for the System Global Area. The shared pool and buffer cache are part of the SGA. For more information on the structure shown here, click on Help.

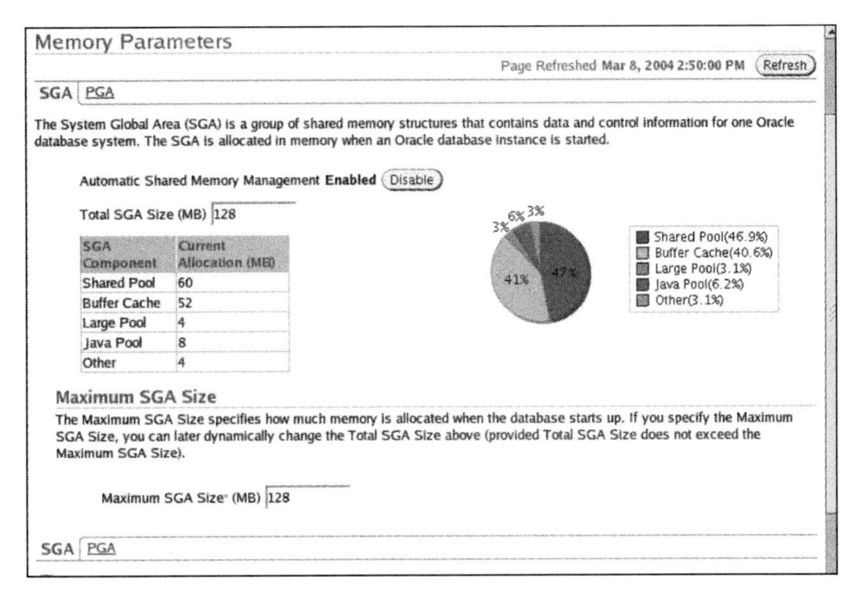

Figure 6.2 - *Memory Parameters*

2. Automatic Shared Memory Management has to be disabled to run the advisor. Choose shared pool or buffer cache and click Advice next to it.

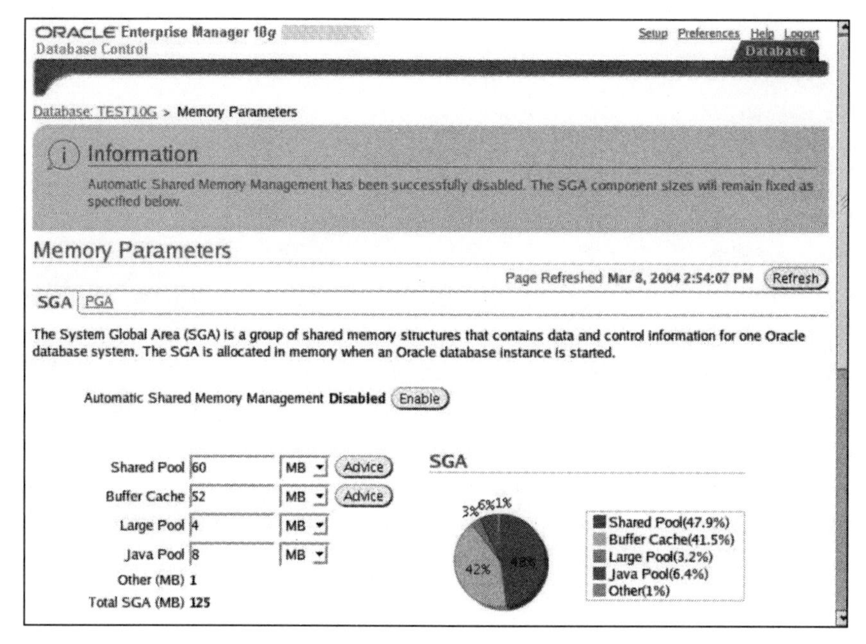

Figure 6.3 - *Memory Advice*

The corresponding graphs appear as shown below.

For Shared Pool size, the graph shows that a shared pool size larger than 60 MB will not improve performance a lot. So the recommended optimal shared pool size is 60 MB.

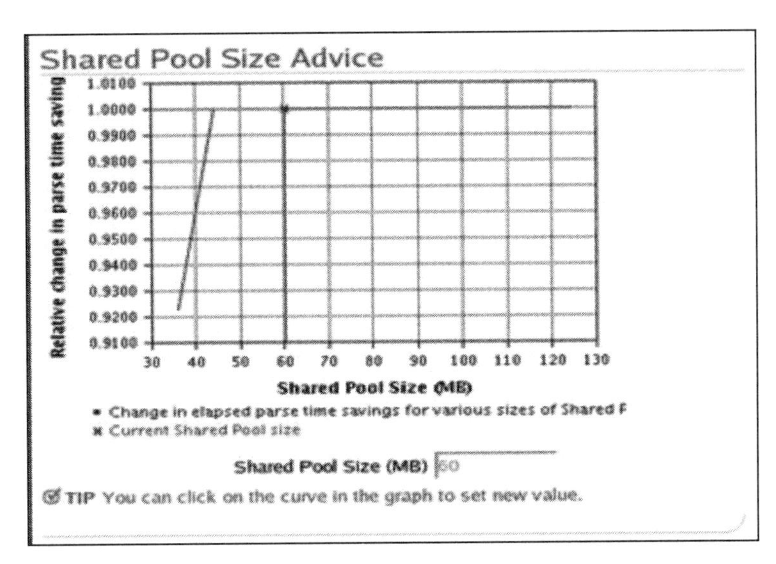

Figure 6.4 - *Memory Advice*

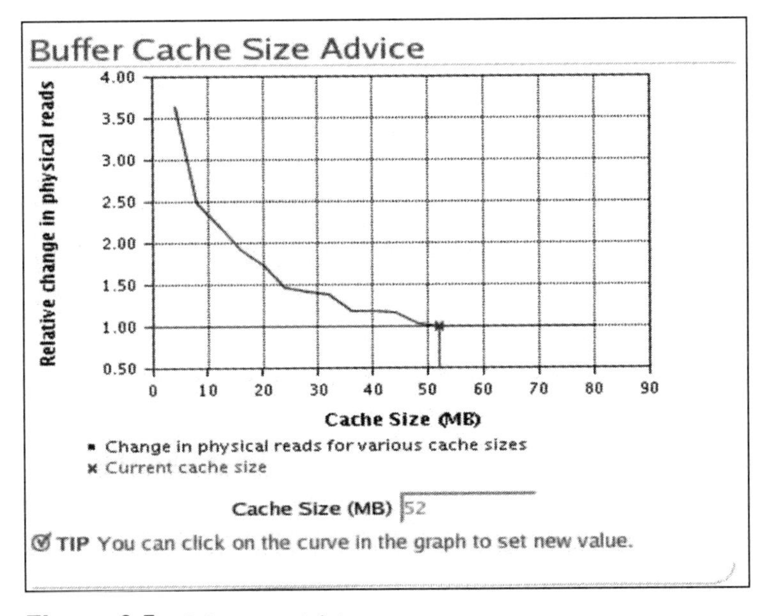

Figure 6.5 - *Memory Advice*

For Buffer Cache, the graph shows that a buffer cache size larger than 52MB will not improve the performance much either. A bigger cache prompts less disk reads and improves the performance. See Guru Conversation for more details.

3. To run the PGA Advisor, click on the PGA property page. This is similar to running the SGA advisors. Cache hit percentage is plotted against memory size. Higher hit ratios in the range of 75% to 100% indicate better cache performance.

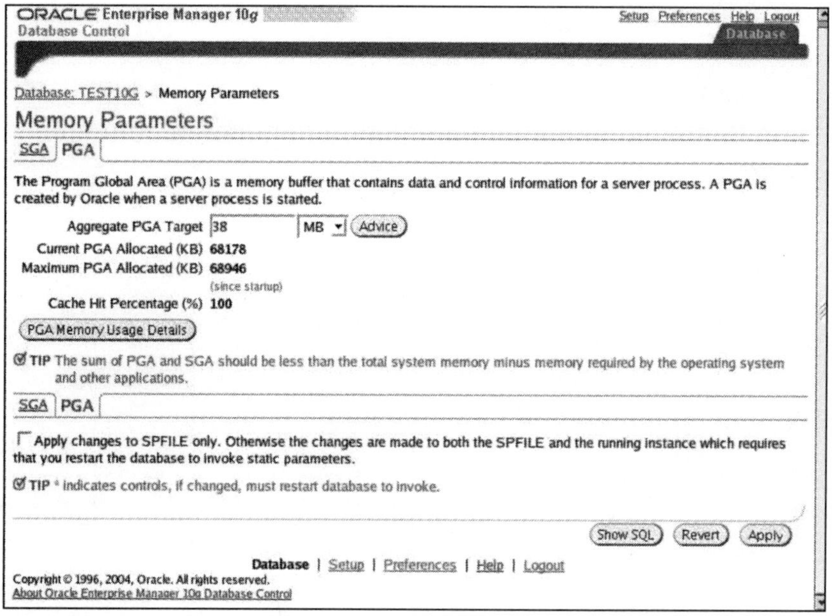

ORACLE Enterprise Manager 10g
Database Control
Setup Preferences Help Logout
Database

Database: TEST10G > Memory Parameters

Memory Parameters

SGA | PGA

The Program Global Area (PGA) is a memory buffer that contains data and control information for a server process. A PGA is created by Oracle when a server process is started.

Aggregate PGA Target 38 MB (Advice)
Current PGA Allocated (KB) 68178
Maximum PGA Allocated (KB) 68946
(since startup)
Cache Hit Percentage (%) 100

(PGA Memory Usage Details)

TIP The sum of PGA and SGA should be less than the total system memory minus memory required by the operating system and other applications.

SGA | PGA

Apply changes to SPFILE only. Otherwise the changes are made to both the SPFILE and the running instance which requires that you restart the database to invoke static parameters.

TIP * indicates controls, if changed, must restart database to invoke.

(Show SQL) (Revert) (Apply)

Database | Setup | Preferences | Help | Logout

Copyright © 1996, 2004, Oracle. All rights reserved.
About Oracle Enterprise Manager 10g Database Control

Figure 6.6 - *PGA Memory*

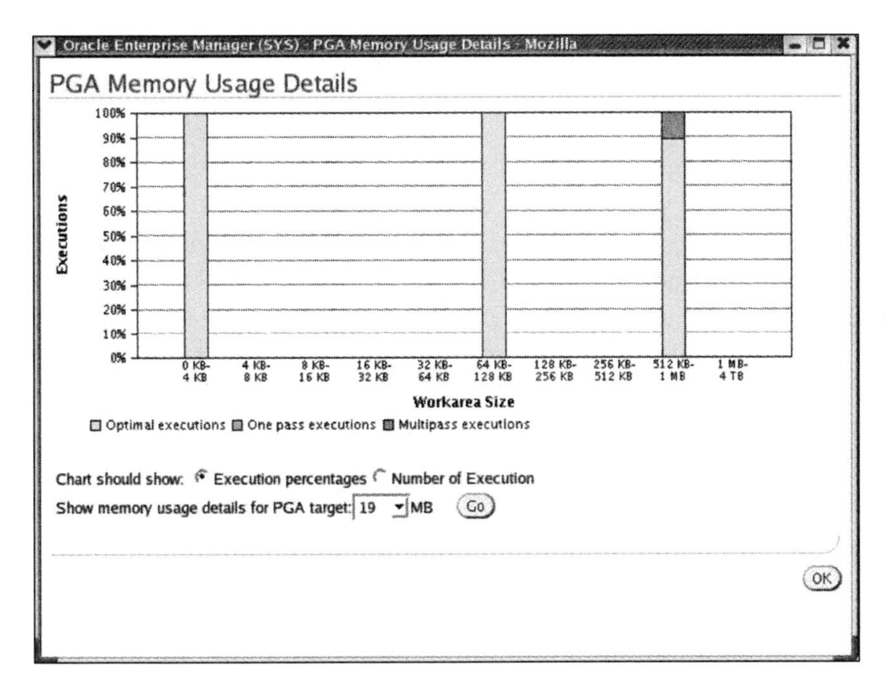

Figure 6.7 - *PGA Memory*

Persistence of Automatically Tuned Values

If using the server parameter file (*spfile*) for the Oracle database, the sizes of the automatically tuned components across instance shutdowns will be retained. Therefore, the system has to learn the characteristics of the workload each time an instance is started. It can start with information from the last instance shutdown and continue evaluating the new workload.

Attention will now be shifted to automated maintenance tasks.

Automated Maintenance Tasks

Oracle Database 10g is designed to handle routine maintenance tasks and schedule them at certain times of the day or week when the system load is low. For the designated time period, a resource plan can be used to control resource consumption of these tasks.

When the time elapses, the database can switch to a different resource plan with a lower resource allocation.

Resource Management

As explained in the previous section, Oracle Database 10g makes use of resource plans for different tasks. At the time of database installation, a Resource Manager consumer group called *auto_task_consumer_group* is predefined. Similarly, a scheduler job class *auto_task_job_class* is also defined based on this consumer group. *gather_stats_job* is defined to run in the *auto_task_job_class* job class.

Guru Conversation for the Senior DBA

AWR in Memory Statistics

Some system and session statistics are stored in *v$sysstat* and *v$sesstat.* The following statistics are the most important statistics that are used by AWR:

- **OS Statistics** - CPU and Memory using *v$osstat.*

Column	Description
STAT_NAME	Statistic name
VALUE	Statistic value at the moment
OSSTAT_ID	Statistic ID

- **Wait Classes** – CPU, application, commit, concurrency, scheduler, I/O, admin, configuration, commit, cluster, and network are available using *v$event_name.*

Column	Description
EVENT#	Number of the wait event

EVENT_ID	Wait event identifier
NAME	Wait event name
PARAMETER1	First parameter description for the wait event
PARAMETER2	Second parameter description for the wait event
PARAMETER3	Third parameter description for the wait event
WAIT_CLASS_ID	Class identifier of the wait event
WAIT_CLASS#	Class number of the wait event
WAIT_CLASS	Class name of the wait event

- **Time Model** - Connection management, PL/SQL compilation, parse, SQL execution, and PL/SQL execution are available using *v$sys_time_model.*

Column	Description
STAT_ID	Statistic Identifier
STAT_NAME	Statistic name
VALUE	Time spent in microseconds for the operation

- **SQL Statistics** – SQL statistics include PL/SQL Java time, wait-class time, bind variables, efficient top SQL based on CPU, elapsed and parse statistics.
- *v$sysstat, v$sql, v$segment_statistics, v$sys_time_model, v$sysmetric_history, v$active_session_history.*

The AWR collects performance data on resources and stored the data inside *wrh$* tables. AWR takes snapshots of the system every 60 minutes Therefore, AWR does not contain enough information to perform current analysis. Typically, the nature of current analysis requires information on activity in the last five to ten minutes.

These tables are viewable through Oracle Enterprise Manager or through the *dba_hist* views. The AWR captures all important SGA metrics about the SGA in the *dba_hist_sga* views and interfaces with the ADDM. SGA advisory functions dynamically optimize the shared pool, data buffer cache, Java pool, and PGA memory areas.

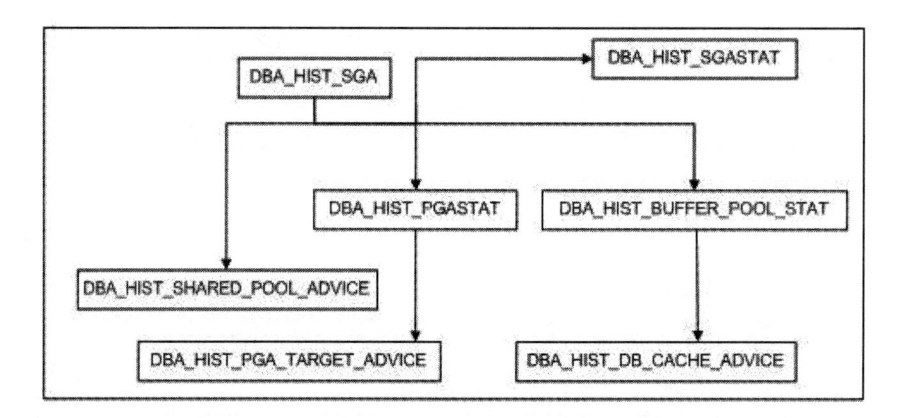

Figure 6.8 - *SGA information in the dba_hist_sga views*

ASH and its influence on memory statistics will be reviewed next.

Active Session History

Oracle Database 10g has upgraded its *v$session* view to include wait events and their durations. However, this view has the values in real time and does not keep track of information to be viewed later. Active Session History (ASH), is very much like AWR, and stores the session performance statistics in a buffer for analysis later. Unlike AWR storage in a table, ASH storage is in memory viewable from *v$active_session_history*. The data on active sessions is polled every second and the older entries are removed from memory to accommodate the latest ones in a circular manner.

The following query is an example of how to get session information along with time waited on events:

```
select session_id||' - '||session_serial# SID, v$event_name.name,
wait_time, time_waited
from v$active_session_history , v$event_name
where v$event_name.event# = v$active_session_history.event#;
```

The above script provides the name of the event and time spent in waiting. A sample portion of the lengthy output is as follows:

```
SID        NAME                           WAIT_TIME TIME_WAITED
---------- ------------------------------ ---------- -----------
134 - 38   SQL*Net message from client          1179           0
165 - 1    db file sequential read                 0       21406
134 - 38   SQL*Net message from client          1457           0
165 - 1    db file sequential read                 0       10179
134 - 38   log file sync                           0       34164
165 - 1    db file sequential read                 0       10964
167 - 1    log file parallel write                 0       33902
134 - 38   log file sync                           0       56131
165 - 1    db file sequential read                 0       24074
167 - 1    log file parallel write                 0       56167
134 - 38   SQL*Net message from client          4773           0
```

The valuable ASH information is flushed to the disk by the MMON slave to the AWR table. This information is visible through the view *dba_hist_active_sess_history*.

Conclusion

In this chapter, the automatic system resource management features of Oracle Database 10g have been reviewed. Here are some of the important points:

- The DBA can set the total amount of SGA memory available to an instance using the *sga_target* initialization parameter. The database will automatically distribute this memory among various sub-components for the most effective memory utilization.

- *sga_target* is set to a non-zero value to enable ASMM.
- Memory Manager (MMAN) is a background process that coordinates the sizing of the memory components and acts as a memory broker to track all memory components and pending resize operations.
- The Memory Advisor which is accessible through OEM has three advisors that provide recommendations: Shared Pool in SGA, Buffer Cache in SGA, and PGA.

In Chapter 7, SQL tuning methods and improvised flashback features of Oracle Database 10g will be explored.

Application and SQL Management

Failure to anticipate Oracle performance problems can lead to panic.

Introduction to Tuning

Two important objectives in tuning any application or database system are to reduce the response time for its end users and to minimize the consumption of resources for the system. Tuning of SQL statements is a major factor in determining the system performance of the database.

SQL tuning is performed by the execution of the following steps:

- Identify the top SQL statements that utilize a major portion of the application workload and system resources.
- Analyze the execution plans from the query optimizer.
- Improve the execution plan of poorly performing SQL statements.

The above steps have to be repeated until performance results are satisfactory for the system. These steps will be examined in more detail in the next sections.

SQL Tuning Features

Top SQL statements or high-load SQL statements are those statements that are poorly performing and resource draining, which in turn slows the entire database and any associated applications. To identify high-load SQL statements, Oracle Database 10g has provided a handful of features, some of which are entirely new to this release. These features are Automatic Workload Repository (AWR), Automatic Database Diagnostic Monitor (ADDM), *v$sql* view, SQL Trace, and Custom Workload.

AWR and ADDM provide services to support automatic SQL tuning. SQL Tuning Advisor and SQL Access Advisor are the SQL tuning tools provided by Oracle.

Automatic Workload Repository

AWR provides services to Oracle Database 10g to collect, maintain, and utilize the statistics for problem detection and self-tuning. The AWR has an in-memory statistics collection facility, which is useful for 10g components to collect statistics. These metrics are stored in memory for performance reasons. The memory version of the statistics is written to disk regularly by a new background process called MMON (Memory Monitor).

Oracle Database 10g captures and retains this historical data without DBA intervention. The default retention period is seven days using a *retention* parameter setting of 10080 which was as described in Chapter 4. The historic data is used for analysis of performance problems that occurred in a certain time period in the past and to do trend analysis.

As a review, some session and system statistics that are retained in *v$sesstat* and *v$sysstat* are as follows:

- Time Model - Connection management, PL/SQL compilation, parse, SQL execution, and PL/SQL execution are available using *v$sys_time_model.*
- SQL Statistics - SQL statistics include PL/SQL Java time and wait-class time, bind variables, efficient top SQL based on CPU, elapsed and parse statistics.

Automatic Database Diagnostic Monitor

Automatic Database Diagnostic Monitor (ADDM) analyzes the information collected by the AWR for database performance problems including top SQL statements. The database automatically captures statistical information from the SGA and stores the information inside the workload repository in the form of snapshots in one hour intervals. These snapshots are written to disk and are similar to STATSPACK snapshots, except they are more detailed in nature.

The ADDM is also scheduled to run the MMON process automatically on every database instance to detect problems proactively. Every time a snapshot is taken, the ADDM triggers an analysis of the period corresponding to the last two snapshots. Although this automatic analysis covers the previous two snapshots, ADDM can analyze across any two snapshots.

This helps the ADDM to proactively monitor the instance and detect bottlenecks before they become catastrophic. The analysis results are stored inside the workload repository. These results are accessible through the OEM console. ADDM can also invoke other advisors, they are as follows:

- SQL Tuning Advisor - provides tuning advice for SQL statements without modifying any statement.
- SQL Access Advisor - provides tuning advice on indexes, materialized views, and materialized view logs for a given work load. It also provides advice on database schema issues and determines optimal data access paths. This advisor is available through OEM.

The SQL Query Optimizer will be examined in the next section.

SQL Query Optimizer

Automatic SQL tuning is offered by the improved Query Optimizer. The improvised features are available through the SQL Tuning Advisor. To prevent the query optimizer from producing inaccurate estimates during SQL tuning, it generates an SQL profile of the statement consisting of auxiliary statistics on sampling and partial execution techniques.

The enhanced query optimizer has two modes, normal mode and tuning mode. In normal mode, the optimizer compiles the SQL and generates a reasonable execution plan, usually in a fraction of a second. In tuning mode, the optimizer conducts additional analysis to check if the normal mode execution plan can be further improved. The output of the query optimizer is not an execution plan. Instead, it is a series of actions, along with their rationale and expected benefits for producing a significantly superior plan.

When the query optimizer is called in tuning mode, it is referred to as the Automatic Tuning Optimizer. The tuning performed by the Automatic Tuning Optimizer is called Automatic SQL Tuning. For more information on the automatic tuning process, please refer to the documentation, *Oracle Database Performance Tuning Guide 10g* from Oracle.

SQL Tuning Advisor

SQL Tuning Advisor provides automatic tuning advice for SQL statements. It takes one or more SQL statements as input and invokes the automatic tuning optimizer to perform SQL tuning without actually modifying any statement. The output is a series of advice or recommendations along with the rationale behind each recommendation and its expected benefits. These recommendations will prompt the user to collect statistics on the affected objects, create new indexes, restructure the statements, or create new profiles. The user can accept the recommendations or reject them.

For tuning multiple SQL statements, a SQL Tuning Set (STS) is created. An STS is nothing but a database object to store SQL statements with their execution context. STS can be created from a command line or the new and improvised Enterprise Manager. For the hands-on DBA, SQL Tuning Sets can be managed with *dbms_sqltune* package procedures.

To manage SQL Tuning Sets through Oracle Enterprise Manager, do the following steps:

1. Select Related Links
2. Choose Advisor Central
3. Choose SQL Tuning Advisor
4. Choose SQL Tuning Sets

SQL Tuning Advisor obtains its inputs from a variety of sources including ADDM, top SQL statements from AWR, Cursor Cache, SQL Tuning Set and user inputs.

Automatic Database Diagnostic Monitor (ADDM) runs periodically as explained earlier and analyzes the key statistics accumulated by AWR over the last hour of operation. By looking at these statistics, ADDM can identify any performance-related problem including top SQL statements. Once it identifies resource intensive SQL, ADDM will recommend the use of the SQL Tuning Advisor against it.

Another source of input for the SQL Tuning Advisor is the high load SQL statements captured in the Automatic Workload Repository. AWR takes regular snapshots of the database system including top SQL statements ranked by relevant statistics like CPU consumption and wait time. This data is retained for seven days, and this retention period can be increased as needed. The user can view these top SQL statements in the AWR and run the SQL Tuning Advisor on them. This implies that the top SQL statements that ran during a specific retention period in the AWR can be tracked and tuned accordingly.

Cursor Cache is used for tuning recent SQL statements that are not yet captured by AWR. Remember that AWR captures them periodically and may not have yet captured the last resource intensive statement. So when used in conjunction with the AWR, the developer or the DBA can identify and tune the top SQL statements.

The last input set for the SQL Tuning Advisor is user-input statements or SQL Tuning Set. This could include untested SQL statements, or a set of SQL statements currently under development. For tuning a set of SQL statements, a SQL Tuning Set (STS) has to be constructed and stored, and fed to the SQL Tuning Advisor.

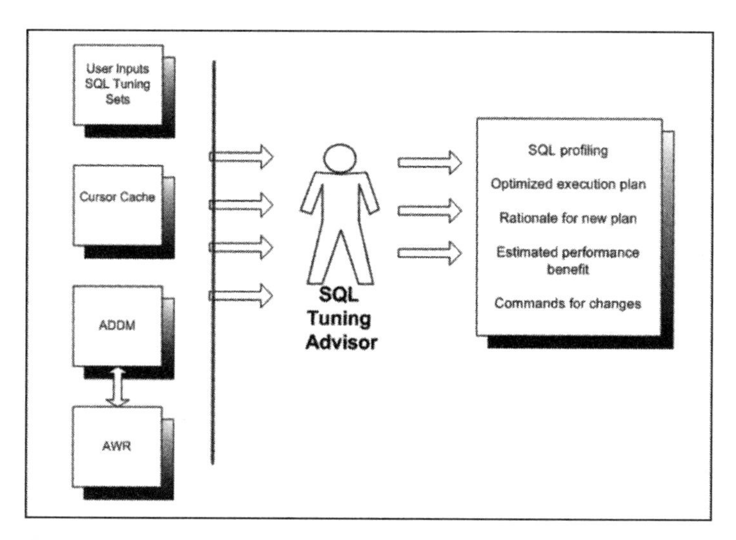

Figure 7.1 - *SQL Tuning Advisor*

The scope and duration of a tuning task done by the SQL Tuning Advisor can be controlled. The scope of the task can be set to limited or comprehensive. With the limited option, the SQL Tuning Advisor produces recommendations based on analysis of statistics, access paths, and SQL structure. SQL Profile recommendations are not generated when the comprehensive option is chosen. The SQL Tuning Advisor does everything under the limited scope and SQL profiling. In the comprehensive option, the user can set the time limit of a tuning task, which has a default value of 30 minutes.

SQL Tuning Advisor provides advice based on optimizing the execution plan, the rationale for the new plan, estimated performance benefit, and commands for the changes. As explained earlier, the DBA or developer has to make a choice on whether to accept or reject the recommendations to optimize the SQL statements.

To access the SQL Tuning Advisor through the Oracle Enterprise Manager, go to the Advisor Central - SQL Tuning Advisor link as shown below.

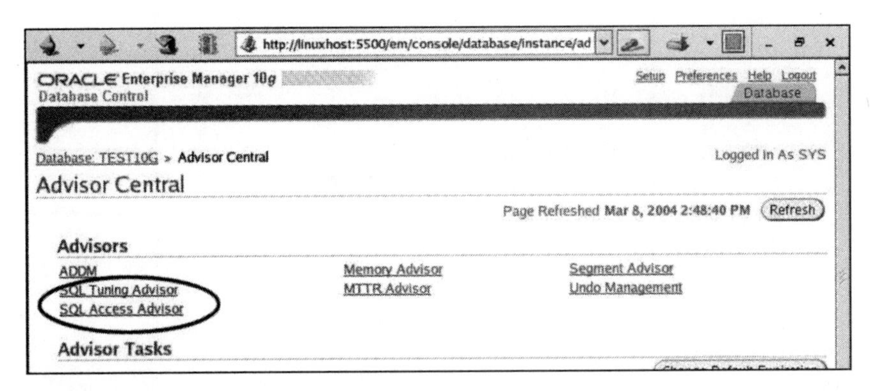

Figure 7.2 - *SQL Tuning Advisor - OEM*

The SQL Tuning Advisor can also be invoked through the *dbms_sqltune* package by anyone with DB role and ADVISOR privilege.

Next, invoking the SQL Tuning Advisor through OEM will be examined.

Using SQL Tuning Advisor through OEM

To access the SQL Tuning Advisor through the Enterprise Manager, do the following steps:

1. Go to Advisor Central and click the SQL Tuning Advisor link as explained above.
2. In the SQL Tuning Advisor page, the advisor gives the choice of running from the following sources:
   - Top SQL – this consists of recently active top SQL statements from the Cursor cache or historical top SQL from AWR.

- SQL Tuning Sets – this consist of SQL statements provided by the user.

3. Choose Top SQL. The Top SQL page appears as shown below. (The page had to be captured in two separate screenshots as it had to be scrolled down for a complete view.) This page has two tabs: Spot SQL and Period SQL. Spot SQL lists the top SQL from the cursor cache, while Periodic SQL from AWR.

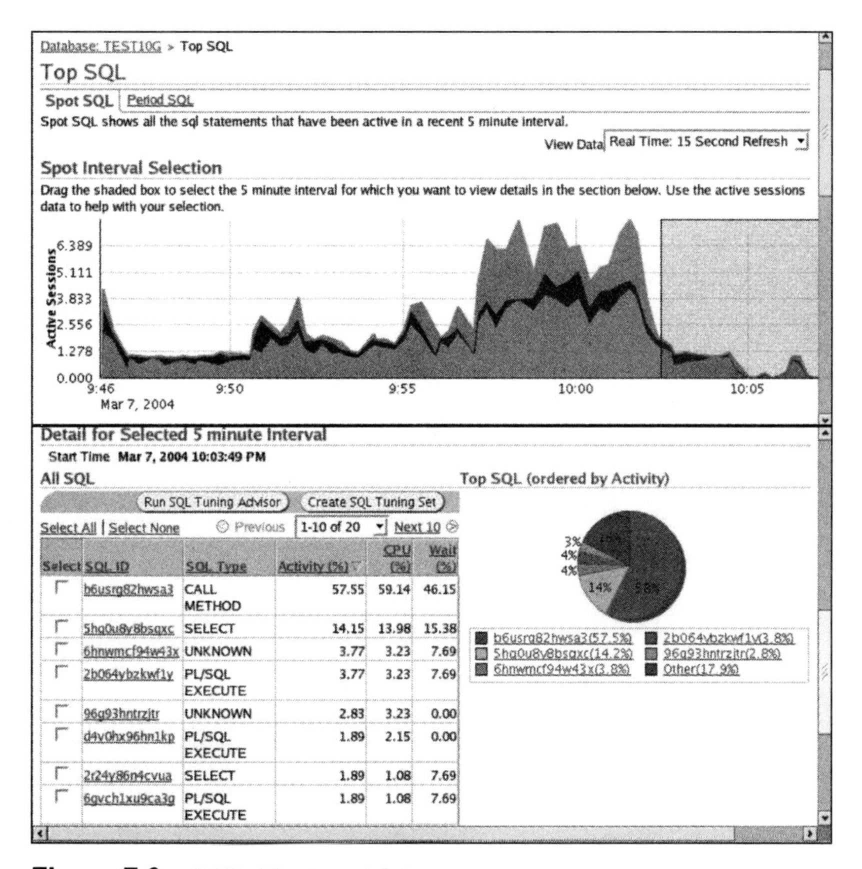

Figure 7.3 - *SQL Tuning Advisor*

4. Select the Top SQL statement by checking the box to the left of the statement and clicking the Run SQL Tuning Advisor button.

5. The following screen (three screen shots) appears with the SQL tuning options page. On this page, the name of the task can be entered along with a description, the scope and analysis methods can be selected (Comprehensive or Limited), and a start time for the task provided. Choose Immediately and click *OK*.

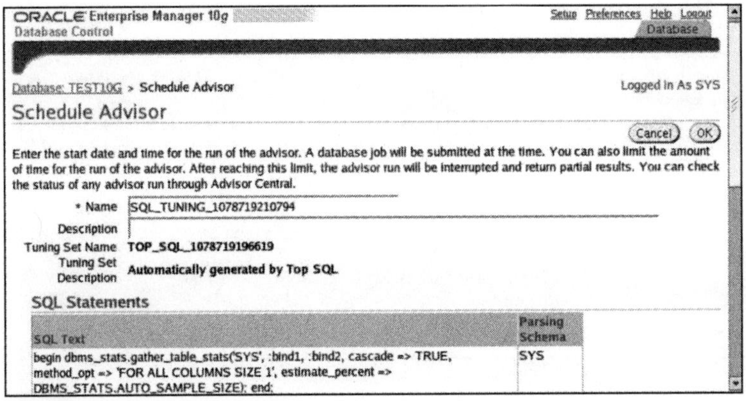

ORACLE Enterprise Manager 10*g*
Database Control
Setup Preferences Help Logout
Database

Database: TEST10G > Schedule Advisor
Logged in As SYS

Schedule Advisor

(Cancel) (OK)

Enter the start date and time for the run of the advisor. A database job will be submitted at the time. You can also limit the amount of time for the run of the advisor. After reaching this limit, the advisor run will be interrupted and return partial results. You can check the status of any advisor run through Advisor Central.

* Name SQL_TUNING_1078719210794
Description
Tuning Set Name **TOP_SQL_1078719196619**
Tuning Set Description **Automatically generated by Top SQL**

SQL Statements

SQL Text	Parsing Schema
begin dbms_stats.gather_table_stats('SYS', :bind1, :bind2, cascade => TRUE, method_opt => 'FOR ALL COLUMNS SIZE 1', estimate_percent => DBMS_STATS.AUTO_SAMPLE_SIZE); end;	SYS

Figure 7.4 - *SQL Tuning Advisor*

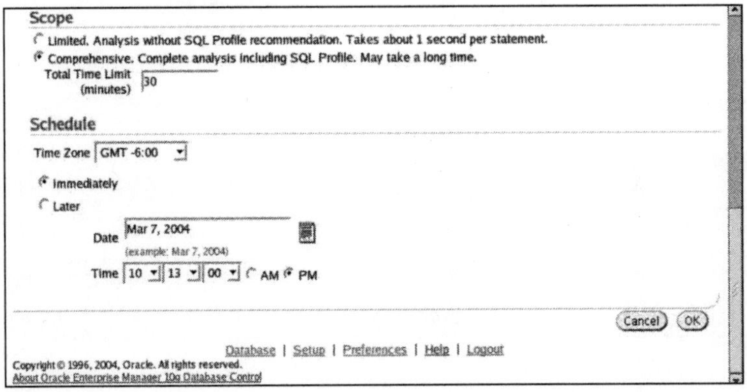

Scope
Limited. Analysis without SQL Profile recommendation. Takes about 1 second per statement.
Comprehensive. Complete analysis including SQL Profile. May take a long time.
Total Time Limit (minutes) 30

Schedule
Time Zone GMT -6:00
Immediately
Later
Date Mar 7, 2004
(example: Mar 7, 2004)
Time 10 13 00 AM PM

(Cancel) (OK)

Database | Setup | Preferences | Help | Logout
Copyright © 1996, 2004, Oracle. All rights reserved.
About Oracle Enterprise Manager 10g Database Control

Figure 7.5 - *SQL Tuning Advisor*

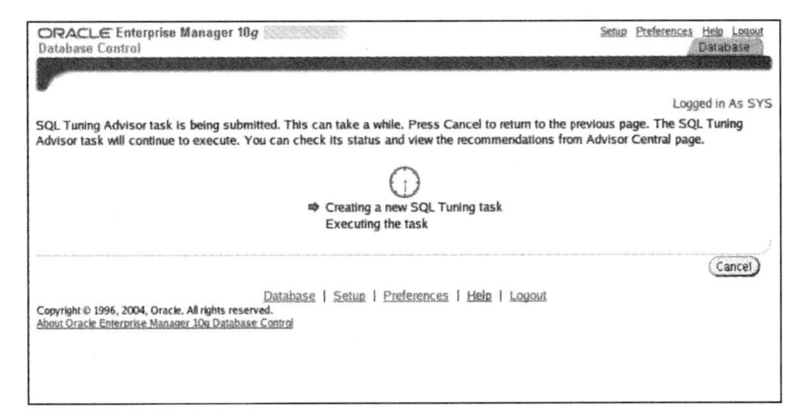

Figure 7.6 - *SQL Tuning Advisor*

6. Go back to the Advisor Central Page. The status for the advisor tasks are listed here. Wait until the task status changes to COMPLETED. Refresh the browser to view the updated status. When the task status is COMPLETED, select the task and click View Result. The following is a representative figure:

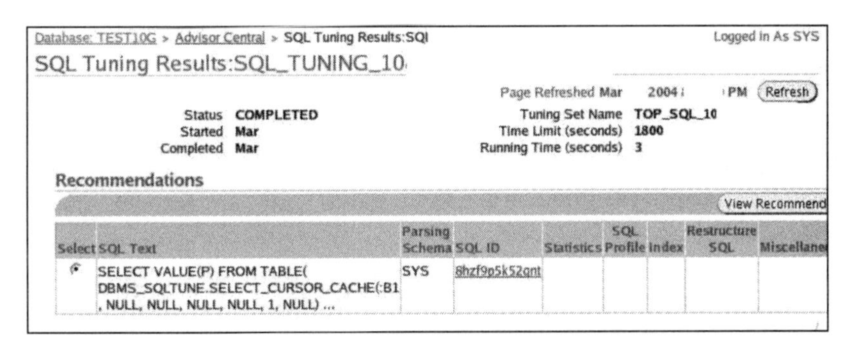

Figure 7.7 - *SQL Tuning Advisor – Tuning Results*

7. On the SQL Tuning Result page, select the SQL statement and click on View Recommendations.

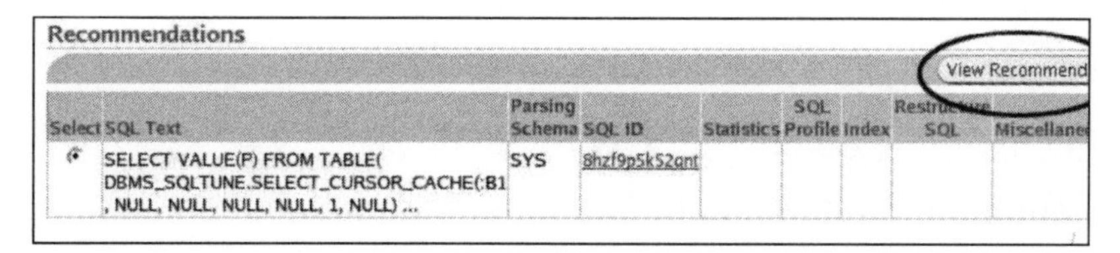

Figure 7.8 - *SQL Tuning Advisor - View Recommendations*

Now that the review of the SQL Tuning Advisor is completed, attention will now be shifted to exploring the SQL Access Advisor.

SQL Access Advisor

When there is an application with complex queries on large sets of data, SQL Access Advisor comes in very handy. For improving performance, it will recommend a combination of indexes, materialized views, and materialized view logs. These structures can result in significant performance improvements; though they require a considerable amount of time and space to create and maintain.

The SQL Access Advisor recommends how to optimize materialized views to be refreshable and benefit from general query rewrites. It also recommends the use of bitmap and B-tree indexes. B-tree indexes are used mainly in data warehouses or large databases to index unique or near-unique keys.

Bitmap indexes are used to create indexes on fields like the DATE field in a SALES table of a retail store database. Bitmap indexes improve the response time for adhoc queries and take up very little space compared to conventional indexes.

The SQL Access Advisor can be run from OEM using the SQL Access Advisor Wizard or by invoking the *dbms_advisor* package.

Using the SQL Access Advisor, the DBA can tune SQL statements, manage workloads, recommend materialized views and indexes, mark, update and remove recommendations, and manage materialized views.

SQL Tuning with SQL Access Advisor

To use the SQL Access Advisor for tuning, perform the following four steps:

1. Create a task.
2. Define the workload.
3. Generate the recommendations.
4. Implement the recommendations.

Task Operations

A task has all the information relating to the recommendation process and its results. To automatically create a task, use the wizard in OEM or *dbms_advisor.quick_tune.* After creating a task, the DBA has to execute the task in preparation for the tuning process:

```
BEGIN
     DBMS_SQLTUNE.EXECUTE_TUNING_TASK (task_name =>
'dba_tuning_task_v1' );
END;
/
```

For the Senior DBA or those who prefer the hands-on approach, use the *dbms_advisor.create_task* procedure. To view the tasks associated with any specific user or application schema, use the following command:

```
SELECT TASK_NAME FROM DBA_ADVISOR_LOG WHERE OWNER = 'owner' ;
```

Similarly, the *dba_advisor_log* can be used to find the status of a tuning task:

```
SELECT TASK_NAME FROM DBA_ADVISOR_LOG WHERE task_name =
'dba_tuning_task_v1' ;
```

The execution progress can be checked with the *v$session_longops* view, which gives the status of various operations that run longer than six seconds (in absolute time). Table 7.1 describes the columns available in this view.

Column	Description
SID	Session identifier
SERIAL#	Session serial number
OPNAME	Description about the operation
TARGET	Object on which the operation was carried out
TARGET_DESC	Target description
SOFAR	Work done so far
TOTALWORK	Total units of work
UNITS	Unit of measurement
START_TIME	Starting time of operation
LAST_UPDATE_TIME	Time of last update for statistics
TIME_REMAINING	Estimated time remaining (in seconds) for completing the operation
ELAPSED_SECONDS	Elapsed seconds from start of operations
CONTEXT	Context
MESSAGE	Statistics summary message
USERNAME	UserID performing the operation
SQL_ADDRESS	Address to identify the associated SQL statement
SQL_HASH_VALUE	Hash Value to identify the associated SQL statement

Column	Description
SQL_ID	SQL identifier of the associated statement
QCSID	Session identifier for parallel coordinator

Table 7.1 - *v$session_longops view*

To view the results of the task execution, use the *report_tuning_task_function*:

```
SELECT DBMS_SQLTUNE.REPORT_TUNING_TASK( 'dba_tuning_task_v1') FROM
DUAL;
```

This report contains all the results and recommendations of the automatic SQL tuning. For each proposed recommendation, the rationale and advantages can be found, along with the SQL commands needed to implement the changes.

There are other useful APIs to be used along with the *dbms_sqltune* package for managing SQL tuning tasks. They are as follows:

- *drop_tuning_task* – used to drop a task and remove all associated results.
- *reset_tuning_task* – used to reset a task during execution to its initial state.
- *interrupt_tuning_task* – used to interrupt a task and exit with intermediate results.
- *cancel_tuning_task* – used to cancel a task execution and remove all results.

Next, the use of workload with SQL Access Advisor will be examined.

WorkLoad

The Workload consists of one or more SQL statements and various statistics and attributes for each statement. The workload is considered a full workload if it contains all SQL statements from a target application. Otherwise, for a subset of SQL statements, a workload is considered partial.

For a full workload analysis, the SQL Access Advisor may recommend dropping some of the existing materialized views and indexes that are not being used effectively. Though the workload may contain a variety of statements, the SQL Access Advisor will rank the contents according to a specific statistic, business importance, or a combination of both.

The SQL Access Advisor can be used without a workload; thereby, generating and using a hypothetical workload based on the dimensions defined in the schema. For best results, a workload must be provided in the form of an SQL Tuning Set, a user supplied table, or imported from SQL Cache.

The recommendation process including types and naming conventions, and workload customization including duration and filtering are controlled by SQL Access Advisor parameters. The values of these parameters are valid for the life span of the task or workload object and can be set using *set_task_parameter* and *set_sqlwkld_parameter*.

Once a task exists and is linked to a workload, use the *dbms_advisor.execute_task* procedure to generate the recommendations. They are in-turn stored in the SQL Access Advisor repository. The status of this job can be viewed with *dba_advisor_log*. To view the recommendations, use the catalog views: *user_advisor_actions*, *user_advisor_recommendations*, and *user_advisor_sqla_wk_stmts*. The user views are for any user who uses the advisor tool. A DBA can look at the *dba_* version of these views or get a script using use *dbms_advisor.get_task_script* procedure. OEM can also be used to get recommendations.

All the recommendations are stored in the SQL Access Advisor repository, which is a part of the Oracle database dictionary. This repository has many benefits such as being managed by the server, support of historical data, and etc.

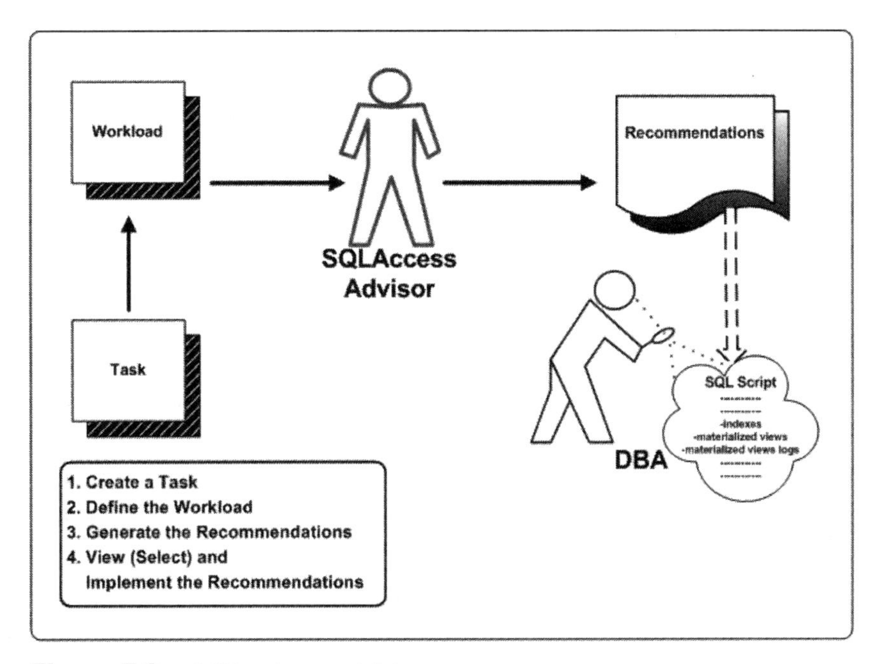

Figure 7.9 - *SQL Access Advisor*

In the next section, automated task scheduling of tuning efforts will be explored.

Automated Task Scheduling

Oracle Database 10g scheduler helps the DBA to schedule routine administration tasks such as gathering optimizer statistics.

The availability of valid statistics on the database objects helps the cost-based optimizer (CBO) generate optimal execution plans. This feature reduces the occurrence of poorly performing SQL statements due to stale or invalid statistics and enhances SQL execution performance.

The *dbms_scheduler* package enables the DBA to control when and where various tasks take place. By automating the routine tasks, human error can be minimized resulting in reduced operating costs.

Unfortunately, Oracle does not provide a defined process to migrate a *dbms_jobs* job to *dbms_scheduler*; the DBA must perform this manually. The scheduler does not guarantee that a job will execute on an exact time because the system may be overloaded and resources unavailable.

A *program* is a collection of metadata about what will be run by the scheduler. The programs can be PL/SQL block, PL/SQL procedure, Java code and C programs. A schedule specifies when and how many times a job is executed. A job specifies what needs to be executed, when to be executed, and with what parameters.

For prudent allocation of resources among competing jobs, the Scheduler makes use of a job class and a window. A job class is a category of jobs that share the common resource usage requirements and other characteristics. Using a database resource plan, the DBA can control resources for each job and prioritize them.

A window is an interval of time with a well-defined beginning and end time. The window helps to prioritize among job classes based on a schedule. The *gather_stats_job* is automatically created during database creation. This task executes the *dbms_stats.gather_database_stats_job_proc* procedure and uses the Scheduler.

Two windows are defined automatically:

- WEEKNIGHT_WINDOW between 10pm and 6am from Monday through Friday.
- WEEKEND_WINDOW between Friday and Sunday midnight.

Changing the time interval, repeat frequency, and resource plan can customize the windows. These two windows belong to a pre-defined group called *maintenance_ window_group*.

The *gather_stats_job* uses a specific scheduler class called *auto_task_job_class*. This class is also created by the database and is associated with a specific resource group called *auto_task_consumer_group*. To control resources used by *gather_stats_job*, the DBA has to define a resource plan and specify the resource to allocate to the *auto_tasks_consumer_group*. Then the resource plan has to be associated with the *maintenance_window_group*.

Next, invoking SQL Access Advisor through the Oracle Enterprise Manager will be examined.

Using SQL Access Advisor through OEM

To access the SQL Access Advisor through the Enterprise Manager, do the following steps:

1. Go to Advisor Central and click the SQL Access Advisor link.

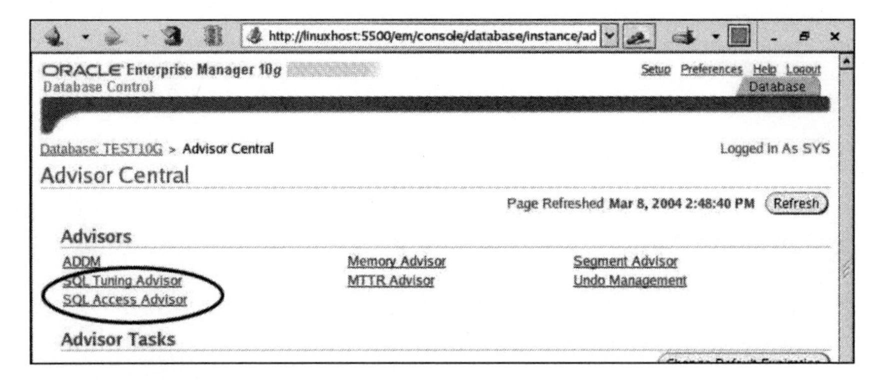

Figure 7.10 – *SQL Access Advisor*

2. This starts a wizard. It will prompt for a workload source.

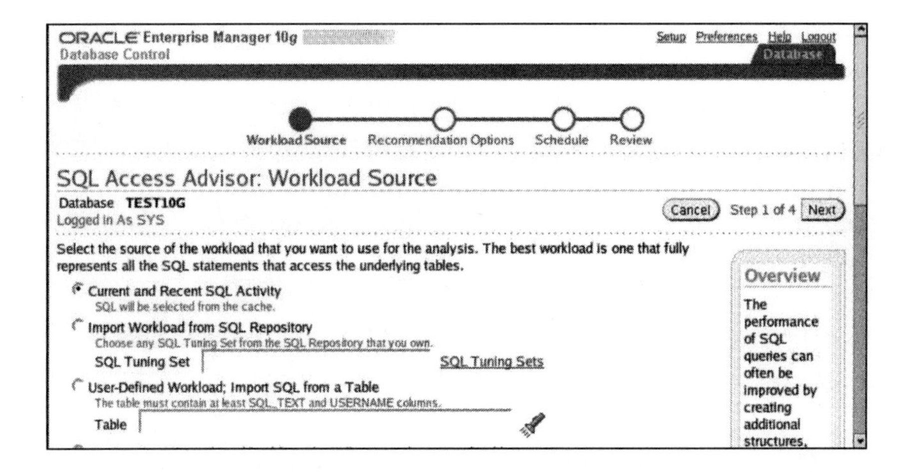

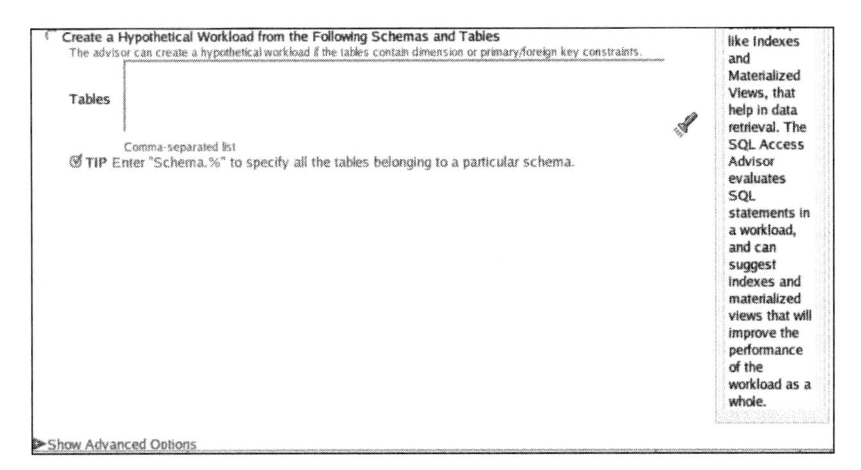

Figure 7.10 – *SQL Access Advisor*

3. Select the Advisor to run in Comprehensive or Limited mode.

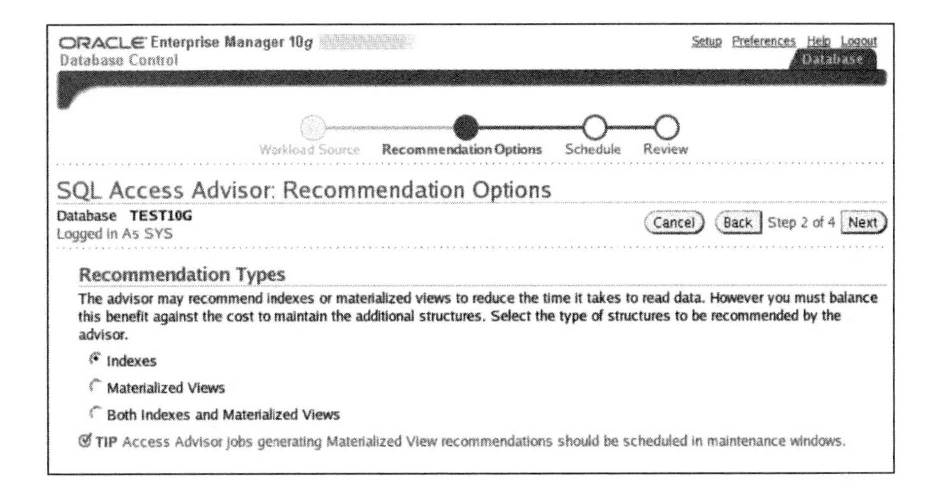

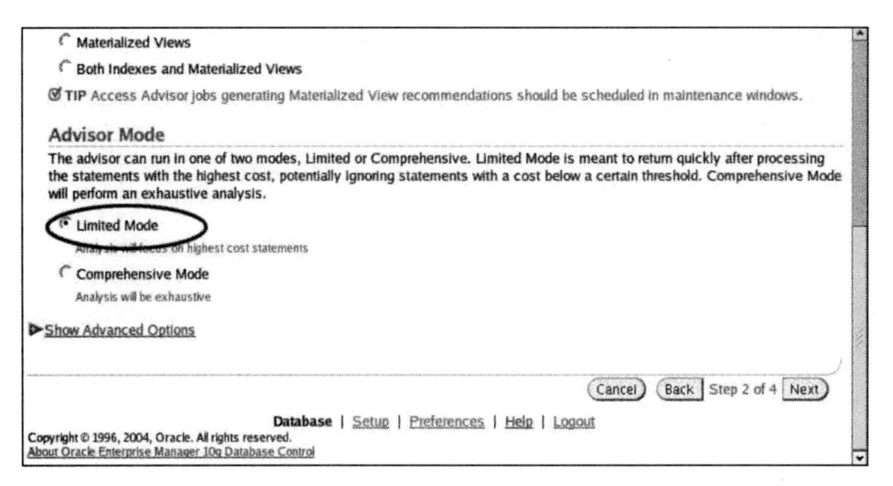

Figure 7.11 *SQLAccess Advisor*

4. Click on Show Advanced Options to show the following screen:

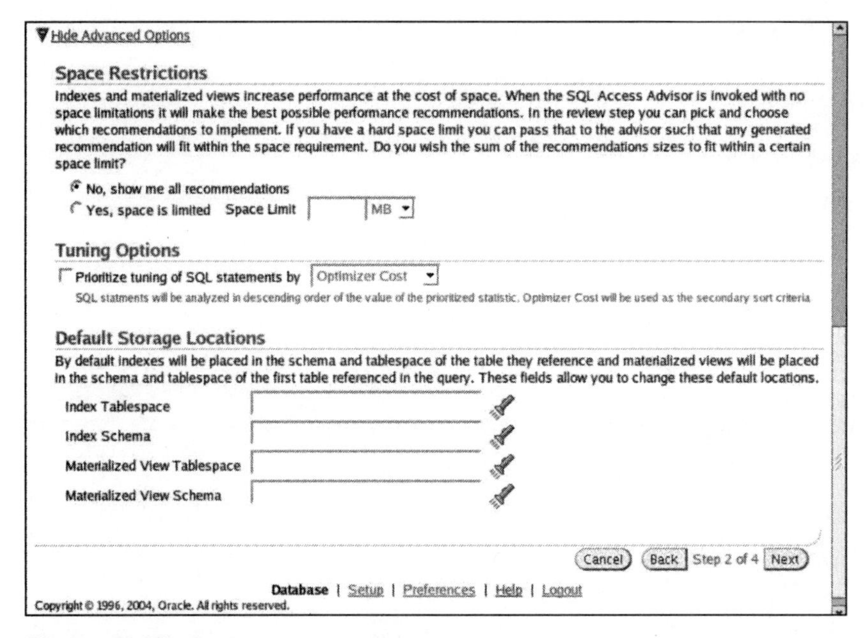

Figure 7.12 – *SQL Access Advisor*

5. Schedule and submit the job.

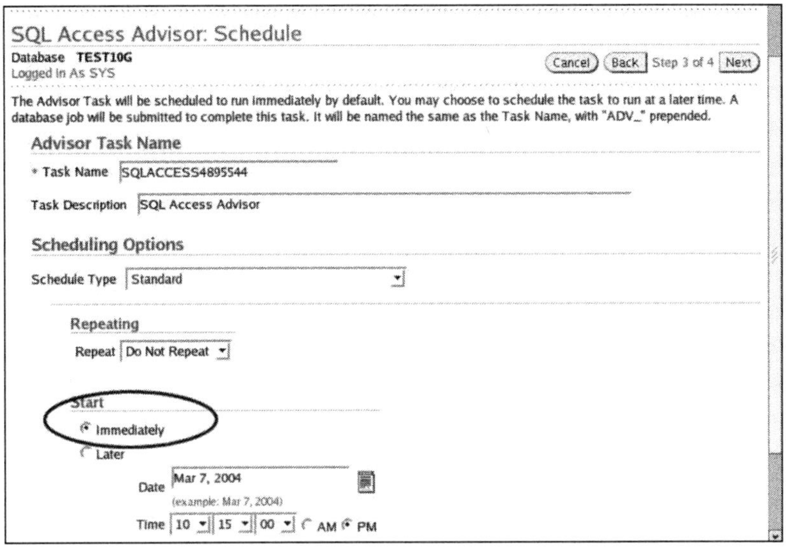

SQL Access Advisor: Schedule

Database TEST10G
Logged In As SYS

Cancel | Back | Step 3 of 4 | Next

The Advisor Task will be scheduled to run immediately by default. You may choose to schedule the task to run at a later time. A database job will be submitted to complete this task. It will be named the same as the Task Name, with "ADV_" prepended.

Advisor Task Name

* Task Name SQLACCESS4895544

Task Description SQL Access Advisor

Scheduling Options

Schedule Type Standard

Repeating

Repeat Do Not Repeat

Start

Immediately

Later

Date Mar 7, 2004
(example: Mar 7, 2004)

Time 10 15 00 AM PM

Figure 7.13 – *SQL Access Advisor*

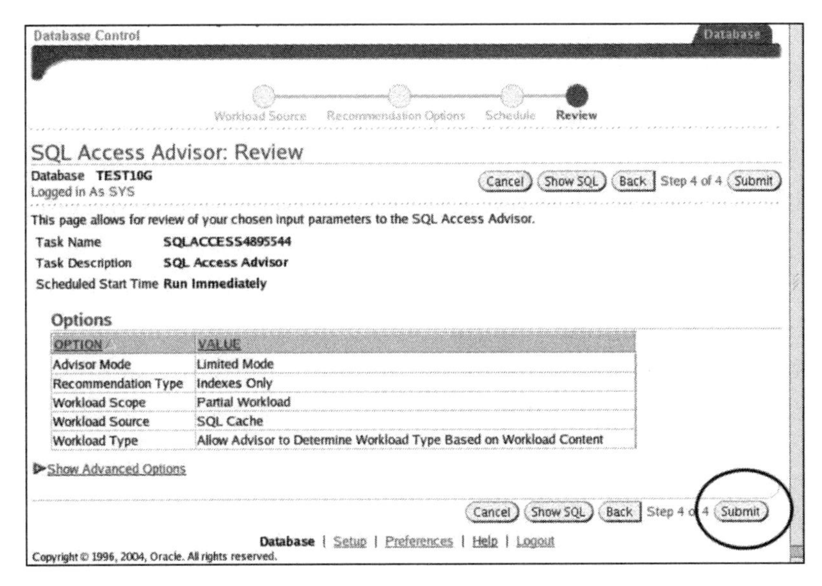

Figure 7.14 – *SQL Access Advisor*

6. Results are available through the Advisor Central Page. Implement recommendations by clicking Schedule Implementation.

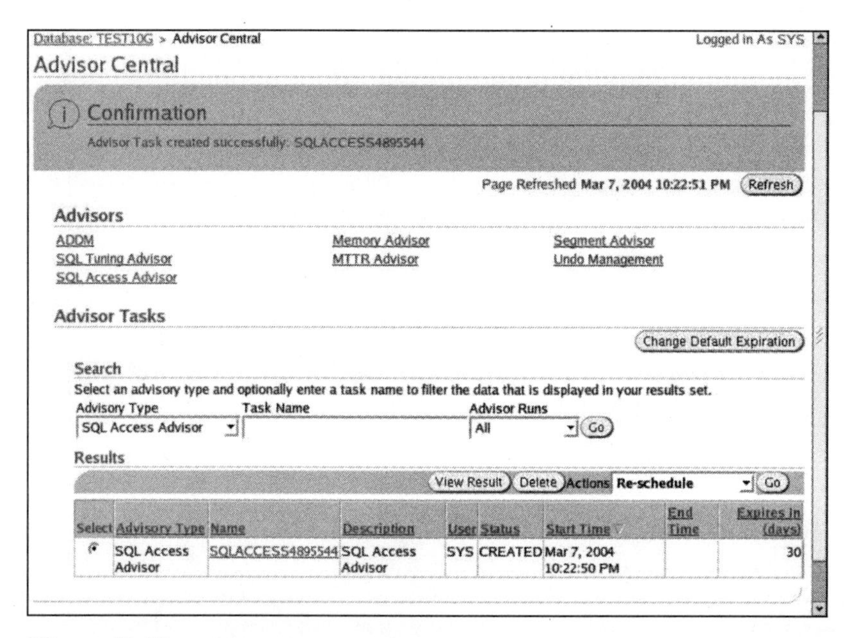

Figure 7.15 – *SQL Access Advisor*

This completes the review of SQL Advisors. Another important feature of Oracle Database 10g is the improvised flash back feature.

Flash Back Corrections

Flashback Query was introduced in Oracle 9i. In Oracle Database 10g, this functionality has been expanded from the AS OF clause in 9i. The DBA can use the VERSIONS BETWEEN clause to retrieve all versions of the rows that existed between the two time points. Flashback Versions Query retrieves all committed occurrences of the rows. However, the VERSIONS BETWEEN clause is not applicable for querying the views.

The Flashback Versions Query can be used to audit a table and retrieve information about the transactions that changed any of the rows. The Transaction ID obtained from Flashback Versions Query can be used to do transaction mining using LogMiner. Similarly, Flashback Transaction Query can be used to get additional information about the transaction.

The Flashback Versions Query returns the versions of the rows and validity range of the version, the transaction ID of the transaction that created the version, and the operation that created that version. The validity range is closed at the lower end and opened at the upper end. This range information is stored in pseudo columns. These pseudo columns can be used in the SELECT clause to display their values or in the WHERE clause to retrieve specific versions of the rows.

All Flashback features rely on undo information to recreate a state in the past. For an undo tablespace, the tablespace retention clause can be used to control preservation of unexpired undo data. The RETENTION GUARANTEE clause of the CREATE UNDO TABLESPACE and CREATE DATABASE specifies that unexpired undo data should be retained in all undo segments in the tablespace even if the undo generating operations fail. The default value of RETENTION GUARANTEE is NO GUARANTEE. When this option is enabled, the database never overwrites unexpired undo data. By default, this option is disabled so that the database can overwrite the unexpired undo data in the undo tablespace.

The default value for the *undo_retention* parameter, which is set in seconds, is 900. The *undo_retention* parameter can be changed in the initialization parameter file to be used by the database startup process or at any time by using the ALTER SYSTEM statement. In the initialization parameter file, put *undo_retention* = 1500 for 25 minutes, or issue the following SQL command:

```
ALTER SYSTEM SET UNDO_RETENTION = 1500;
```

This takes effect immediately, as long as there is free space in the current undo tablespace. The undo retention period for the current undo tablespace is obtained by querying the TUNED_UNDORETENTION column of the *v$undostat* dynamic performance view. The RETENTIONcolumn is set to GUARANTEE when the tablespace has RETENTION GUARANTEE. Use this GUARANTEE clause with caution, as it may affect any existing or long running DML operations.

The retention value can be viewed from the RETENTION column of *dba_tablespaces.* The possible values are GUARANTEE, the default which is NOGUARANTEE, or NOT APPLY which is used for other tablespaces.

Oracle Database 10g has come up with new SQL functions to convert an SCN data type number to a corresponding TIMESTAMP value and vice versa. This function is useful in flashback operations and will be explained in more detail later.

The SCN_TO_TIMESTAMP function will convert SCN to the corresponding TIMESTAMP value while TIMESTAMP_TO_SCN function will convert a string representing a TIMESTAMP data type to the corresponding SCN value of the NUMBER data type.

Flashback Transaction Query

One of the important new features of Oracle Database 10g is the Flashback Transaction Query. It is a diagnostic tool to view the changes made to the database at the transaction level. This feature will help diagnose problems, analyze and audit transactions, and recover from user or application errors. The undo SQL generated by the flashback transaction query can be used to rollback the changes made by a transaction.

Flashback Transaction Query uses an indexed access path to get to the undo data. It is faster than the LogMiner, which mines the redo log files to obtain the undo information.

The *dba_transaction_query* view stores the changes made by a transaction and the nature of changes made during a specified time. Using the transaction identifier or a time range as part of the query, this dictionary view provides information on changes made to the database by any query at any time. When there is insufficient undo data for a transaction, the *dba_transaction_query* will return a row with a value of UNKNOWN in the OPERATION column.

The FLASHBACK ANY TRANSACTION system privilege is needed to issue a query against the *dba_transaction_query* view.

Flashback Table

The Flashback Table allows the DBA to recover database tables to a specific point in time without restoring from a backup. With this feature, the data in the tables and all associated objects including indexes, constraints, triggers etc. are restored. This statement is executed as a single transaction. All the tables must be flashed back successfully or the entire transaction is rolled back.

The Flashback Versions Query and Flashback Transaction Query can be used in tandem to determine the appropriate flashback time. The SCN should always be noted before issuing a

FLASHBACK TABLE command. The effects of a FLASHBACK TABLE command can be undone by issuing another FLASHBACK TABLE command with the appropriate SCN or timestamp. The *v$database* view can be queried to obtain the current SCN value represented in the CURRENT_SCN column.

Triggers are disabled by default for the duration of a Flashback Table operation. After the Flashback Table operation is completed, the triggers are returned to the state prior to the flashback operation.

The Flashback Table is an efficient operation to easily and quickly recover from erroneous user modifications done without DBA involvement. This is significantly better than media recovery in terms of speed, availability, and ease of recoverability.

Flashback Table operations consider the integrity of data before doing any changes to the database tables. When a FLASHBACK TABLE command is issued, the database checks for referential integrity constraint violations and aborts the operation if any are found. This can be avoided by flashing back multiple tables to the same point using a single FLASHBACK TABLE command.

The DBA can use the ENABLE TRIGGERS option of the FLASHBACK TABLE command to override the default disabling of triggers. This will enable all the triggers for the table. The ALTER TRIGGER command can be used to selectively disable triggers before using the ENABLE TRIGGERS option of the FLASHBACK TABLE command. Triggers that are disabled with ALTER TRIGGER remain disabled.

If a DDL operation has altered the structure of any tables in the database, flashback operations cannot be used to undo those operations. DDL operations that cannot be flashed back include upgrading, moving or truncating a table, adding a table to a cluster, dropping or altering a column; and adding, dropping, splitting, coalescing or truncating a partition or sub-partition. DLL operations that change the storage attributes for the table are not impacted by the FLASHBACK TABLE command.

If a transaction is processing, it will be necessary to COMMIT or ROLLBACK the operation before using the FLASHBACK TABLE command.

Flashback Drop

In previous releases of Oracle database, dropping the tables was an irrecoverable operation without restoring from media. This was time consuming and often resulted in loss of work and database changes made during this period.

In Oracle Database 10g, when a table is dropped, it is placed in a recycle bin. The extents allocated to the table are not deallocated until they are purged. The tablespace counts the space used by these objects against its quota until they are purged. Constraints and triggers are preserved even after moving an object to the recycle bin.

For implicit database operations like DROP TABLESPACE INCLUDING CONTENTS or DROP USER CASCADE, objects are not placed in the recycle bin. All objects belonging to the dropped tablespace or user in the recycle bin are purged.

The DROP TABLE PURGE command is used to drop objects. When this command is used, the objects are not placed in recycle bin and discarded permanently. This is similar to the drop feature in previous releases of Oracle database.

Information about all the objects that have been dropped can be viewed from USER_RECYLEBIN or DBA_RECYCLEBIN. The SQL Plus command SHOW RECYCLEBIN will give a list of all objects in the recycle bin.

Objects in the recycle bin remain there until permanently dropped with the PURGE command or recovered with the FLASHBACK TABLE <table_name> .. TO BEFORE DROP command. Similarly, objects remain in the recycle bin until there is no room for new rows or updates in the tablespace or until the tablespace has to be extended for tablespaces with the AUTOEXTEND ON option.

When an object is dropped and moved to the recycle bin, the name of the object is changed to avoid conflicts with objects in the recycle bin that has the same name. This also helps in creating a new object with the same name and dropping it again.

The tables in the recycle bin can be queried by issuing a SELECT command. Also, flashback query operations are possible on objects in the recycle bin, if the undo information is still available. It is not possible to INSERT, UPDATE or DELETE against tables in the recycle bin.

The PURGE command removes the object completely from the database and removes the entry from the recycle bin. When the PURGE command is issued, the object name also has to be specified. The PURGE TABLESPACE command purges all objects from the specified tablespace in the recycle bin. If there are some dependent objects such as LOBS, nested tables, or partitions in the tablespace, then that base table itself stored in a different tablespace will be purged because it cannot exist without these required segments.

The PURGE RECYCLEBIN command removes all objects from the recycle bin and frees up the space. The PURGE DBA_RECYCLEBIN will remove all objects from the system wide recycle bin. SYSDBA privileges are needed for this operation, though.

When the DROP TABLESPACE INCLUDING CONTENTS command is issued, the objects in the tablespace are not placed in the recycle bin. Any objects in the recycle bin belonging to this tablespace are also purged.

When DROP USER — CASCADE is issued, the user and all its objects are dropped. Any objects in the recycle bin belonging to the user are also purged.

Tables can be recovered from the recycle bin when issuing the FLASHBACK TABLE <table_name>.. to BEFORE DROP command. The RENAME clause can be used to give a new name for the table. Any recovered triggers, indexes, or constraints retain their system generated recycle bin names.

In Oracle Database 10g, flashback functionality has been extended for the entire database. Using this functionality, a database can be reverted to a state at a past point in time. This will help to recover from changes due to user errors or logical data corruptions.

It is faster than point in time recovery using backups and redo log files. The database must be mounted in an exclusive state to perform the flashback operation.

Guru Conversation for the Senior DBA

SQL tuning packages and their access through OEM have been reviewed. SQL Tuning Information views and *dba_hist* views will be examined in this section.

The major views for reviewing the information gathered by SQL tuning processes are as follows:

- SQL Tuning Views - *dba_sqltune_statistics, dba_sqltune_binds, dba_sqltune_plans.*
- SQL Tuning Set Views - *dba_sqlset, dba_sqlset_binds, dba_sqlset_statements, dba_sqlset_references.*
- SQL Profile View - *dba_sql_profiles.*
- Advisor Information Views - *dba_advisor_recommendations, dba_advisor_tasks, dba_advisor_findings, dba_advisor_rationale.*
- Other Dynamic Views - *vsql, vsqlarea, v$sqlbinds.*

The AWR data structures are really complex and capture all aspects of Oracle historical performance. The AWR captures complete instance-wide metrics and tracks important details for use by Oracle Enterprise Manager as well as through tuning scripts. Use the following figure to get a pictorial view of the relationship between tables:

System Statistics History - The AWR keeps detailed metrics for more then 250 separate instance-wide metrics in the *dba_hist_sysstat* view. This information is used by EM to compare instance-wide performance to individual components.

File Performance History – A very high I/O is common in many Oracle databases. So the AWR keeps detailed information on file-level statistics (*dba_hist_filemetric_history*) and segment-level

I/O performance metrics (*dba_hist_seg_stat*) for the DBA to review them and take corrective actions.

SQL Performance History – This component makes Oracle Database 10g surpass all other commercial database management systems. For all important SQL statements, the AWR collects the full text of the SQL statement in *dba_hist_sqltext*, the execution plan for the SQL in *dba_hist_sqlplan*, and all of the important run-time performance statistics in *dba_hist_sqlstat*. This allows EM to easily display top SQL statements and allows ADDM to apply artificial intelligence to recommend changes to sub-optimal SQL.

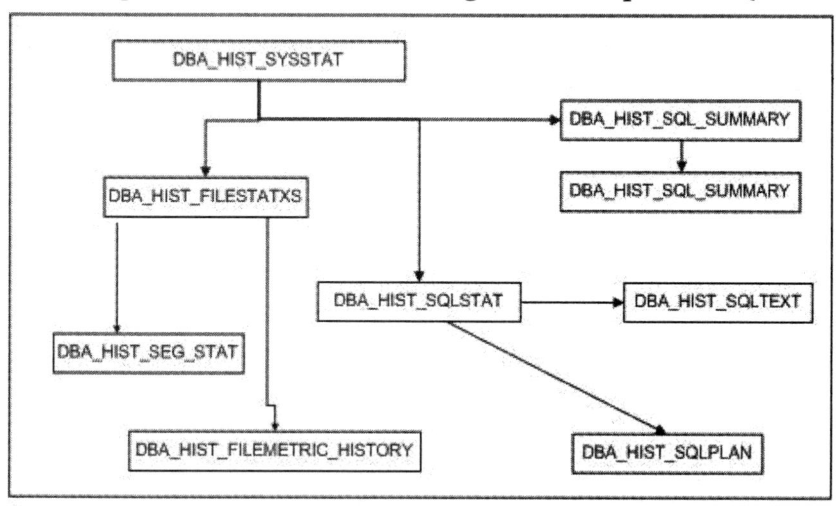

Figure 7.16 - *Some dba_hist views used by AWR for SQL tuning*

The next section will review the manual implementation process of SQL Access Advisor recommendations.

Implementing SQL Access Advisor Recommendations Manually

If inclined to run the tuning steps manually after using *dbms_advisor* packages with SQL Access Advisor, use the following scripts:

- The following query shows each recommendation, order of importance, and the improvement in optimizer cost. Substitute the TASK_NAME value where appropriate:

```
SELECT REC_ID, RANK, BENEFIT FROM USER_ADVISOR_RECOMMENDATIONS
WHERE TASK_NAME = my_task;
```

- The following query shows the SQL statements in the workload affected by the recommendations and the optimizer cost of these queries before and after the recommendations are implemented and the cost improvement as percentage value. Substitute the values for TASK_NAME and WORKLOAD_NAME where appropriate:

```
SELECT SQL_ID, REC_ID, PRECOST, POSTCOST,
(PRECOST-POSTCOST)*100/PRECOST FROM USER_ADVISOR_SQLA_WK_STMTS
WHERE TASK_NAME= my_task AND WORKLOAD_NAME = MY_WORKLOAD;
```

- The following query gives a list of recommended action items from the SQL Access Advisor as a result of the tuning activity. This will give a list of commands truncated at 45 characters along with its REC_ID and ACTION_ID:

```
SELECT REC_ID, ACTION_ID, SUBSTR(COMMAND, 1, 45) AS COMMAND
FROM USER_ADVISOR_ACTIONS WHERE TASK_= my_task
ORDER BY REC_ID, ACTION_ID;
```

Conclusion

This chapter explored the SQL tuning features of Oracle Database 10g. Information was presented about the different flashback features. The important points from this chapter to remember are:

- To identify high-load SQL statements, Oracle Database 10g has features like Automatic Workload Repository (AWR), Automatic Database Diagnostic Monitor (ADDM), *v$sql* view, SQL Trace, and Custom Workload.
- AWR and ADDM provide services to support automatic SQL tuning.
- SQL Tuning Advisor and SQL Access Advisor are the SQL tuning tools provided by Oracle.
- An SQL Tuning Set includes untested SQL statements, or a set of SQL statements, which is fed to the SQL Tuning Advisor.
- SQL Access Advisor is used when there is an application with complex queries on large sets of data.
- All Flashback features rely on undo information to recreate a state in the past.
- The Flashback Transaction Query is a diagnostic tool to view the changes made to the database at the transaction level.
- The Flashback Table allows the DBA to recover database tables to a specific point in time without restoring from a backup.
- Using Flashback Database, a database can be reverted to a state at a past point in time, faster than point in time recovery using backups and redo log files.

The final Chapter focuses on features and functionalities to monitor and communicate database issues and Data Pump technology.

Automatic Performance Monitoring – Utilities

CHAPTER 8

Like a detective, Oracle10g always searches for potential problems.

Automated Performance Monitoring – Utilities

Details about using SQL Advisors were presented in Chapter 7. In this chapter additional features and functionalities included in the Oracle Database 10g will be examined that proactively monitor database health, identify performance problems, and communicate these problems to the administrator along with taking remedial corrective actions. Data Pump technology will also be reviewed, which boosts the data movement speed by several factors over prior export and import commands.

Proactive Database Monitoring

Oracle Database 10g proactively monitors the health and performance of the database by making use of vital health signs (metrics) as examined in Chapter 4. It automatically identifies any issues that need attention by the administrator and sends them as alerts in the Enterprise Manager and will email or page the administrator. The performance monitoring features are handled by alerts and by using ADDM.

Database Alerts

Alerts help the database administrator to monitor the databases proactively. Most database alerts are notifications generated on reaching or exceeding particular metric threshold values. As presented before, critical and threshold values for each metric can be set. Whenever the metric values exceed these boundary values, the system identifies that it is in an undesirable state and generates an alert.

The DBA should ensure that the *statistics_level* initialization parameter is set to TYPICAL or ALL for proper alert notification.

Other alerts are generated when the database experiences events such as Snapshot Too Old or Recovery Area Low on Space. These kinds of notification alerts indicate the occurrence of a significant event. Alerts can also be set to start a script on meeting certain conditions. Examples would include a script that shrinks tablespaces or archives records from a SALES table to a SALES_HISTORY table on nearing a set limit of tablespace usage.

Oracle enables the following alerts by default: Tablespace Usage (warning at 85% full, critical at 97% full), Recovery Area Low on Free Space, Snapshot Too Old, and Resumable Session Suspended. Setting their metrics to non-default values can modify these alerts. Similarly, other types of alerts are enabled by setting their metrics. Database Control (OEM) also automatically sets thresholds on server metrics with object type SYSTEM.

With the introduction of the new monitoring process MMON, internal components can schedule regular monitoring activities. Components that detect a problem may generate an alert message upon which the DBA can act.

Both user and system defined alerts take 10 minutes to appear via the alert event. Also the 10 minute interval is only specific to the tablespace alerts as other alerts can have different values. For example, if the alert is matrix based then the interval is every 1 minute, since MMON collects metrics every one minute and will compare them to their thresholds.

Alerts Management Using OEM

Alerts can be managed easily from the Oracle Enterprise Manager console. The following sections describe how to manage the different alerts using OEM.

Reviewing Metrics and Thresholds

As reviewed previously, Oracle defines Metrics as a set of statistics for certain system attributes. These statistics are calculated and stored by the Automatic Workload Repository (AWR). These results are displayed in OEM through the All Metrics page under Related Links on the Database Home page.

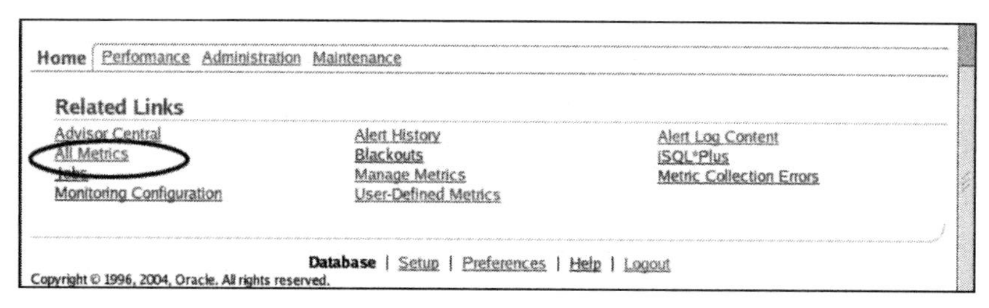

Figure 8.1 - *All Metrics*

The following figure shows a typical display of the All Metrics page. The screen has to be scrolled down to get a complete view. Hence, this page is presented here in two screenshots. More details can be obtained on each metric by clicking on the specific link. An online help feature provides a description of the metric.

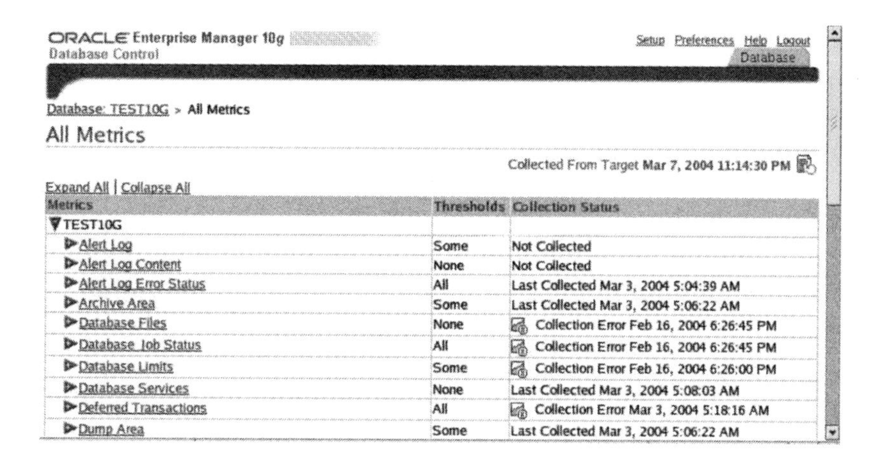

Metrics	Thresholds	Collection Status
TEST10G		
Alert Log	Some	Not Collected
Alert Log Content	None	Not Collected
Alert Log Error Status	All	Last Collected Mar 3, 2004 5:04:39 AM
Archive Area	Some	Last Collected Mar 3, 2004 5:06:22 AM
Database Files	None	Collection Error Feb 16, 2004 6:26:45 PM
Database Job Status	All	Collection Error Feb 16, 2004 6:26:45 PM
Database Limits	Some	Collection Error Feb 16, 2004 6:26:00 PM
Database Services	None	Last Collected Mar 3, 2004 5:08:03 AM
Deferred Transactions	All	Collection Error Mar 3, 2004 5:18:16 AM
Dump Area	Some	Last Collected Mar 3, 2004 5:06:22 AM

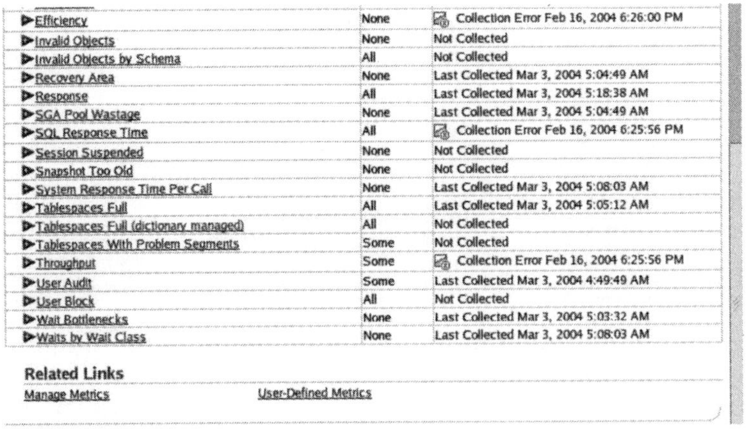

▶Efficiency	None	Collection Error Feb 16, 2004 6:26:00 PM
▶Invalid Objects	None	Not Collected
▶Invalid Objects by Schema	All	Not Collected
▶Recovery Area	None	Last Collected Mar 3, 2004 5:04:49 AM
▶Response	All	Last Collected Mar 3, 2004 5:18:38 AM
▶SGA Pool Wastage	None	Last Collected Mar 3, 2004 5:04:49 AM
▶SQL Response Time	All	Collection Error Feb 16, 2004 6:25:56 PM
▶Session Suspended	None	Not Collected
▶Snapshot Too Old	None	Not Collected
▶System Response Time Per Call	None	Last Collected Mar 3, 2004 5:08:03 AM
▶Tablespaces Full	All	Last Collected Mar 3, 2004 5:05:12 AM
▶Tablespaces Full (dictionary managed)	All	Not Collected
▶Tablespaces With Problem Segments	Some	Not Collected
▶Throughput	Some	Collection Error Feb 16, 2004 6:25:56 PM
▶User Audit	Some	Last Collected Mar 3, 2004 4:49:49 AM
▶User Block	All	Not Collected
▶Wait Bottlenecks	None	Last Collected Mar 3, 2004 5:03:32 AM
▶Waits by Wait Class	None	Last Collected Mar 3, 2004 5:08:03 AM

Related Links

Manage Metrics User-Defined Metrics

Figure 8.2 - *All Metrics*

Warning and critical threshold values can be defined for each of these metrics. Whenever the threshold is crossed, Oracle issues an alert, which can be propagated as explained earlier. Alerts are displayed on the Database Home page under the Alerts section in OEM. Non-database alerts are displayed under Related Alerts.

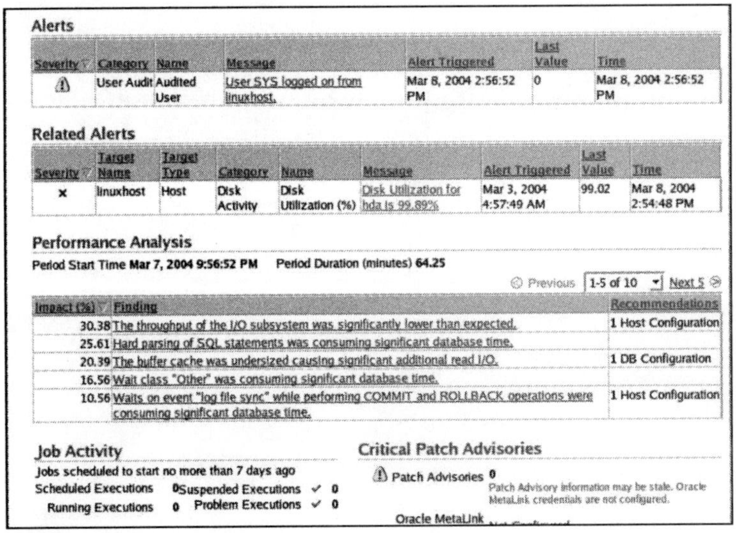

Alerts

Severity	Category	Name	Message	Alert Triggered	Last Value	Time
⚠	User Audit	Audited User	User SYS logged on from linuxhost.	Mar 8, 2004 2:56:52 PM	0	Mar 8, 2004 2:56:52 PM

Related Alerts

Severity	Target Name	Target Type	Category	Name	Message	Alert Triggered	Last Value	Time
×	linuxhost	Host	Disk Activity	Disk Utilization (%)	Disk Utilization for hda is 99.89%	Mar 3, 2004 4:57:49 AM	99.02	Mar 8, 2004 2:54:48 PM

Performance Analysis

Period Start Time **Mar 7, 2004 9:56:52 PM** Period Duration (minutes) **64.25**

Previous 1-5 of 10 Next 5

Impact (%)	Finding	Recommendations
30.38	The throughput of the I/O subsystem was significantly lower than expected.	1 Host Configuration
25.61	Hard parsing of SQL statements was consuming significant database time.	
20.39	The buffer cache was undersized causing significant additional read I/O.	1 DB Configuration
16.56	Wait class "Other" was consuming significant database time.	
10.56	Waits on event "log file sync" while performing COMMIT and ROLLBACK operations were consuming significant database time.	1 Host Configuration

Job Activity

Jobs scheduled to start no more than 7 days ago

Scheduled Executions 0 Suspended Executions ✓ 0

Running Executions 0 Problem Executions ✓ 0

Critical Patch Advisories

Patch Advisories 0

Patch Advisory information may be stale. Oracle MetaLink credentials are not configured.

Oracle MetaLink

Figure 8.3 - *Alerts*

As soon as the condition or conditions that triggered the alert are resolved and the metric's value is within its predefined boundary, Oracle clears the alert. Hence, metrics are vital inputs for self-tuning of the database and tuning recommendations made by Oracle advisors.

Managing Metric Thresholds

Oracle has provided a set of predefined metrics, with predefined thresholds for some of them. When the database system needs metrics outside of these predefined values, the thresholds have to be set to different values. These thresholds can be edited using OEM as described below:

1. Go to the Database Home page on OEM. Click on the Manage Metrics link under Related Links.

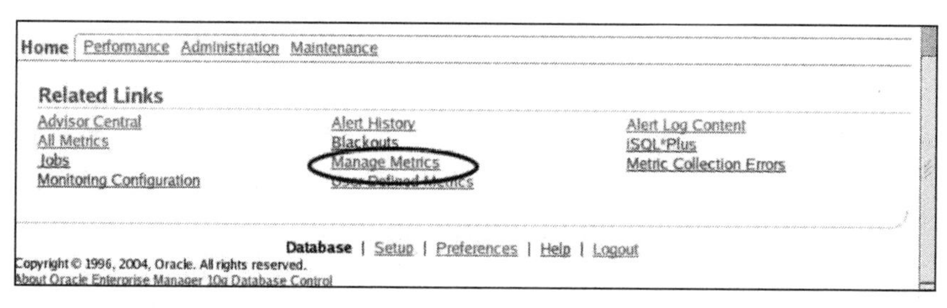

Figure 8.4 - *All Metrics*

This will display the Manage Metrics page. It displays existing thresholds for metrics with response actions, if any. Review the thresholds and identify those values that need editing.

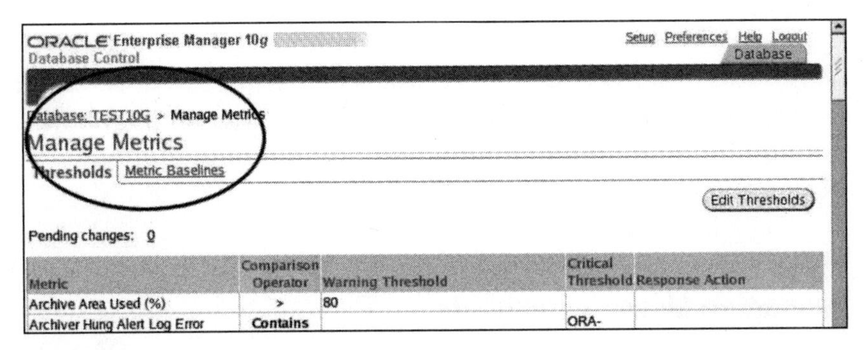

Figure 8.5 - *Manage Metrics*

2. Click the Edit Thresholds link. On this page, the new Warning Threshold and Critical Threshold values can be entered, or the existing values can be modified. In the Response Actions field, a script's name can be added or an operating system command to be executed when a threshold is crossed and an alert is issued.

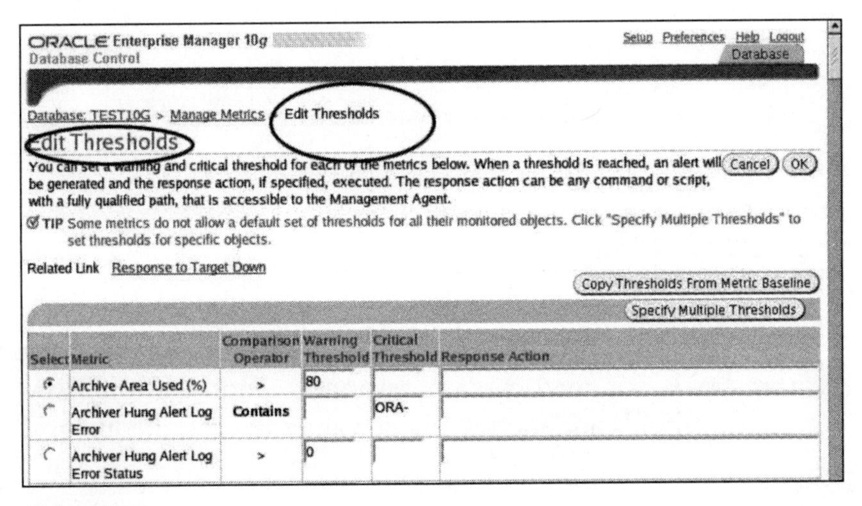

Figure 8.6 - *Edit Thresholds*

3. Click OK to save changes made on this screen.

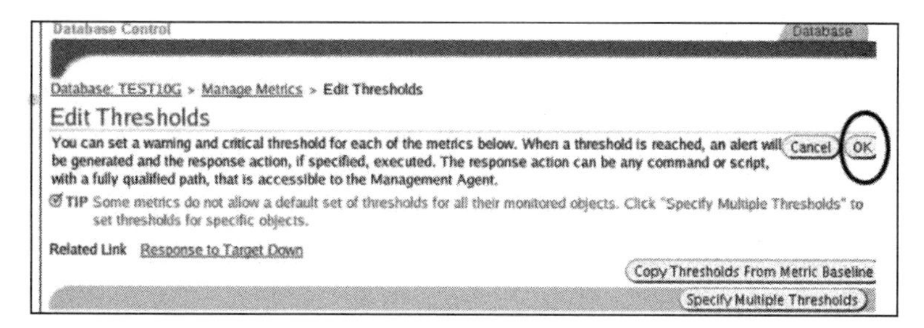

Figure 8.7 - *Edit Thresholds*

Oracle provides a list of alerts that are not enabled by default. Those alerts can be enabled by specifying the threshold values.

OEM also allows for comprehensive management of threshold settings for various alerts. To do it, proceed as follows:

1. On the page under the Edit Thresholds link, click the radio button in the Select Metric column for that metric.

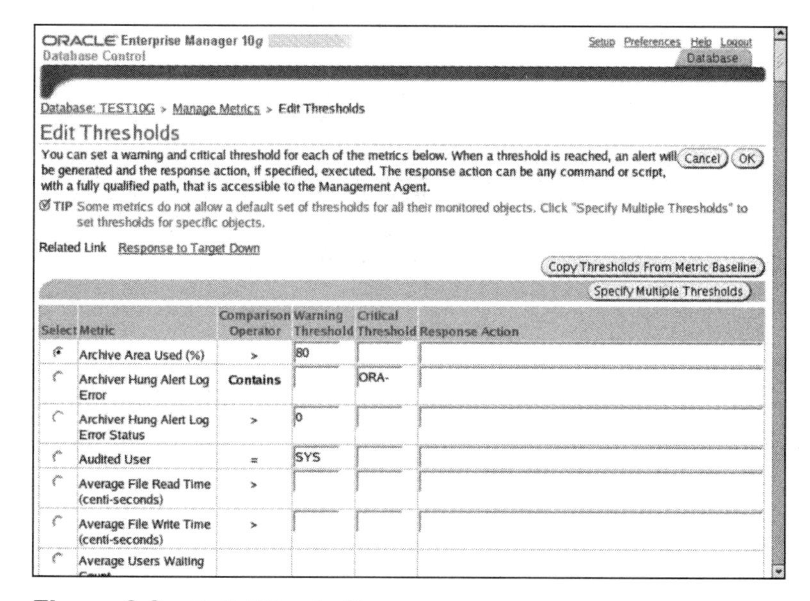

Figure 8.8 - *Edit Thresholds*

2. Click Manage Metric Indexes. The Manage Metric Indexes: metric_name page is displayed. This is where specific threshold and response action settings can be added or deleted. For example, the Table Space Used (%) metric for thresholds for individual tablespaces can be set. To change the thresholds, select this metric; then click Manage Metric Indexes. Enter the tablespace name and its warning and critical values.

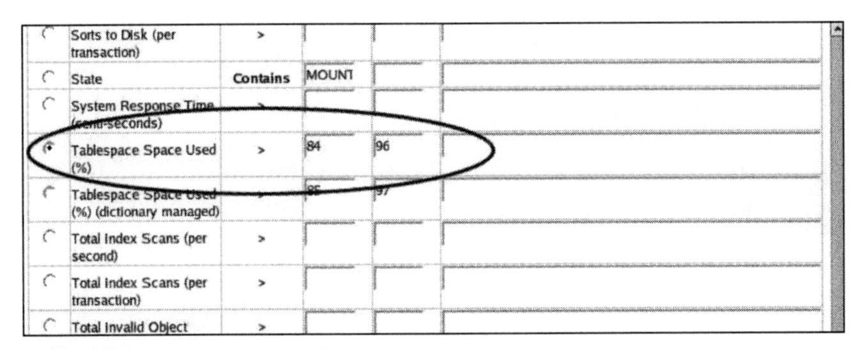

Figure 8.9 - *Change Metric Thresholds*

3. Click *OK* to save these changes.

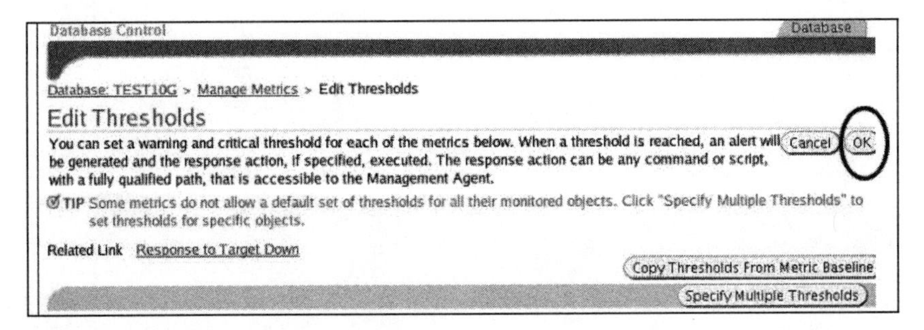

Figure 8.10 - *Save New Values*

Alerts Notification and Setup

Oracle Enterprise Manager can be used to send alert notifications to the DBA by pager or email. Here is an example of setting up an email notification for critical alerts using OEM.

1. From the *Database Control* page, click the *Setup* link visible in the header as well as footer areas.

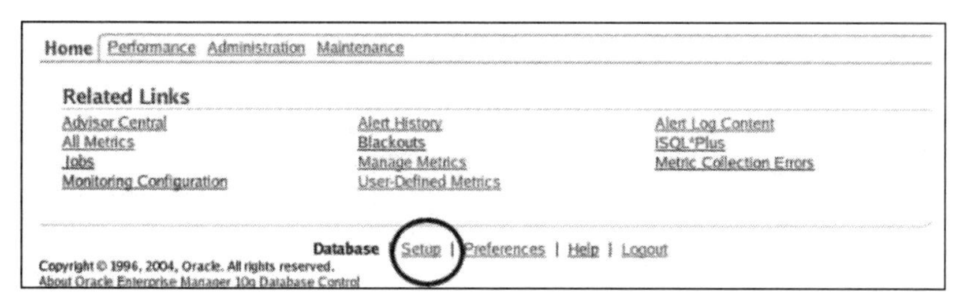

Figure 8.11 - *Setting Up Alerts*

2. Click *Notification Methods* on the Setup page. See figure below.

   Complete the information needed for the Mail Sever portion on this page. Seek help from a network administrator or refer to online help for more information regarding mail server names; as discussion on mail server names is beyond the scope of this book.

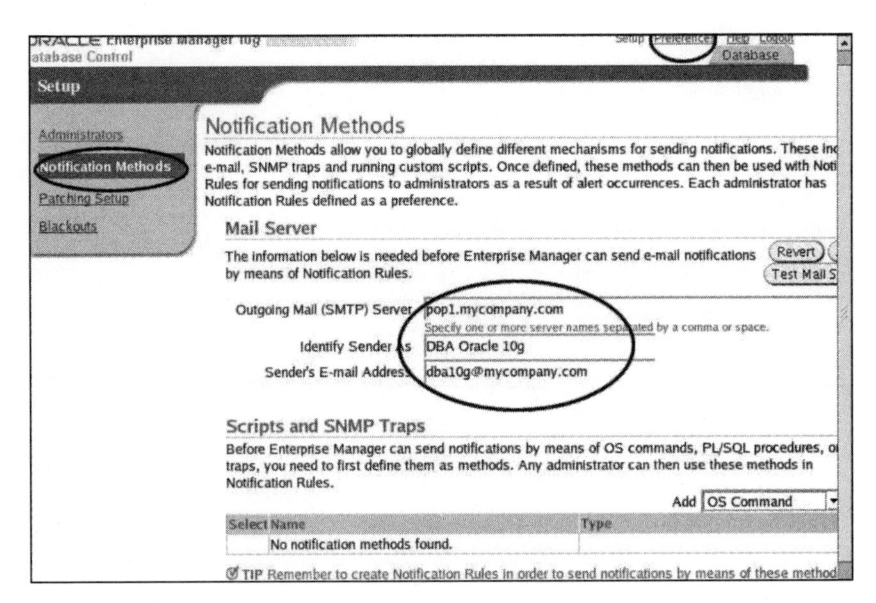

Figure 8.12 - *Alert Notification*

3. From any Database Control page, click on the Preferences link visible in header or footer areas. See Figure 8.12 above.

4. Select General and enter the appropriate email address in the E-mail Address section.

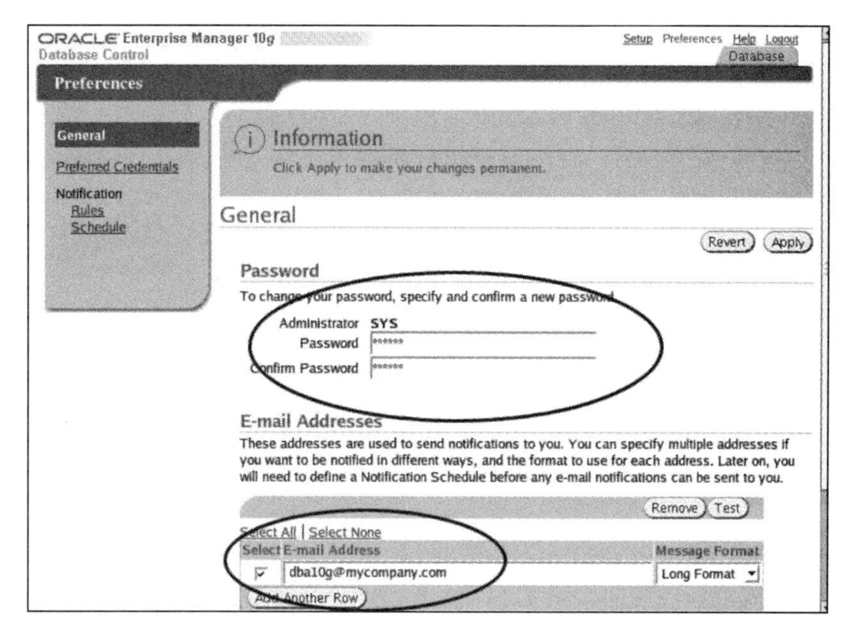

Figure 8.13 - *Alert Notification*

5. Select Notification Rules to modify any default notification rules. This page will help with changing the severity settings for receiving notification.

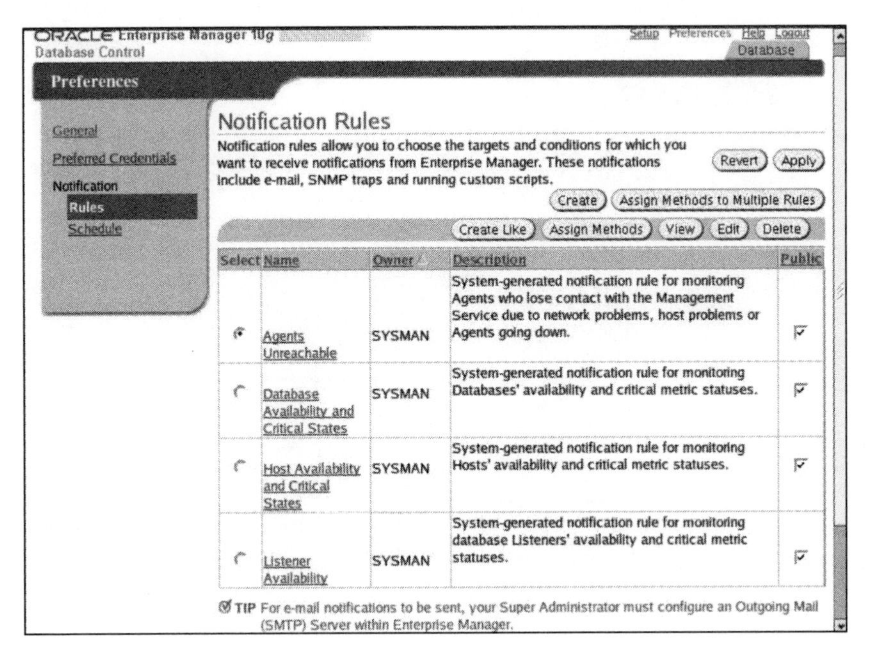

Figure 8.14 - *Notification Rules*

This concludes the review of alert set up and management, the next will explore how to respond to them.

Responding to Alerts

Whenever an alert is received, follow the recommendations it provides or run ADDM or another advisor as needed to get a more detailed diagnostics of system or object behavior. The DBA can also opt to run a corrective script to run on receiving an alert as mentioned in Managing Metric Thresholds section.

If a Tablespace Space Usage alert is received, take remedial actions by running the Segment Advisor on the tablespace to identify objects for shrinking. Those objects can then be shrunk to free space.

The next section goes into how to clear the alerts part of alert management.

Clearing of Alerts

Oracle clears most of the alerts automatically when the cause of the alert disappears. But, there are certain alerts that need to be acknowledged by the DBA, and alerts that require corrective measures. After taking the necessary corrective actions, acknowledge the alert by clearing it or purging it. Clearing an alert sends it to the Alert History, which is viewable from the home page of OEM under Related Links; whereas, purging an alert removes it from the Alert History.

To clear an alert, choose the Alerts link in the Home page. Click the Alert link and the Alert Log page appears. Select the alert to be cleared and click Clear or click Purge to purge the alert. It is also possible to Clear Every Open Alert or Purge Every Alert using these buttons, though it is not recommended as a good practice.

Data Pump

No database is complete without data loading and unloading. The new data movement tools in Oracle will be briefly explained in the following paragraphs.

Oracle Database 10g provides a new high-speed infrastructure for data and metadata movement called Data Pump aka DBMS_DATAPUMP. The data pump infrastructure provides a dramatic improvement in performance over the original export and import utilities. It provides high-speed data load and unload capability to existing tables. Using a robust proprietary format, platform independent flat files can be moved between multiple servers. It is also possible to use the new network mode to transfer data using database links. Although their commands are similar to Export and Import, they are separate products.

Oracle Database 10g introduces new tools that support this infrastructure as well as new command line export and import clients, expdb and impdb. Parallelism for Data Pump is only available in the Enterprise Edition

This diagram shows the major components of Data Pump architecture.

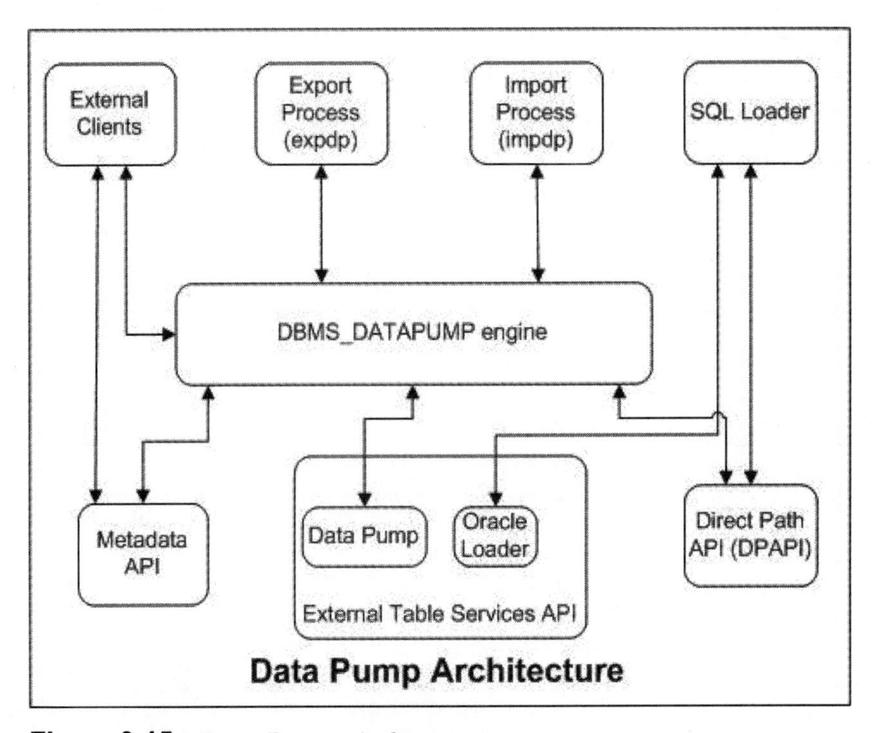

Figure 8.15 - *Data Pump Architecture*

The major components of Data Pump are as follows:

- *Direct Path API (DPAPI)* - Row data is read or written to dump filesets as a DPAPI stream. This reduces the duration of data conversion and parsing while executing load and unload processes.

- External Tables Services Data Pump - uses the following external table access drivers:
    - ORACLE_LOADER - provides external table read-only access (originally debuted in Oracle 9i).
    - ORACLE_DATAPUMP - a new access driver that provides external table read/write access using DPAPI streams.
- DBMS_METADATA package - provides database object definitions to an expert worker process for the entire database or the requested subset in proper creation order. It recreates all objects from XML representations at import time.
- DBMS_DATAPUMP package - provides the API for high speed export and import utilities for bulk data and metadata movements.
- SQL Loader client - has been integrated with external tables to provide automatic migration of loader control files to external table access parameters.
- New export and import clients (*expdp* and *impdp*) - While remaining compatible with original export and import clients, these provide thin layer connections making calls to the DBMS_DATAPUMP package to initiate and monitor Data Pump operations.
- SQL Plus - can be used as a client of DBMS_DATAPUMP for simple status queries against ongoing database operations.
- Miscellaneous Applications - OEM, User applications.

Data Pump Export (*dpexp*) is a utility for unloading data and metadata into a set of operating system files called dump file sets. Data Pump Import (*dpimp*) is used to load data and metadata stored in these export dump file sets to a target database.

The Data Pump API accesses its files on a server rather than on the client. In network mode, these utilities can be used to export data from a remote database to a dump file set, or load a target database directly from a source database with no intervening files. This network mode is helpful to export data from a read-only database and import into another database.

At the heart of every Data Pump operation is the master table (MT), which is a table, created in the schema of the user running a Data Pump job. The MT maintains all aspects of the job. The MT is built during a file-based export job and is written to the dump file set as the last step. The MT is the key to Data Pump's restart capability in the event of a planned or unplanned job stoppage. The MT is dropped when the Data Pump job finishes normally.

Some benefits of Data Pump Export and Import are as follows:

- It is possible to detach from a long running job and reattach without affecting the job. This enables the DBA to monitor jobs from multiple locations, stop the jobs and restart them later. The space needed for an export job can be estimated using the ESTIMATE ONLY attribute. This prevents the destination directory from running out of space.
- Data Pump also supports fine-grained object selection using the EXCLUDE, INCLUDE, and CONTENT attributes. This helps in scenarios such as exporting and importing a subset of a large data warehouse to datamarts etc. The version of database objects can be specified through the VERSION attribute.
- the number of threads working for the Data Pump job can also be controlled. Parallel is available only in Enterprise version of the database.

- Another benefit of Data Pump is the remapping of data during export and import processes. With this, the names of source data files, source schema names, and source tablespaces can be changed to different names at the target system.

Process Flow in Data Pump Implementation

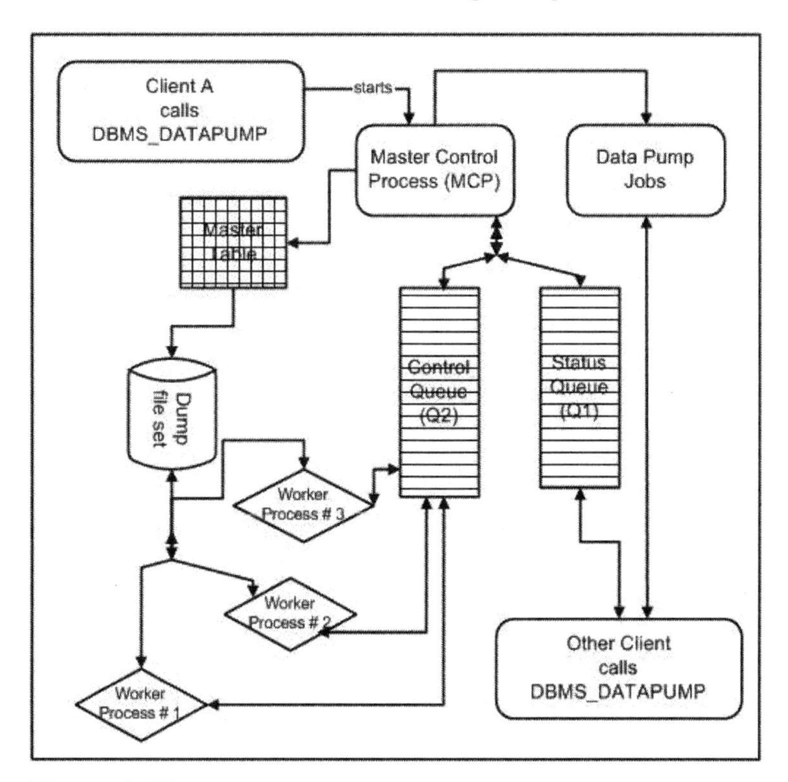

Figure 8.16 - *Data Pump Implementation*

Client C1 starts a Data Pump Export operation by calling the DBMS_DATAPUMP package. This starts the Master Control Process (MCP) and establishes two queues. One of these queues sends status, logging, and error information to clients interested in this operation (Status Queue - Q1). The second queue controls the work process established by the MCP. The second queue is also used by the client to post dynamic commands to the MCP.

Client C1 calls DBMS_DATAPUMP to start the job. The MCP starts 'n' processes that registers with the command and Control Queue Q2. The MCP establishes 'n' initial files for each stream to make up the dump file set. More files are created as the job progresses depending on the space consumption.

Using the DBMS_METDATA package, the MCP directs one of the worker processes to initiate retrieval of metadata. All metadata is written to the dumpfile set as XML. This will help in metadata transformations on import process.

During this operation a master table is maintained in the schema of the user starting this operation. When metadata is retrieved, size and location of each object is written in individual rows to the master table. When the entire operation is finished, the master table is loaded into the dump file set.

During import, the first step is loading the master table from the dump file set. This master table has all the sequencing information for the entire import job and enables the restart for both export and import.

To unload row data, the MCP checks for a worker process to perform unload operations for the current table. If it finds a process, it will send a request to it to unload the table. Each row of unload data will be unloaded in DPAPI stream format into a file and byte offset supplied by the MCP. Only one active thread of unload writes to a file at a given time. During this process, the worker and master processes communicate via the command and control queue to track progress, space requirements, and errors, if any.

While the export job is running, the original client can detach from the job without aborting the job. More than one client may be attached to a job at any time. Other clients can use SQL*Plus to execute scripts to monitor this job at the same time. After all objects are successfully exported and the master table is unloaded to the dump file set, the processes are stopped and the job terminates.

As explained earlier, Data Pump supports direct path API and external tables to access table data. These two methods can be used interchangeably for import and export.

Data Pump uses direct path load and unload when a table's structure allows it and maximum single stream performance is desired. The Data Pump uses external tables over direct path when it works with the following: clustered tables, tables with active triggers or referential integrity (constraints), tables with fine grained access control enabled in insert and select modes, and existence of global indexes in single partition loads. Also, if a table contains encrypted columns, domain index exists for LOB column or loading tables that are partitioned differently at load time and unload time.

All files are accessed relative to server paths, as Data Pump is Server based. It cannot work with absolute paths. DATA_PUMP_DIR is an environment variable created for the purpose of specifying a directory object name rather than the *directory* parameter. If no explicit directory object is specified, Data Pump looks at the DATA_PUMP_DIR variable. The user must have appropriate access privileges to the directory object for the operation attempted.

There are three types of files that are managed by the Data Pump jobs. These files are - dump files to contain the data and metadata that is being moved, log files to record the messages associated with an operation, and SQL files to record the output of a SQLFILE operation.

Data Pump Jobs

This section is intended as a high-level summary on Data Pump Jobs. For more information on using expdp and impdp commands and detailed examples, see *Oracle Database Utilities* documentation or Rampant's *Oracle Database 10g New Features* book. Oracle Database 10g keeps dictionary views for the Data Pump utilities such as DBA_DATAPUMP_JOBS, DBA_DATAPUMP_SESSIONS, and etc. Longer running jobs are tracked through *v$session_longops.*

Data Pump utilities can be invoked from the Command line interface, the parameter file interface, and the interactive command interface. All file-related parameters (LOGFILE, DUMPFILE, and SQL FILE) require a directory object. This can be embedded in the specific file parameter or by the *directory* parameter. Parallel Full export and imports can be enabled by adding parallel = 'n' in the scripts. Also, selected schemas, objects, or tablespaces can be exported by specifying their names during the operation.

If there is more than one export job running, the job name has to be specified to attach to any particular job and to be monitored. If there is only one job, the ATTACH command will attach to it by default.

A job can be stopped with the STOP_JOB command. The client session is terminated and the job winds down in a controlled fashion. The job can be restarted as long as the dump files are not disturbed. The user can restart the job using START_JOB command. The job can be killed by the KILL_JOB command. In order to exit a client, use the EXIT_CLIENT command.

External Tables

In previous releases, external tables were read only. However, as of Oracle 10g, external tables can also be written to. Although neither Data Manipulation Language (DML) operations nor index creation is allowed on an external table, it is possible to use CREATE TABLE AS SELECT .. to populate an external table composed of Direct Path API flat files that are operating system independent.

Loading data refers to reading data from an external table and loading into a table in the database. Unloading data refers to reading data from a table in the database and inserting the data into an external table. Loading and Unloading data can be done with external tables using the new Data Pump access driver.

The advantage of loading and unloading data is to unload tables to flat files and load the flat files to target system, which is helpful for large data volumes. For larger tables, parallel loads can be done. ETL operations are not possible with Data Pump.

The status of external tables can be queried from the PROPERTY column of the *dba_external_tables* view. The following views list the specific attributes of external tables in the database:

- *dba_external_tables*
- *all_external_tables*
- *user_external_tables*

A list of data sources for external tables can be obtained from:

- *dba_external_locations*

- *all_external_locations*
- *user_external_locations*

A detailed explanation of external tables is beyond the scope of this book. For more information regarding the use of external tables and detailed examples on these tables, see *Oracle Database Utilities* documentation or Rampant's *Oracle Database 10g New Features* book.

Conclusion

This chapter reviewed database alerts, alert metrics, alert monitoring, and communicating them to the DBA and use of OEM to set these correctly. Information was also presented about the new Data Pump technology for high-speed data and metadata movement. The important review points are as follows.

- Alerts help the DBA to monitor the databases using the notifications generated on reaching or exceeding particular metric threshold values.
- Oracle defines Metrics as a set of statistics for certain system attributes which are calculated and stored by the Automatic Workload Repository (AWR).
- Oracle Enterprise Manager can be used to send alert notifications to the DBA by pager or email.
- The data pump infrastructure provides a high-speed data load and unload capability over the original export and import utilities.
- Data Pump Export (*dpexp*) is a utility for unloading data and metadata into a set of operating system files called dump file sets.
- Data Pump Import (*dpimp*) is used to load data and metadata stored in these export dump file sets to a target database.

- Data Pump also supports fine-grained object selection using the EXCLUDE, INCLUDE and CONTENT attributes.
- Using Data Pump, data can be remapped during export and import processes.

Book Conclusion

This book was the culmination of a genuine attempt to explain all the intricacies of Oracle Database 10g automatic administration features. While it is impossible to explain all these features in detail in such a conscise book, an attempt has ben made to explain almost all important points in a clear and lucid style for novice as well as veteran DBAs. For more information on any of these database features, please refer to the materials mentioned in the references. The hope is that this book will be really helpful for a smooth voyage through the seas of Oracle Database 10g.

Index

E

F

G

I

J

L

M

O

P

R

S

T

U

V

W

About the Author

Arun Kumar R. is an expert in architecting, implementing, and trouble-shooting large-scale, highly complex systems using Oracle technologies. This includes a decade experience in Oracle Database Administration including multidimensional, decision support systems and ERP software. He has worked on a wide variety of projects and environments ranging from client-server, E-Business to managed services across multiple relational database systems in telecommunications, retail and health care industries.

Arun serves as the Associate Editor for SELECT Journal published by IOUG and as the Chairman of an IEEE Dallas chapter. He is a columnist on "Oracle Data Strategies" in Database Trends and Applications magazine. He also serves as a faculty member for Database Technologies and E-Business at a renowned private university. He has published several papers for many technical journals in the US and Asia and spoken at Oracle technology conferences and international seminars.

Arun has Ph.D. in Business Administration, and M.S. majoring in Computer Science. He is an alumnus of Louisiana State University. He is a Systems Architect for Enterprise Data Services at a major wireless carrier in Dallas.

About Mike Reed

When he first started drawing, Mike Reed drew just to amuse himself. It wasn't long, though, before he knew he wanted to be an artist.

Today he does illustrations for children's books, magazines, catalogs, and ads.

He also teaches illustration at the College of Visual Art in St. Paul, Minnesota. Mike Reed says, "Making pictures is like acting — you can paint yourself into the action." He often paints on the computer, but he also draws in pen and ink and paints in acrylics. He feels that learning to draw well is the key to being a successful artist.

Mike is regarded as one of the nation's premier illustrators and is the creator of the popular "Flame Warriors" illustrations at **www.flamewarriors.com**. A renowned children's artist, Mike has also provided the illustrations for dozens of children's books.

Mike Reed has always enjoyed reading. As a young child, he liked the Dr. Seuss books. Later, he started reading biographies and war stories. One reason why he feels lucky to be an illustrator is because he can listen to books on tape while he works. Mike is available to provide custom illustrations for all manner of publications at reasonable prices. Mike can be reached at **www.mikereedillustration.com**.

Oracle In-Focus
Oracle Dataguard
Standby Database Failover Handbook
Bipul Kumar
RAMPANT
Don Burleson

Oracle Data Guard

Standby Database Failover Handbook

By: Bipul Kumar

ISBN 0-9745993-8-7
Retail Price $27.95 / £19.95

This book is an essential guide for planning a disaster recovery strategy. Covering all areas of disaster recovery, standby database and automatic Oracle failover, this book explains how the use of Oracle10g Data Guard provides a comprehensive solution for disaster recovery. This book covers all aspects of Oracle Data Guard in detail and provides an overview of the latest Data Guard features in Oracle10g.

Written by a working Oracle DBA, this text covers the concepts and the architecture of standby databases and provides a detailed description of the implementation and management of data guard. Expert tips are revealed for success in configuration and first-time implementation of Data Guard. Advance topics such as "Using RMAN to create Data Guard Configuration" and "Data Guard Broker" have been explained in detail to assist production DBAs managing multiple databases.

http://www.rampant-books.com

Oracle Wait Event Tuning

High Performance with Wait Event Interface Analysis

Stephen Andert

ISBN 0-9745993-7-9
Retail Price $27.95 / £17.95

The Oracle Wait Event Interface is a revolution in Oracle tuning. Unlike archaic tuning techniques, the Oracle Wait Interface provides a complete method for quickly locating and fixing even the most perplexing Oracle performance problem.

Stephen Andert is a practicing Oracle tuning expert and shares his secrets for fast and reliable Oracle tuning. The Oracle Wait Interface is very complex, and Andert provides step-by-step guidance though the process of identifying and correcting Oracle performance issues.

This is not a beginner book. This text is targeted at the working Oracle professional who must quickly and reliably locate problems and tune databases. Best of all, Andert reveals little-known tips and tricks for capturing external information relating to Oracle performance including disk, network and CPU bottlenecks.

http://www.rampant-books.com

Oracle Streams

High Speed Replication and Data Sharing

Madhu Tumma

ISBN 0-9745993-5-2
Retail Price $16.95 / £10.95

Oracle Streams is a high-speed tool that allows synchronization of replicated databases across the globe. It is an indispensable feature for any company using Oracle for global eCommerce. A noted and respected Oracle author, Madhu Tumma, shares his secrets for achieving high-speed replication and data sharing. Using proven techniques from mission-critical application, Tumma show the front-line secrets for ensuring success with Oracle Streams. From installation through implementation, Tumma provides step-by-step instruction to ensure success with these powerful Oracle features.

Tumma walks you safely through the myriad of complex Oracle Streams tasks including the set-up of the staging area queue, propagation through data hubs, customized apply functions, rule-based data propagation, Oracle Streams transformation, and lots, lots more. Best of all, Tumma shares working code examples that allow easy management of even the most complex Oracle Streams implementation.

http://www.rampant-books.com

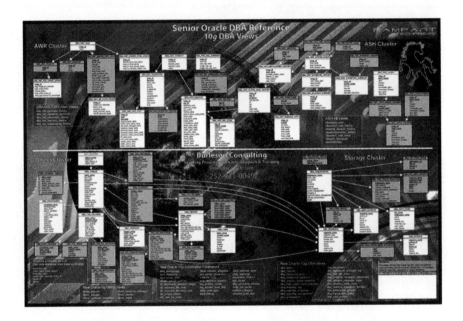